To
Jane, Jeff and Claire;
Mom, Dad and Mike;
and
My brothers and sisters
(even though "Cliff" likes golf more than tennis)

Contents

Acknowledgments

I began working on this book about a year ago, but it actually originated on June 24, 1971. That was the day I reluctantly accompanied my father to Wimbledon at age 15.

Until then, my interest in tennis was marginal. My father had introduced me to the sport, but I remained a novice. Like many other beginners, I spent most of my time picking up balls, which failed to amuse me. But then, I had never seen a match between accomplished players. I had no role models.

Until Wimbledon. I sat transfixed for six hours at Centre Court watching third-round matches. Roger Taylor of Great Britain vs. Cliff Richey of the United States. Top-seeded Rod Laver of Australia vs. Clark Graebner of the United States. Julie Heldman of the United States vs. a 19-year-old Australian named Evonne Goolagong. Tom Okker of the Netherlands vs. Nikki Pilic of Yugoslavia.

Even I had heard of Laver. He would lose to future U.S. Davis Cup captain Tom Gorman in the quarterfinals, clearing the path for fellow Aussie John Newcombe to win his second straight Wimbledon singles title. Goolagong would win the ladies' title to become the youngest Wimbledon champion since Karen Susman in 1962.

Pilic would spark the infamous Wimbledon boycott two years later by failing to participate in a Davis Cup series to which he had allegedly committed himself. When Wimbledon honored his suspension by the Yugoslav Tennis Federation, 79 members of the year-old Association of Tennis Professionals (including 13 of the 16 seeds) withdrew.

As I watched the players, I was captivated by the beauty of their strokes and the spins they put on the ball. Finally, my father dragged me away from Wimbledon.

I followed the rest of the tournament on television (which was almost as good as being there, thanks to the knowledgeable, dignified commentators of the British Broadcasting Corporation), eagerly filling in the draw each day. I've been filling in draws ever since.

I still have the program we bought that day at Wimbledon. My only regret is that we didn't go to Wimbledon five or 10 years earlier. I might have become a poor man's Michael Chang — small, quick and determined. OK, a *very* poor man's Michael Chang.

I settled for becoming a tennis writer and received the opportunity to write this book.

So, thank you, Dad, for taking me to Wimbledon.

My mother, father and stepfather have always supported me in whatever I wanted to do.

I am also indebted to my wife and two children for sacrificing so I could write this book. They did so because they knew how important this was to me. Andre Agassi is the best story I've encountered in my 16-year newspaper career, and there's no way someone who loves writing and tennis can resist that. My wife also helped edit the book and translated a lengthy French article.

Many others helped make this book possible.

Lois Kern, Kim Nader and both sets of grandparents took care of the kids while my wife and I were working.

Aaron Cohodes, Alex Greenfeld, Sid Fleischman and Karl Kistner provided invaluable advice and support. Adrian Cacuci helped with research. Bonus Books editors Andrea Lacko, Carey Millsap-Spears, Rachel Drzewicki and Deborah Flapan were patient and understanding.

Of the many people I interviewed, the following were especially helpful:

- Wendi Stewart, Agassi's former girlfriend.
- Rita Agassi, Andre's oldest sister.
- U.S. Davis Cup captain Tom Gullikson.
- Professional players Jeff Tarango, Luke Jensen, Mark Woodforde, Mark Knowles, Richey Reneberg and Guy Forget.
- Weller Evans, executive vice president of player services for the ATP Tour.
- Chuck Kellogg, the former head professional at the Spanish Oaks Tennis Club in Las Vegas.
- Marty Hennessy Sr., the tennis director at the Desert Inn Resort & Casino in Las Vegas.
- Hans Riehemann, the fitness/tennis coordinator at the Spanish Trail Country Club in Las Vegas.
- Journalists Bud Collins, John Feinstein and Richard Evans.
- Racket stringers David Mindell and George Kylar.

Providing valuable information were Greg Sharko and Joe Lynch of the ATP Tour, Art Campbell and Brian Walker of the United States Tennis Association (USTA), Becky Lenhart and Donna Lamb of the Intermountain Tennis Association and Peter Herb of USTA Northern California.

Jim Fossum, the sports editor of the *Las Vegas Review-Journal*, and Allen Leiker, an assistant sports editor at the *R-J*, graciously gave me as much time as possible to work on the book even though we were often shorthanded. The sports staff as a whole took great interest in the book. Hardly a week went by without Leiker asking me sympathetically, "Got it done yet?" Or, "You still working on that thing?"

Well, my wife and kids are virtual strangers, the cars look as if they've just completed the Baja 1,000, the back yard looks like the Amazon rainforest, I have a stack of magazines as tall as my daughter to read, I've forgotten how to grip a tennis racket and my physical condition has deteriorated to the point that I get winded bending over to pick up the newspaper. But yes, the book is finally finished.

Foreword

It was the strangest interview I have ever conducted. Andre Agassi was the subject. Sort of.

Agassi, his older brother Phillip and I sat on the deck of the Lakeridge Tennis Club overlooking Reno, Nev., on a pleasant evening in early May 1986.

Andre, who had just turned 16, was playing in his first full tournament as a professional — the $10,000 Nevada State Open. The singles champion would earn $1,600. That's pocket change for Andre now, but it was a big deal to him then. Phillip, 23, was also entered.

I was covering the tournament for the *Reno Gazette-Journal*, where I worked as a sportswriter.

Even before we sat down to talk, it was apparent that Andre wasn't your ordinary interview subject.

First, there was Andre's hair. Yes, he had some back then. A lot of it. His naturally brown hair was bleached blond on top, short on the sides and shaggy in the back.

Then there was Andre's fingernail. The nail on his right little finger was about an inch long and painted red. All of his other fingernails were cut short and unpainted.

(Andre had no earrings, as he does now.)

Phillip, on the other hand, looked . . . well, normal, even though his hair was already thinning. Even then, Andre was unique.

I spoke to the Agassi brothers for about 30 minutes for a feature story in that Sunday's newspaper. The story was on both of them, but Andre was the focus.

And here's the most unusual part of all: Andre uttered three sentences during the entire interview. Phillip spoke for him the rest of the time.

Andre broke his silence only when asked about his first Grand Prix tournament earlier that year and about his father. Both answers were revealing.

Andre had lost to Mats Wilander, then ranked third in the world, 6-1, 6-1 in the second round of the $405,000 Pilot Pen Classic at La Quinta, Calif., in late February 1986.

"There was a crowd of 4,000 people," Andre said. "I was so nervous, I couldn't hit the ball."

Andre also insisted that he never felt pressure from his devoted, demanding father and coach, Emmanuel (Mike) Agassi. If Andre had been completely open, we would have been there for hours. Instead, he looked me directly in the eye and said with a straight face, "I always wanted to make him happy and proud."

That is unquestionably true. Unfortunately for Andre, almost nothing would ever be quite good enough for Mike. Not winning Wimbledon. Not dating Brooke Shields. Talk about hard to please.

Nine years later, Andre admitted in a penetrating interview on *60 Minutes* that his father put enormous pressure on him "to not accept losing."

Andre's reticence in the Reno interview was probably due to cockiness. He was not, however, one of those snotty athletes who look everywhere but at you, tap their finger impatiently and otherwise act bored. Andre listened intently. He just let Phillip do most of the talking.

Believe it or not, Andre was still obscure at this point. It wasn't difficult to get an interview with him and Phillip — such as it was. There were no autograph hounds hovering over us that day on the Lakeridge deck. It was just the three of us having a cordial chat — OK, the two of us.

You knew — you just knew — that it would never be like this again. Agassi would become not only a top-10 player but a phenomenon. He had the game — nobody blasted forehands and returns of serve the way this kid did, even in the pros — and the charisma. He was Tiger Woods before Tiger Woods and, as we'll see, Dennis Rodman before Dennis Rodman.

Several players in the tournament disagreed about Agassi's future. Although he won the tournament, he struggled against club pros and aspiring touring pros, and his behavior was poor.

But the other players probably didn't know that Agassi, at 15, was already beating veteran touring pros.

Or that Agassi was just coming off of a grueling five-week satellite circuit (equivalent to the low minor leagues in baseball) in Florida and South Carolina.

Or that Agassi had to adjust not only from sea level to Reno's 4,498-foot altitude (so did the other players, most of whom came from Northern California), but from the Southeast's humidity to Reno's dry air.

In any case, Agassi quickly made a splash on the pro tour and would go on to achieve just about everything in tennis: win Wimbledon, the U.S. Open, the Australian Open, an Olympic Gold medal and the ATP Tour World Championship; reach No. 1 in the rankings; and play on three Davis Cup championship teams.

Agassi was so good that he felt he could win with a diet from hell and little or no preparation. To a large degree, he was right. His hand-eye coordination is extraordinary. His return of serve is considered the best ever and his backhand textbook perfect.

On the court or off, it seems Agassi is always doing something spectacular. Winning a Grand Slam tournament. Losing listlessly in the first round. Losing his temper. Playing tennis on a San Francisco street in a Nike commercial. Dangling from a helicopter in a Mountain Dew ad. Becoming a born-again Christian. Introducing denim tennis shorts. Wearing baggy pajama-style shorts. Growing his hair down to his shoulders. Bleaching it. Cutting it off. Undergoing career-threatening wrist surgery. Befriending Barbra Streisand. Marrying Shields. Buying a 727. And on and on.

Yet for all of Agassi's fame, the public does not really know him. Not even avid tennis fans. People think they do. Agassi was — and still is to a degree — the victim of several misconceptions. Early in his career, he was considered a choker, stupid and all style, with no substance. He is, in fact, a survivor, bright and exceedingly complex.

Agassi is also enormously generous. His charitable foundation in Las Vegas is only the most public example. Privately, he has gone out of his way many times to help others: making a large donation to a children's hospital, paying for friends' educations, building houses for his parents and conditioning coach, arranging outings for other players, etc.

Before I began researching this book, I thought Agassi was an enigma with his extreme highs and lows. I still don't have all the answers. I don't think Andre does, either, though God knows he tries. But it all makes a lot more sense than it did, and the key is Mike Agassi.

Andre and Mike are more alike than Andre would probably care to admit. Both have two sides. They are great guys off the court who can be terrors on it.

Mike has been described as "a genius" and "innovative," "warm," "gentle," "tender," "sweet" and "generous." He has also been described in less than flattering terms.

I saw both sides of Mike when I wrote a four-part series about Andre for the *Las Vegas Review-Journal* after Andre won Wimbledon in 1992. Mike submitted to the longest interview I've ever done — three or four hours. He showed me the court behind his house and all the ball machines he used to drill Andre and his other kids. Then we went into the kitchen. Mike offered me a soda on a typically blazing summer day in Las Vegas, and we continued to talk.

A few days later, I received a call from Mike at the *Review-Journal*. Saying he had been burned by other reporters, he demanded to read the series before it was published. When I told him that would be impossible, he threatened never to talk to me again. It was a mild threat compared to others he has made.

The series contained both glowing praise and harsh criticism of Mike. After it was published, he called me at home. Uh oh, I thought, here it comes. However, Mike thanked me for the series, invited me to lunch and talked to me for another hour. Afterward, Mike drove me to the lot where Andre was building a house for his parents.

That's Mike Agassi. Fascinating guy. So is his youngest son.

Good As Gold

Thousands of Olympians arrived in Atlanta for the 1996 Games on Boeing 727s. Only Andre Agassi, however, came on his own 727.

Whereas other athletes crammed themselves into their coach seats on carriers such as Atlanta-based Delta Airlines, the then-26-year-old tennis star/pop icon stretched out in luxury on "Air Agassi."

Agassi had recently replaced his 10-seat Lockheed JetStar with a 98-seat 727. You and I upgrade from Ford Escorts to Ford Tempos. Agassi upgrades from small jets to big ones. What's next, a 747? Maybe Bill Clinton, of whom Agassi is a big fan, will sell him a used Air Force One.

Agassi customized the 727, reducing its capacity to 32 seats, according to his father. The interior is basically a penthouse apartment, featuring a living room, a long table with seats for 12 to 15 people, easy chairs and a master bedroom.

The purchase of the jet was very hush-hush. Few reporters knew about it, and Agassi wasn't about to tell the others. He doesn't like to flaunt his considerable wealth or discuss his personal life. Nobody was saying how much the jet cost, but golfer Greg Norman bought a customized Boeing 737 in June 1997 for $30.5 million. And held a news conference to announce it.

Agassi was coming to Atlanta determined to earn one of the few prizes that had eluded him — an Olympic gold medal.

"To me, it's a no-brainer, one of the greatest opportunities an athlete could ever have," he said after arriving in Atlanta. "Winning a gold medal is what we're all here for, but the good part is the experience in and of itself."

Most top professional tennis players could not have cared less about the Olympics because it didn't offer the two things around which their world revolves: money and ranking points (which lead to money). Only three of the world's top 10 men — No. 6 Goran Ivanisevic of Croatia, No. 7 Agassi and No. 10 Wayne Ferreira of South Africa — played in the tennis event in the new $20 million complex at Stone Mountain Park, 16 miles from the Olympic village in downtown Atlanta.

Agassi, who has never been like most players, would be the first to admit that the tennis calendar is too crowded, even without the Olympics. But he wasn't going to let that stop him from competing.

"I can't comprehend the feeling of being inconvenienced by the Olympics," Agassi said. "To me, being here is worth the whole year."

Agassi conceded that he would have preferred a stronger Olympic field.

"You want to feel like you earn it, no question," he said after beating Jonas Bjorkman of Sweden in the first round. "Winning big matches against the best players is ideal, but I will take a gold medal any way I can get it."

Several factors made the Olympics a priority — if not an obsession — for Agassi. Most importantly, he desperately wanted to please his father, a former Olympian who taught Andre how to play tennis, after a lifetime of trying.

"My father is as proud, if not prouder, of my being at the Olympics than anything I have ever accomplished," the 1992 Wimbledon champion said before the tennis event in the Games began. "It's a special moment."

Emmanuel "Mike" Agassi boxed for his native Iran in the 1948 Olympics at London and the 1952 Games at Helsinki, Finland.

"I would give my right arm for Andre to win the gold medal," said Mike, who still has a delightfully thick Middle Eastern accent despite living in the United States for 45 years. "I didn't do it."

Several weeks before the Olympics, Mike and his wife, Elizabeth "Betty," had gone out to dinner with Andre and his fiancé, Brooke Shields, in Las Vegas.

"I asked him to win the gold medal for me," Mike said. "He said, 'I'll try.' "

Andre is a patriot who has succeeded John McEnroe as the United States' staunchest supporter of the Davis Cup, the men's international team competition. This patriotism, too, is probably related to his father. U.S. servicemen introduced Mike to tennis at an American mission church in Iran when he was a child. Mike later fell in love with the game and immigrated to Chicago in 1952.

Then there was the influence of Brad Gilbert, Agassi's coach. Although Gilbert had cracked the top 10 as a player and earned $5.5 million in career prize money, he said winning a bronze medal in the 1988 Olympics at Seoul, South Korea, was the highlight of his career.

"There was no more important tournament for me than the Olympics," said Gilbert. "A gold medal is a gold medal. You can't buy it, and you have to wait four years to win it again."

Andre did not grow up dreaming about competing in the Olympics, though. The Games were never discussed much in the Agassi household when Andre was a child.

First of all, Mike concealed his boxing past from his children.

". . . They found out when the media did research on me," Mike said. "I never wanted them to box. I never believed you should put your head in front of a punch."

Secondly, tennis withdrew from the Olympics from 1924 until 1988, except as a demonstration sport in 1968 at Mexico City and 1984 at Los Angeles. By the time tennis officially returned in Seoul, Agassi was 18 and had long since left home.

Tired of what it perceived as tennis' second-class status in the Olympics, the International Lawn Tennis Federation ('Lawn' was dropped from the title in 1977) pulled the sport out of the Games after 1924 in Paris. The courts in those Games were unplayable, the men's changing facilities were ½ mile from the courts, and the women's consisted of a wooden hut that was locked for much of the competition. Similar problems had plagued tennis in previous Olympics. When the International Olympic Committee rejected several proposed changes, the ILTF had had enough.

Seeking to increase tennis' exposure and prestige, International Tennis Federation (ITF) executives David Gray and Philippe Chatrier successfully spearheaded a movement in the 1980s to readmit tennis into the Olympics.

There are still those, however, who believe tennis shouldn't be in the Olympics.

". . . For tennis players, Wimbledon, the U.S. Open, the French Open — these are much more important than the Olympic Games," said Germany's Michael Stich, a gold medalist in doubles with Boris Becker in 1992 at Barcelona, Spain. "Track and field athletes and swimmers train for four years to go to the Olympic Games, and that's the highlight of their careers. For tennis players, it's not."

Free-lance journalist Joel Drucker agreed.

"With neither money nor ranking points at stake, Olympic tennis has been little more than flag-waving that's heavily underexposed and adds yet another burden on the already overbooked tennis calendar," Drucker wrote before the 1996 Games in a *Tennis* column entitled, rather bluntly, "Get tennis out of the Olympics."

Agassi felt differently, but he was not ranked high enough to earn a berth on the 1992 U.S. Olympic team. Twenty-two at the time, he was mired in one of his trademark slumps that spring, when the U.S. Olympic team was chosen for the Barcelona Games. The United States Tennis Association (USTA) named Jim Courier, Pete Sampras and Michael Chang, none of whom would win a medal in the clay-court tournament.

Ironically, Agassi won Wimbledon before the Olympics began, but the team could not be changed.

"The last thing you'll find me doing is trying to convince someone I'm the man they need," Agassi said after capturing the Wimbledon title. "I'm not going to complain about it. They chose the team when I was at a low professionally and personally. The next [Summer] Olympics is in four years, and they'll pick me."

He was right. The U.S. named Sampras and Agassi — ranked No. 1 and 2 in the world, respectively — to play singles in Atlanta, and Richey Reneberg and MaliVai Washington to play doubles.

Injuries knocked out Sampras before the 1996 Olympics and Reneberg during the event, but Agassi finally had his chance to win a gold medal. Maybe his only chance. He would be 30, retirement age in men's professional tennis, during the 2000 Summer Olympics at Sydney, Australia.

". . . And it won't be the same in Australia," Gilbert said. "This one is in America. It doesn't get any better."

The only problem was that Agassi had lapsed into another funk, winning only three matches in the previous 3 ½ months. The crowd in Monte Carlo had jeered him during a 6-2, 6-1 third-round loss to Alberto (now Albert) Costa of Spain on clay in late April. Then Agassi had lost to 72nd-ranked Chris Woodruff in the second round of the French Open and to Doug Flach, a qualifier ranked No. 281, in the first round at Wimbledon.

On a scale of 1 (lowest) to 10 (highest), Mike Agassi rated Andre's performances against Woodruff and Flach a 2.

"He didn't care," Mike said at the time, stating what everyone could plainly see. "You could see it in his eyes. He has a lot on his mind: the marriage, [customizing] the airplane, [a new] house and several other problems. [Tennis] is not his first priority. But he's coming out of it. He'll be all right."

Mike would not elaborate on Andre's "other problems."

As Mike spoke on the telephone, Andre was practicing with Gilbert on the court at Mike's new house — a gift from Andre — in an exclusive west Las Vegas development.

"I haven't seen him practice like this [for a long time]," Mike said. "He's excited. He didn't practice at all for Wimbledon, the French or the Australian [where Andre reached the semifinals before losing in straight sets to fellow Southern Nevadan Chang]. People are not supermen. When you don't practice, you're not going to play well."

Actually, Andre is notorious for playing well without practicing. But it catches up with even him after a while.

"If the Olympics are important to [Andre], it's a good sign," Mike said. "With his talent, if he wants to win, he will win."

Andre's chances received a big boost when Sampras withdrew a week before the Olympics with an Achilles tendon injury. Reneberg, ranked 21st in singles, replaced Sampras in the draw and remained in the doubles field.

Andre and Shields stayed in a rented house with a tennis court and a pool near Stone Mountain, rather than in the Olympic village.

"Being a tennis player, traveling your whole life as an individual and doing things the way I wanted, I felt my main duty was to give myself the best shot to win," Agassi said. "And I didn't want to stick myself in an arena that I may end up not being used to or comfortable with. I chose to prepare myself the way I do [for] all the events, 52 weeks a year for the last 10 years."

Nor did Agassi venture to any Olympic venues, where he would have been mobbed and expended energy. Instead, he stayed in the house and watched the Olympics on television, although his former girlfriend, Wendi Stewart, said he is not an avid sports fan.

Agassi ate a late-night dinner one night at Shoney's, an inexpensive chain restaurant, and Shields went grocery shopping at Kroger's.

The conditions in Atlanta were favorable for Agassi. The Olympic tournament was on hard courts, his favorite surface. And Agassi, who trains in 110-degree heat in Las Vegas, wasn't likely to wilt in Atlanta's upper-90s temperatures (although the heat is bone dry in Las Vegas and dripping wet in Atlanta).

As it turned out, the Olympics were a microcosm of Agassi's career. The Games illustrated his patriotism, wild popularity, wittiness, vulgarity, struggles, brilliance and father's influence.

Agassi drew a tough first-round assignment against Bjorkman in the 64-player tournament. Bjorkman, 24, had defeated former world No. 1 Stefan Edberg en route to the quarterfinals of the 1994 U.S. Open and extended Agassi to five sets in the fourth round of the 1996 Australian Open in January.

This time, Agassi escaped with a 7-6 (8-6), 7-6 (7-5) victory over Bjorkman before 12,000 fans, many of them chanting "U-S-A."

"It was close," Agassi said afterward. "Definitely a close call. I feel pretty good about getting through that one."

Shields, watching nervously in the second row, peeked through her hands as Agassi fell behind 4-1 in the first set. Bjorkman had two set points at 6-4 in the first-set tiebreaker and led 4-3 in the second-set tiebreaker, but Agassi prevailed by ripping service returns and groundstrokes.

"If it goes to three sets, I think I have a little advantage," Bjorkman said. "I think I'm in a little bit better shape."

The drama was only beginning.

Agassi had the next day off, but two developments affected him. Reneberg retired from his first-round match with an injury, and Ivanisevic, erratic as always, fell in the first round.

Reneberg trailed Leander Paes of India 6-7 (2-7), 7-6 (9-7), 1-0 when the American aggravated a weeks-old groin muscle injury in his left leg. Reneberg said he doubted he would be able to play doubles in two days, leaving the possibility that the U.S. would not be able to field a doubles team. No players could be added to the U.S. squad at that point, meaning that Agassi was the only possible player to team with Washington.

Agassi hadn't played doubles since that March at Indian Wells, Calif. He and fellow American Patrick Galbraith, ranked No. 1 in the world in doubles in 1993, lost to eventual runners-up Brian MacPhie of the U.S. and Michael Tebbutt of Australia in the first round, 6-3, 5-7, 7-5. In Agassi's last doubles appearance before that, he and Petr Korda of the Czech Republic won the title at Cincinnati in 1993.

Reneberg speculated that Agassi would decline to play doubles in the Olympics to conserve energy for singles.

"Andre Agassi is here to do well in singles," Reneberg said. "Unfortunately, it may end up being we just don't have a doubles team."

But Reneberg underestimated Agassi's patriotism and loyalty — or perhaps public-relations skills. Agassi agreed to play doubles, although he and Washington were unlikely to win a gold medal with Australians Todd Woodbridge and Mark Woodforde in the field. "The Woodies," as they are known on the tennis circuit, had won a record four straight Wimbledon doubles titles.

"The [U.S.] team took a hit," Agassi explained. "You've got to adjust to it. As far as I'm concerned, if it calls

for you to give more, you've got to give more. It's as simple
as that. Even if it costs me a medal, it is still something that
you've got to do."

Meanwhile, Ivanisevic lasted all of 60 minutes in the
Olympic singles event, further clearing the way for Agassi.
The Croatian, who had lost to Agassi in a thrilling five-set
Wimbledon final in 1992, committed 42 unforced errors in a
6-2, 6-4 loss to 104th-ranked Marcos Ondruska of South
Africa.

The *Atlanta Journal-Constitution* reported that Ivanisevic skipped practice with his team in Mississippi to spend
most of the previous three weeks on a boat in the islands.
He said he had not practiced except for two days at the
Stone Mountain Tennis Center.

"I had no energy, and I'm thinking I'm going to kill
myself unless I slow down and take some time off," Ivanisevic said. "I came here to represent my country, but it
was poor."

Agassi continued to advance, beating 86th-ranked
Karol Kucera of Slovakia 6-4, 6-4 in the second round and
No. 38 Andrea Gaudenzi of Italy 2-6, 6-4, 6-2 in the third
round.

In between, Agassi and Washington outlasted Mexico's Alejandro Hernandez and Oscar Ortiz 6-3, 4-6, 6-4 in
the first round of the 32-team doubles event before 5,000
fans packing Court 1 at Stone Mountain.

Agassi and Washington nearly collided once at the
net and blew three set points and one match point. They
also eschewed the fancy hand signals behind their backs
favored by many experienced doubles teams.

"I'd rather walk back and say, 'Hold on, tell me what
you are thinking,' " Agassi said. "Forget that hand signal.
As long as we are from the same country, speaking the same
language, I'd rather [he] keep his hands in front of him on
the racket.

"Plus, it is never my idea to look at Mal's ass when I
am about to serve anyhow," he said. "It kind of distracts me
a little bit."

"Distracts you because it is good-looking, or distracts you because . . . I mean, elaborate there," Washington wondered.

"We will talk about that one later," Agassi said, eliciting laughter from the media.

That night, the mood at the Olympics turned from festive to somber. A pipe bomb exploded at Centennial Olympic Park, killing one person and injuring more than 100.

"I think they should hang the guy by the nuts and execute him publicly if they catch him," Agassi said.

Agassi added that he wasn't concerned about his own security.

". . . I try not to . . . start feeling like I have to live in a hole of some sort," he said. "That is the last thing you want to do is get yourself that concerned about it because then you miss out on what life is about, and it is not right. . . ."

The Games continued as planned, and a bizarre scene took place at Stone Mountain. Tennis fans in the U.S. (except New York) have never been known as rowdy, but riot police were called in to stop what the *Journal-Constitution* called "a noisy but peaceful revolt" after a doubles match featuring Agassi and Washington was moved off Center Court in rain-related rescheduling.

Fans whose tickets for the 12,000-seat Center Court would not allow them access to the 5,000-seat Court 1, where the match was moved, chanted, "Change it back!"

At least 35 riot police officers were called in as fans streamed out of the stadium and demanded to be allowed into Court 1. Many had waited through a rain delay of more than three hours.

There were no arrests or injuries, and Olympic organizers relented and moved the Agassi-Washington match back to Center Court. Agassi and Washington acknowledged the fans with a wave as they entered around 7 P.M., and the crowd chanted, "Thank you! Thank you!"

Organizers had no idea that moving the doubles match would create such a furor, said referee Ken Farrar.

The idea was to get the doubles played as quickly as possible because more bad weather was feared, he said.

Agassi and Washington said they were unaware of the fans' protest when they entered the stadium. Agassi called their reaction "the ultimate compliment."

The crowd eventually saw the Americans lose to sixth-seeded Ellis Ferreira and Wayne Ferreira (no relation) of South Africa 7-5, 6-7 (3-7), 6-0 in the second round.

"For two guys who almost never play doubles together, [Agassi and Washington] did very well," said U.S. coach Tom Gullikson. "They lost to a very good doubles team."

Agassi added: "It's never easy to lose, especially when you're playing for your country. But the main thing is leaving the court knowing you've done your best, and we did that."

Having done his patriotic duty, Agassi could focus on his quarterfinal match against Wayne Ferreira. Agassi had never lost a set to Ferreira in five matches, but this time the American eked out a 7-5, 4-6, 7-5 victory in 90-degree heat and 77 percent humidity.

Both players complained vociferously about line calls from the beginning of the match. Agassi finally lost his temper after the first game of the second set, receiving a warning and then a point penalty for verbal abuse.

"I honestly believe he should be kicked off the court for the things he was saying," said the strawberry-blond Ferreira. "They were pretty rude and actually the worst I've ever heard anybody say. I'm surprised the umpire [George Rustscheff] took it so lightly. If I was sitting in the chair, I probably would have done something different."

Agassi laughed at Ferreira's suggestion that he should have been defaulted. "It was about the only way he was going to beat me," Agassi said.

Ferreira wouldn't repeat Agassi's remarks, but Bud Collins, who was covering the match for NBC-TV and *The Boston Globe*, said, "It was 'Fuck you' and 'Fuck this' and that sort of thing."

The controversy and the crowd's overwhelming support gave needed inspiration to Agassi, whose interest seemed to wane in the second set. Fans chanted "Andre! Andre!" at each changeover and "U-S-A" after every game Agassi won.

As Julie Cart of *The Los Angeles Times* wrote: "Ferreira found out that when playing an American in the Olympics in the United States, it's not going to be Wayne's world, but Andre's."

Agassi struggled again in the semifinals, beating No. 127 Paes of India, 7-6 (7-5), 6-3. The American survived two set points in the 12th game of the first set.

Paes, who twice hit drop shots while returning first serves in the opening game, played what Agassi called a "very strange" match.

"He hit like maybe 25 drop shots," Agassi said. ". . . I stopped guessing and started using a simple philosophy. If I think it's ridiculous, I'm going to plan on him doing it."

Agassi's opponent in the final would be his Spanish friend Sergi Bruguera, who defeated Fernando Meligeni of Brazil 7-6 (11-9), 6-2 in the other semifinal. Bruguera, once a guest at Agassi's house in Las Vegas, won the French Open on clay in 1993 and 1994.

But Bruguera tore two ligaments in his right ankle while training on December 22, 1995. Bruguera returned to the circuit in February 1996 and was unseeded entering the Olympics. His ranking, as high as No. 3 in 1994, had plummeted to No. 70.

Agassi was 5-2 against Bruguera entering the match, with both of the Spaniard's victories coming on clay.

"If we were on clay, I'd be stressing a little bit," Agassi admitted. ". . . To me, this is a huge match on Saturday. It's as big a match as playing in a Grand Slam final."

To Mike Agassi, winning a gold medal "would probably be the greatest accomplishment I could have in this sport — besides winning every match I play," Andre said with a smile. "He might prefer that."

Andre, though, scoffed at the notion that a silver medal would be unacceptable.

"If the silver medal is a disappointment, you're a [jerk]," he said. "Certainly the gold is a great accomplishment, but a silver is a wonderful thing."

There was no stopping Agassi now, though. With scalpers getting up to $175 for a seat, he crushed Bruguera 6-2, 6-3, 6-1 in 77 minutes.

"The way I was playing today, it didn't matter who was on the other side of the net," said Agassi, who became the first American gold medalist in men's singles since Vincent Richards in 1924.

Bruguera agreed.

"I think when he's on, he's the best player in the world on this surface," he said. "He played too good for me today."

By the end of the first set, a Spanish reporter had seen enough. As he left the press box, he muttered, "Bruguera is only interested in silver. He will lose within an hour."

The reporter was off by four minutes.

Asked to compare his gold medal to his three Grand Slam singles trophies, Agassi said: "I think to win a Grand Slam in the sport of tennis is the biggest thing you can accomplish inside your sport. But I think that the Olympics is the biggest thing you can do in all of sports. To win a gold medal is what it is all about. If you can't come here and give everything to win the medal for your country, then I think you're really missing out. I'll keep this over all of them."

Paes took the bronze medal, and Woodbridge and Woodforde — Who else? — won the gold medal in doubles.

As soon as he defeated Bruguera, Agassi turned to the ponytailed Shields and pumped his fist. Then, like an Olympic boxer in the ring, Agassi faced each section of the stadium, blew kisses and bowed.

Suddenly, a stocky 65-year-old man with glasses appeared from a stadium tunnel, ran onto the court and hugged Agassi.

It was his father.

"I didn't know he was going to be here," Andre said. "After the match, I gave him a chance to get closer to gold than he's ever been. It was just a memorable embrace that we'll have forever."

Mike had developed Andre into one of the greatest players in tennis history — but also perhaps the most insecure and erratic champion ever.

Betting The House

2

Mike Agassi was obsessed with developing his children into tennis champions.

Not champions of the Mickey Mouse Junior Invitational.

Not collegiate champions.

Not U.S. champions.

World champions.

What else but obsession would you call it when someone:

- Shovels snow off the courts in Chicago for four hours so he can play?
- Gets a job with a construction company for the sole purpose of learning how to build a tennis court?
- Moves from Chicago to Las Vegas so he can teach his children, some of whom haven't been born yet, the game year-round in warm weather?

- Buys a house in Las Vegas without stepping inside it, inspecting only the back yard to make sure there's enough room for a tennis court?
- Grooms his children literally from birth to play tennis?
- Works at his casino job until 7 A.M. Saturday and awakens at 9 A.M. to give lessons to his kids and others?
- Teaches tennis to his kids for thousands of hours in heat suitable for broiling chicken?
- Customizes 13 ball machines to simulate every conceivable shot and increase their capacity?
- Buys 200 balls a *week* and throws 200 out?
- Spends every spare dime and devotes every spare minute to his childrens' tennis careers?
- Surreptitiously climbs a tree to watch his daughter's match?
- Rages if his children receive bad line calls?
- Throws second- and third-place trophies in the garbage?

"Every parent has a dream for his child," Mike once said. "The child is going to be the president, or the best doctor or lawyer. I thought my four kids were going to be world [tennis] champions. You know it's never going to happen, but it's a dream. It makes it easy to go on the court and work with a kid."

First came Rita, then Phillip, then Tami. All of them became accomplished tennis players, but none reached his or her potential and none became a world champion. Then came Andre.

"[Mike] was hell-bent on having a champion, and he *lucked* out with Andre," said Wendi Stewart, who grew up with Andre in Las Vegas and traveled with him on the professional tennis circuit for 2½ years as his girlfriend. "He lucked out, because he tried it with Rita, he tried it with Phillip, he knew he couldn't try it with Tami. He saw what happened with Rita."

Marty Hennessy Sr., the longtime tennis director at the Desert Inn Resort & Casino in Las Vegas, has known the Agassis for 25 years. He paused when asked how hard Mike was on his children.

"This guy's life was dedicated to those kids, period," he said. "He moved out here from Chicago so the kids could play tennis because the weather was good. And he saved money, not so he could buy these kids a fancy car or house, but so they could travel and play tournaments. He had his own little fund for that. He knew what was best for his kids. Most kids have no clue what they want out of life."

Phillip discussed only the positive side of Mike in a 1986 interview.

"Tennis always came first in our family," he said. "My father went out of his way to help us. He'd teach Las Vegas juniors in our back yard for nothing. He's a tennis freak. He loves tennis."

Yet, Stewart, a 1997 journalism graduate of New York University who has known Andre since they were 8, said there was much discord in the Agassi family.

"Their coping mechanisms, their communication skills are just absolutely null and void," said Stewart, who is 27 like Andre. "I think Andre is *the* most functional one, because he works at it. He constantly thinks about this kind of stuff — relationships. He analyzes them and people."

Rita, 37, hasn't spoken to Mike since she was 19, although she said she loves him. She said she despises Phillip and rarely talks to Andre. Rita said she was invited to Andre's wedding in April 1997 but didn't attend. She loves her mother and sister. Phillip and Andre, who are very close, have reconciled with their father after difficult . . . not *childhoods*, because they didn't really have them . . . *upbringings*.

"We weren't raised like a do-things-together family," Rita said. "We're all independent entities who don't cohabitate well together," she added with a laugh.

*   *   *

Mike Agassi, an Armemian, might have inherited some of his traits from his mother.

"My grandmother lived with us [in Las Vegas] for a while," said Rita. "She was a character. She didn't speak English very well, but everyday she pulled out her English books. She'd sit there and have her nose down and be writing in those workbooks trying to learn the language, and she was 70-something. She had a temper, too."

Rita said she never knew her paternal grandfather. Both of Mike's parents are deceased, she added.

Emmanuel "Mike" Agassi was born on December 25, 1930, in Iran. U.S. soldiers introduced him to tennis at an American mission church in Iran when he was 9. He watered and rolled the two dirt courts behind the church while the soldiers squeezed in a game. Occasionally, he played himself.

There was another side to the young Emmanuel, though.

"I was a street fighter," said Mike, a stocky 5 feet 6 inches today. "We had a gang of 12 kids and fought one-on-one with kids from other neighborhoods. I had a pretty good punch."

It was good enough for Mike to box for Iran in the 1948 Olympics at London and 1952 Games at Helsinki. He lost in the first round each time, as a bantamweight in 1948 and as a featherweight in 1952. Even so, he was forming ideas that he would use later to train his children in tennis.

Mike said his Olympic experience "made me more mature, more sure of myself. It showed me how to go about a sport and become great at it. You have to have vision and work hard [at] it. Things may be impossible now but not in the future. For instance, in basketball in the 1970s, nobody was shooting from 3-point distance. If you had a kid in the 1950s and taught him that, he'd be a superstar today. You try to predict how a sport will be 10, 15, 20 years from now.

"I spent every [free] minute watching other sports: track and field, soccer, swimming. I never wanted to be a prize fighter. My bones are too small and break too easily. Many times I broke my finger and wrist."

After immigrating to Chicago in 1952 at age 21, Mike took a job waiting tables at the Ambassador Hotel and once served Australian great Rod Laver.

Mike became a fixture on the public tennis courts, even in the winter. "We'd start shoveling at 7 A.M.," he said. "By 11 it would be ready. Of course, we had no net."

Mike got his construction job the following year. Characteristically, he had his own ideas about how things should be done and wasn't shy about expressing them.

"One day, my boss said, 'If I hear one more word from you, you're fired,' " Mike said.

Mike was soon scanning the want ads. But he had accomplished his goal of learning how to build a tennis court.

Mike's pro boxing career ended before it started in the middle 1950s. Just before his pro debut, at Madison Square Garden, his opponent withdrew on doctor's orders with a fever. The promoter found a replacement 30 minutes later.

"He had 35 or 40 knockouts in 46 fights," Mike said. "The fight was six rounds, and I had never fought four rounds."

Mike did what any sensible person would do. He ran.

"I've never touched a glove since," he said.

Mike immersed himself in tennis, learning everything he could about the sport. He read books, rented films and visited factories.

Boxing and tennis are more similar than they might appear. Tennis journalist Bud Collins, in fact, once referred to tennis as "boxing without blood." Both involve slugging between two athletes. In tennis, however, players bash a ball instead of each other.

Mike knew he had to get to warmer weather to pursue his dream. He intended to move to Los Angeles "because it was tennis country," but couldn't find work. He and his wife, Betty, went to Las Vegas in 1962, and Mike found jobs at two casinos. He eventually rose to showroom captain at Bally's-Las Vegas. Betty worked for 27 years as an alien certification specialist for the state before retiring in 1992.

It's difficult to imagine a greater personality contrast than between Mike and Betty Agassi.

"[Betty] has always been very quiet," Hennessy Sr. said. "She was always in the background, and Mike was running the show. I don't even remember hearing her talk for the first few years I saw her. She wasn't one who would stand out in a crowd. You would know Mike was coming even before he got there. You wouldn't know she was there even if she was sitting next to you."

The stark contrast is understandable. If Betty were like Mike, there would be a nuclear meltdown in their house. Which is essentially what happened with Rita.

Betty, a stout woman, looks more like your house-keeper than the mother of one of the most glamorous athletes in the world. Once, while Mike was being interviewed for a newspaper article in the kitchen of their former Las Vegas home, Betty sat in the living room doing crossword puzzles and watching a soap opera. There is nothing pretentious about her.

Interview requests petrify Betty.

"I want out of the public [eye]," she explained sheepishly. "It's a mental block on my part."

When asked once for an interview about Andre, Betty said, "Oh, I don't have anything to do with that."

What she meant was that she didn't have anything to do with Andre's tennis career. And she didn't (except driving him to tournaments). That was Mike's job.

When the Agassis moved to Las Vegas, Nevada's population was about 300,000. Today, it is more than five times that amount.

"I remember we didn't have 50 tennis players in the state of Nevada," Mike said. "We used to play at a senior citizens center that had four courts. I was introduced to some of the Desert Inn bosses, and they allowed me to play at the Desert Inn. I gave them some free lessons.

"There was no tennis patrons association. We tried very hard to build one. But it was very difficult because there were only 30 to 35 tennis players. There were two or three tournaments in town and one Nevada championship. Anyone was allowed to come [to the Nevada tournament], but nobody did."

An association was finally formed in 1968. Mike was accepted as a member and — ironically, considering his later conflicts — put in charge of linesmen and umpires.

Mike and longtime adversary Chuck Kellogg, a local pro, feuded over whether Southern Nevada should be in the weak, sprawling Intermountain Tennis Association (ITA) with Utah, Colorado, Wyoming, Idaho and Montana or in the strong, relatively close Southern California Tennis Association. Driving times from Las Vegas are about five hours to Los Angeles, seven to Salt Lake City, 12½ to Denver, 14 to Cheyenne, Wyo., 10½ to Boise, Idaho, and 16 to Billings, Mont. The best players from each section in the country go to the nationals.

"He said our kids are never eligible to go to the nationals, so we should get in the weakest section," Mike said. "Then every parent would take their kid to Kellogg [for lessons] because he'd have a higher ranking. They don't know that the final in the Intermountain section is weaker than the first round in Pasadena [Calif.].

"It's gonna cost me a fortune to go to Intermountain sectional tournaments. If I go to California, I can take 30 kids in a bus, chaperone the kids, put them in a motel and the most it's gonna cost each kid is $70 to $80. The other way, the parent has to leave his job [during the week]. You are hitting the pocket of poor people. He said, 'The kid is not gonna improve if he doesn't go to the nationals.' I say, 'Every tournament in Southern California is like the nationals.'

"They put it to a vote, and it went through [to join the Intermountain section]. It was the biggest disaster for the game of tennis in Las Vegas. . . . After 12 or 13 years, when Las Vegas was put on the [tennis] map by Rita Agassi and Andre Agassi with national rankings, the Intermountain agreed to [hold sectional championships] here every year or other year. Parents learned this is a good place, and they could have a lot of fun. [Kellogg] has been very proud of this big mistake."

Kellogg's response to Mike's statements?

"At one time, I wanted to move [Las Vegas] in the [Southwest] section with Arizona," he said. "[Las Vegas] is so far from the [rest of the] Intermountain section and too far from California. I don't know that Mike was ever involved in that discussion."

Phoenix, however, is just as far from Las Vegas as Los Angeles.

Mike taught all of his children to play the same way — hit the hell out of the ball from the backcourt.

"The game was pretty much molded from Rita to Phillip all the way down," Hennessy Sr. said. "They all did pretty much the same pattern of working on their ball machine for 'X' amount of hours, and then their father would take them in their van and drop them off at different facilities to have matches.

"It kind of reminded me of somebody working out in a gym, a boxer working on the speed bag and the heavy bag and jumping rope and doing different kinds of workouts and then doing some sparring. Mike's mentality looked like to make sure they got into the 'gym' everyday, and they all had a nice aggressive game.

"We've all seen Andre play, but geez, if you had a chance to see Rita hit the ball or Phillip or even little Tami or [cousin] Suzi, they all have tremendous games. They have weapons off of each side. But when the big points came up, they seemed to lean a little more in Andre's favor compared to the other kids. He was a big-point player.

"I also noticed that he didn't really feel like, even at a younger age, he needed to practice that much. Possibly, he hit so many balls at a young age that the timing was almost innate."

If there was discord in the Agassi family, you'd never know it talking to Hennessy Sr.

"The main thing about the whole family is they were competitors," he said. ". . . It was a team effort. The Agassis stuck together. Every match these guys played, they all sat in the stands and rooted for each other."

Nobody was more dedicated than Mike.

"Behind all great kids — [Monica] Seles, [Michael] Chang, [Jim] Courier, Agassi, everyone — are parents who gave everything," Mike said. "They don't mind spending the money and standing behind them."

Even if you're dead tired.

"He slept maximum four or five hours a night," Rita said. "He had no life [of his own]."

Sometimes, Mike had too much on his mind to sleep. He was thinking about — What else? — tennis.

"I used to lie awake at night thinking of how tennis was going to be played when Andre was 22 or 23," he said. "Speed is the key — power forehand, power backhand, no weaknesses. The most important thing is to be inside the court, to hit the ball on the rise and not let the other guy hit the ball."

Mike elaborated.

"If you hit the ball 60 mph, that's 88 feet per second — less than one second from one end of the court to the other," he said. "If you hit the ball 90 mph, that's 120 feet per second. If you hit the ball inside the baseline a split second early, the other guy has to go so fast to reach that ball."

This — along with Andre's incomparable return of serve — has made him one of the greatest players in history.

Mike, an iconoclast, is disdainful of tennis pros. Of course, tennis pros try to teach their students to play the game. Mike had a somewhat loftier goal.

"It's easy to get people's money by telling them to bend their knees and get the racket back," he said. "There are 12 to 15 [tips] that all the pros know. But there's nobody to teach you how to hit a ball 125 mph or with no pace."

Mike can and did. Especially the former.

"He knew what he was doing," Rita said. "He's an incredible guy. He has a lot of knowledge in a lot of areas. If he wanted to raise kids who could graduate from college by 14, he could have done it. He's very innovative."

According to conventional tennis wisdom, the last thing you want to do when learning to play is hit hard. After all, what good is a shot if it goes out?

Mike took the opposite view. He reasoned that "at some point, you'll learn to control it," said Mary Rowan, who trained with the Agassi children under Mike — free, of course — for six years. "Most coaches emphasize control, but in a pressure situation, that player is going to gag.

"When you get nervous, your arm gets tight. Then you tend not to follow through, the balls get shorter, and you invite your opponent to drill it. I've seen Andre lose plenty of matches, but never because he was unwilling to hit out and through the ball."

The secret to power, Mike said, is timing and the breaking of the wrist.

"If I throw a hanky 180 mph, it will do nothing," he said. "If I snap it at you, it can make you bleed.

"Until Andre came on the circuit, nobody hit 100 mph on his groundstrokes. If you take a slow-motion picture [of his forehand], you'll see what he's doing. He makes a circular motion with his racket on the backswing, which gives him momentum to go forward. His wrist is back. He breaks his wrist, elbow and hip. All three snaps get maximum speed on the ball. It's something pros don't teach. [They say,] 'Hit harder.' What does that mean?"

Nor did pros use ball machines as much as Mike. He estimated that his older children hit 7,000 to 8,000 balls a week and that Andre hit 14,000 (Andre said 21,000) — first at the Tropicana Hotel, and later on the court at their house.

"We loved the rain," Phillip said. "It meant one day when we didn't have to play."

Bad news for Phillip: Las Vegas has the least precipitation (4.19 inches of rain a year) of any metropolitan area in the country. But good news for Mike.

"I always knew practice makes perfect," Mike said. "I thought if a kid started early enough, liked the game and had the proper training and coaching, you could lead him or her to the world championship."

*   *   *

Rita was the "guinea pig," as she put it, in Mike's grand experiment.

"She had a chance to become a world champion, but she was always against me," Mike said. "She could have been the youngest Wimbledon champion — better than Billie Jean King and Chris Evert. But she didn't want it."

Mike was not alone in his glowing assessment of Rita.

"Two hands off both sides, like Seles, but hit flat bombs, just *rockets* in the corner," Hennessy Sr. said. "She wasn't real fast, but it didn't really matter because of the shots she was hitting. . . . You couldn't rally with the girl. She hit the ball too hard and too deep, like a [Jimmy] Connors with two hands."

Rita's biggest junior rival in Las Vegas was Lani Wilcox. Her father coached boys' and girls' tennis for 25 years at Clark High School in Las Vegas. Among his players was David Pate, who would go on to rank No. 1 in the world in doubles in 1991.

"My honest opinion is that Rita Agassi, had things worked out right, could have played on the women's pro tennis circuit," said Bob Wilcox. "She could have played with Martina Navratilova and all the rest of them because she could hit a ball almost as hard as Andre does. She was strong, boy. . . . I think she definitely could have been top 10 in the world."

Mike motivated his children negatively, especially Rita. If she won, he'd praise her to others, but tell her nothing.

"He just expected [winning]," she said. "It wasn't an option."

If Rita lost, she'd receive a tongue lashing.

"If you weren't up to what you were expected to do, you'd hear about it," she said. "So it's like, 'No news is good news.' "

Rita dished it right back to Mike — and paid for it.

"I'd say, 'Shut up,' to him," Rita said, "and *whack!*"

Mike's philosophy was reminiscent of Vince Lombardi's: "Winning isn't everything. It's the only thing." They both produced champions and even looked alike with their stocky builds and glasses. But Rita said her father never mentioned the legendary Green Bay Packers coach.

"My dad was more like, if you hated to lose, you never would," Rita said.

There were two major differences between Lombardi and Mike Agassi:

- Lombardi was dealing with men and Mike with children.
- Lombardi was a master psychologist. Mike was not.

Rita, now a tennis coach, said her father "would never be a psychology major. He didn't understand that there are two kinds of kids: kids who are not motivated and kids who are self-motivated. If you have kids who are self-motivated, you don't have to push them as hard. You can kick them in the butt once in a while, but you don't have to push them. If you do, it gets ugly.

"I was very self-motivated, and he pushed. There were some really ugly fights about that because I'd push right back. If he was dealing with kids who were totally unmotivated, maybe he wasn't too pushy."

Were Phillip, Tami and Andre self-motivated?

"Phillip, I'd have to say no," Rita said. "I don't think Phillip was interested in playing tennis. Neither was I, but I liked competing. Tami wasn't competitive, but she liked to play. Andre was most definitely self-motivated, but by the time he came around, I don't think [Mike] was pushing as hard."

Mike was especially hard on Rita, though, because she came first and she was a girl. In the first case, he didn't know any better. In the second case, he could have been influenced by his staunchly conservative Middle Eastern culture.

"He was really overprotective, and he just pushed too hard in practice," Rita said. "The problem I had with him was the overdoing of stress in practice and his lack of knowledge at the time. He learned a lot about tennis through the years when Phillip and I were growing up, but when we started, he knew nothing. When you have someone who's got a lot of drive and ambition, and the knowledge hasn't caught up with that, it's very hard."

Mike was "hard as hell" on Rita, according to Stewart.

"She got the worst of it," Stewart said. "She got the worst of it. . . . [Mike] just didn't know how much kids could handle. And Rita's got a spirit like Andre. She's headstrong and feisty. That wasn't going to work, and it didn't. Tami and Phillip are more laid-back."

Sources said Mike pestered Rita and his other children during their tournament matches. Rita, 12 or 13 at the time, said she threatened to lose intentionally if he came to an event at Redlands, Calif. Naturally, Mike couldn't bear to stay away. What happened next was comical.

"He was watching my match, and he was bothering me," Rita said. "He'd make all these noises like 'Ohhhhh' or 'I can't believe you did that' when you missed a shot. It was like traumatic [for him], like you're not supposed to miss a ball. So I got mad and decided I wasn't going to win, because that's the only way to get even with him. He went away, but then he came back and climbed a tree [to watch the match].

"Then I saw these people staring up at the tree, and I knew he was in there. So I started hitting balls over the fence [during points] . . . served it over the fence, hit the returns over the fence, hit them on the next court, hit them two courts down . . . so he'd go away, and he did. I actually won that match. I think I was playing Lisa Albano or somebody. I remember she was just in shock."

Mike never stayed away for long, though.

"He hid a lot," said Rita, who developed bleeding ulcers by age 13. "I didn't care if he was watching. I just didn't want to have to see him or talk to him or hear him or deal with him. You're trying to play a match. You don't need any pressure from the outside. Besides, I never wanted him to get any satisfaction from me playing tennis."

Mike battled not only with Rita, but with other parents and tennis administrators. Both Agassis paint a harrowing picture of jealous, backstabbing, cutthroat tennis parents.

"There was a lot of jealousy among parents of tennis players, a lot of politics," Mike said. "When making the draw, if I'm your friend, they put me in an area where I'll get through two or three rounds. I didn't care. We wanted to play the best. They were dodging us, not us them. They couldn't destroy the Agassi family, but they did find ways to bother us.

"The week before a final once, [the Intermountain Tennis Association] had meetings. There were a couple of people from each state. They passed a new rule that you had to play four sectionals and one final to go to the nationals. They had already played two, and it was one week before the nationals. Automatically, my kids are out of the nationals.

"Now they say I'm a madman, a maniac. I'm fighting for my kids. It's the biggest blow a person can give to someone like me who has given his life so someone could be a tennis player."

Gene Corrigan, a former president and grievance committee chairman of the ITA, labeled Mike Agassi's conspiracy charge "nonsense, absolute nonsense. The ITA wanted its best players to go to the nationals. We sympathized with his kids. We knew they were under a lot of pressure. Mike says he was fighting for his kids, but he was fighting with people. We were on the kids' side."

When Rita began to dominate in the ITA, she was allegedly the victim of sabotage on several occasions.

"I've been changing in the locker room, and my tennis shoes were stolen because I had a match against somebody that day," Rita said. "I've had rackets with the gut slit. I've had my applications changed [to a higher age group]. I've had my tires slashed."

Rita persevered and cracked the top 100 in the world before quitting tennis in 1981. She married tennis Hall of Famer Pancho Gonzalez, 32 years her senior, in 1984. They had a son, Skylar, in 1985 and divorced in 1990. Gonzalez died of stomach cancer in 1995 at age 67.

Rita worked in real estate for several years before accepting a position as a tennis instructor at Bally's under David Pate, who owns the tennis operation there. Ironically, Mike had been a showroom captain at Bally's when his children were growing up. Rita coaches juniors, which has helped her understand the conflicts between her father and other tennis parents.

"The way parents look at kids who are good [players] is kind of frightening," Rita said. "There's such a hatred and such an envy. It causes ugly situations — not necessarily among rational people, but with somebody who's sleeping six hours a night and working a job and trying to train their kids, and then you've got to put up with someone else. It's just a volatile situation. My dad and Bob Wilcox used to get in [verbal] fights all the time. It was unnecessary, and it was ugly, but it wasn't just my dad."

Rita's marriage infuriated Mike, which of course was part of the plan.

"Pancho was his own man," Rita said. "Nobody could intimidate him or push him around. He was that way until the day he died. He's the only person I ever knew that was stronger-willed than my dad. That bothered [Mike]. That *really* bothered him."

Marrying Gonzalez was actually a three-pronged attack on Mike:

1. Getting married meant Rita was no longer daddy's little girl.

"He never had control over me, but he'd lose the opportunity to even try to have control," Rita said.

2. Mike detested Gonzalez.

"He thought he was an asshole," Rita said.

Why?

"Because he was," Rita responded with her trademark hoarse laugh. "He was hard. Pancho could be mean. He was never mean to me, but he was mean to a lot of people. You could dig up stories on him that would fill a garbage truck. Pancho didn't take any shit from anybody."

3. Gonzalez was so much older than Rita — older, in fact, than his father-in-law.

Gonzalez wasn't crazy about Mike, either.

"It's a personality conflict," Gonzalez said in 1992. "He has a hard time getting along with a lot of people."

Rita didn't marry Gonzalez solely out of spite. She said she loved him. They lived together for four years before getting married.

"We were just so happy, got along really well," Rita said. "Latin guys, as long as you don't marry them, you're fine. You marry them, you're a piece of property, a chair in the house. . . .

"I was on the phone with Phillip one day. He said, 'Dad knows [you're living with Pancho].' I said, 'So what did he say?' 'He said that you were stupid, that Pancho would never marry you. He was just going to use you and throw you out.' I said, 'Oh, did he?' It took me three years, but I finally got married."

It didn't last, though.

"Two things happened," Rita said. "One, I grew up. What you're like in your early 20s is completely different from what you're like in your later 20s.

"Two, age difference is hard when it was *that* much. He was just in a different place in his life. We had discussed it before we got married, how I'd be gearing up to go into different things and he'd be winding down. He said there was no problem with it. But when it came the time where he was winding down, he didn't want me gearing up. He wanted me home."

What did Rita want to do?

"I don't know, but I wanted to go out and see what I wanted to do," she said. "I wanted to go into business or something, because just hanging out at the house wasn't going to hack it."

Gonzalez said he never worked with Andre.

"I talked to him once about his serve," said Gonzalez, perhaps the greatest server in history. "I said it was as good as anybody his size [5 feet 11 inches] would ever have."

Rita said: "Pancho wasn't interested in other people's tennis. He was interested in his own. There was such an animosity between him and my father. I could never understand why my dad would take me [to Caesars Palace, where Gonzalez was the tennis director] for lessons when they didn't like each other. Pancho was giving me lessons when I was 11."

Andre has made conflicting statements about Gonzalez.

In 1987, Andre said Gonzalez was "always too lazy to get out on the court" and play with him.

In 1996, however, Andre said Gonzalez "was one of the few tennis players responsible for the game as it is today and was a champion in so many areas of life. He was a fighter. He absolutely brought a whole new level to the words 'intensity' and 'focus.' He taught me a lot throughout his career and through his fights as a human being."

Andre did not attend Gonzalez's funeral in Las Vegas in 1995 after losing in the Wimbledon semifinals the previous day.

Even though Rita hasn't spoken to Mike, a host at the MGM Grand Hotel/Casino, in 18 years, she insists it's not out of spite.

"It's not an anger thing like, 'Oh, I'm so mad, and I'll never speak to him again,' " she said. "It's more out of common sense. We're never going to agree on anything. My relationship with my dad is not much different than my relationship with Phillip. I have the same kind of distaste for both of them. It doesn't mean you don't love them."

Rita has many conflicting feelings about her father and Phillip.

On one hand, she says of Phillip: "If he died tomorrow, I wouldn't go to his funeral."

On the other hand, she says of him: "If something was wrong and he needed help, I'd help him."

Huh?

"We have never gotten along," Rita said. "We never *will* get along. We look at life completely opposite. I'm very straight to the point and very competitive and probably a much bigger risk-taker in decision making. He's much more conservative, much more practical. Whenever we *are* talking, it's always conflicts."

Rita said she and Andre have a superficial relationship.

"Andre and I don't have much in common, except we're related," said Rita, who's nine years older. " 'How ya doin'? How's life? How are things going?' That's about it."

Rita would not say if Andre has helped her financially. She didn't hesitate, though, when asked if Andre is a good person.

"Yes," Rita said. "Andre doesn't have a malicious, mean bone in his body. He's smart, very smart, empathetic, very intense. I've never even known Phillip — someone I'm not that fond of most of the time — to be malicious."

*   *   *

Phillip Agassi had it rough, too.

"I feel sorry for Phillip," Stewart said. "I really do. He got the raw end of the deal. He was supposed to be a champion, too, but Mike was really hard on him because he couldn't hack it, because he didn't have the killer instinct that Andre had.

"His life was set up just like Andre's. He did nothing but [play] tennis. So when you fail at the one thing you're supposed to do, what the hell *do* you do? He had nothing else, and then his life became Andre's [chaperoning Andre on the pro circuit], and Andre grew up."

Said Rita: "Phillip was really quiet and passive. . . . I don't think [Mike] liked that."

Nick Bollettieri, Andre's former coach, wrote in his 1996 autobiography *My Aces, My Faults* that Phillip's "confidence and self-esteem had been shaken by years of harsh criticism and scant praise from his father."

Andre, Mike and Phillip declined several interview requests for this book. But Phillip, 35, has said: ". . . I've resolved my own ghosts and skeletons, and they're private. I've become good friends with my dad."

Kellogg, the retired head pro at the Spanish Oaks Tennis Club in Las Vegas, recalled a match that Phillip lost when he was 11 or 12. Kellogg said he saw Mike chase Phillip afterward.

"I don't think [Mike] intended him any harm," Kellogg said. "It's just that he wanted to yell at him, and Phillip didn't like it, I guess."

So Phillip started running?

"Phillip started running before Mike ever approached him," Kellogg said. "He knew Mike was coming."

Despite Mike's browbeating — or perhaps because of it — Phillip developed into a strong player. Using a two-handed forehand and a one-handed backhand, the opposite of many players, he played No. 1 singles as a freshman and sophomore at the University of Nevada Las Vegas (1982-1983). He still holds school records for highest season winning percentage (25-2, .926) and highest career winning percentage (55-6, .902).

"He was a dominating serve-and-volley player, in contrast to Andre," said Fred Albrecht, the UNLV men's tennis coach at the time and now the school's director of alumni relations. "Phil had a big serve, over 100 mph, and great groundstrokes. He liked to stay back because that's what he was taught, but we converted him into more of a serve-and-volley player. His biggest weakness was patience. Sometimes he tended to hit out on shots when they weren't there."

Phillip — one of three Agassis who played at UNLV, along with Tami and cousin Suzi — was never chosen to play in the NCAA Tournament, despite his outstanding record.

"I got screwed out of the NCAAs because of politics," he said in 1986. "They [the members of the NCAA selection committee] don't recognize Las Vegas. Three of the people I beat went [to the NCAAs], and I didn't. Explain that to me. It's a bunch of politics. I just quit and turned pro."

Coaches in the Intermountain region instead selected Utah's Greg Holmes, who won the NCAA singles title in 1983.

"We were just developing a tennis program," Albrecht said. "Utah had been top 25 year in and year out. [The coaches] felt the other fellow played a better schedule."

UNLV, founded in 1957, had never sent a player to the NCAA Tournament. Since then, the Rebels have sent Scott Warner (1986-1987), Jolene Watanabe (1990), Swedes Roger Pettersson (1994-1996) and Marianne Vallin (1994-1997) and Australian Luke Smith (1997) to the NCAAs in singles and many players in doubles.

Smith, ranked 65th among collegians in singles and 19th in doubles with fellow Aussie Tim Blenkiron entering the 1997 NCAAs at UCLA, became the second player in 20 years to sweep the titles. Alex O'Brien accomplished the feat in 1992 and also led Stanford to the team title that year.

Phillip was "a very well-behaved kid," according to Albrecht. "Everyone used to say he had a temper in his junior days, but he matured when he came to college. He had a temper, but not one he couldn't control."

Albrecht said there was an incident with Mike, however, at one of Phillip's matches.

"I had to ask his dad to sit down and watch," Albrecht said. "He thought his son was getting hooked on [line] calls. Players called their own lines then and still do. He yelled at the other player. He complied, and Phillip got a line judge. After that, I never had any problems with his dad."

Phillip played briefly on the satellite circuit — equivalent to the low minor leagues in baseball — before abandoning his career to travel with 16-year-old Andre on the Grand Prix circuit (now known as the ATP Tour). Phillip later became vice president of Agassi Enterprises in Las Vegas, handling interview requests and scheduling exhibitions for Andre.

Hennessy Sr. said he practiced "about a thousand times" with Phillip years ago.

"By the time he was 18, 19, he was a world-class player," Hennessy Sr. said. "He just didn't get a chance to go out there and compete. To me, he's better than a Carl Chang [Michael's older brother and coach]. Carl is out there periodically playing some tournaments and winning some matches. I think Phillip was a bigger hitter than this fella.

"But it takes a few years to get out there and groom yourself and get the confidence. By the time he was 19, 20, he pretty much leaned toward working with Andre. That's not to say [Phillip] would have been No. 1 because that's a different ballgame. But he could have possibly supported himself on the circuit."

*   *   *

Tami Agassi won the Nevada state championship and was named a prep All-American as a junior at Bonanza High School in Las Vegas.

She graduated early and briefly attended the Nick Bollettieri Tennis Academy on a scholarship with Andre.

Tami went 24-13 in singles as a freshman at UNLV in 1988 and finished as the runner-up at the No. 2 position in the Big West Conference. All of the Agassis, including Andre, came to watch Tami play, said Craig Witcher, the UNLV women's coach at the time. Andre ended that year ranked third in the world at 18 years old.

Witcher said he never saw Mike get upset during one of Tami's matches. Kellogg said he did, though, during a junior match.

According to Kellogg, Mike was applauding mistakes by Tami's opponent, Laura Gonzalez (no relation to Pancho), at the Las Vegas Country Club in the 1980s. When Mary Ann Rivera, the mother of three tennis-playing children, asked him to stop, Mike "blew up. He called the lady a 'motherfucker.' He threatened to fight both her and her husband and break both their legs."

Mike hinted that the allegations, and others, were true while declining an interview request for this book.

"Maybe I called someone a motherfucker, maybe worse," he said. "Put it in [the book]. I can't give an interview because we're writing our own book."

In 1992, Mike gave his version of the Las Vegas Country Club incident.

"Anytime Tami missed a ball, Mrs. Rivera was shouting," Mike said. "Tami told her not to, and [Rivera] made a wise remark. I told Tami, 'Just pretend whoever is clapping is an idiot. Just play the game.' Mrs. Rivera said, 'Who are you calling an idiot?' Kellogg said, 'This is a respectable place.' I said, 'If this is a respectable place, why do they let a jackass like you in?' Maybe I was wrong, but I have never let anybody come between me and my kids."

However, Mike once called Tami one of the crudest, most vulger epithets because she was struggling in a high school match, according to a witness who requested anonymity.

Diplomatic, Mike is not. He makes Don Rickles look like Mother Teresa.

Rivera declined to discuss the Las Vegas Country Club incident. When asked if she ever had any problems with Mike, she said: "Not that I want to share. The nice thing about Mike is that when he's your friend, he's a *really* good friend. I respect the hell out of him because of what he sacrificed for his kids . . . for all the right reasons. He really believed in them and gave them everything he had."

Tami did not return numerous calls. Gonzalez and her mother said they don't recall the incident. Gonzalez's father never attended her matches, Laura said.

Kellogg said he banned Mike from Spanish Oaks after the Rivera incident, prompting another threat.

"He called me up at two o'clock in the morning and said he was going to 'waste' me," Kellogg said. "I laughed at him. I knew he wouldn't do it. Everything else he says he's going to do, he never does it. He's a very volatile person who's not able to control himself when he loses his temper."

Tami transferred to Tyler (Texas) Junior College after one year at UNLV.

"All along she wanted to go away to school, but not right away," Witcher said. "I knew from day one that she would be at UNLV only one year."

Tami's transfer had nothing to do with Mike, according to Witcher.

"She and her dad got along fairly well," he said. "She was just like any kid. She wanted to get away and be independent. It never seemed that she was unhappy at home."

Tami finished 27-3 as a sophomore at Tyler, won the Flight 4 national championship and helped the school capture the junior-college national title. She played at Texas A & M for her last two years, winning Southwest Conference championships at No. 5 singles as a junior and No. 2 singles as a senior. Her overall singles record for the Aggies was 45-32 (.584).

"She had a ton of talent," said Bobby Kleinecke, the Texas A & M women's tennis coach then and now. "She was a fun girl to coach. One of her downfalls might have been that she played to the level of her opponent. She played just well enough to win, but she came up with some great wins for us."

Tami was a baseliner — naturally — and used two hands on both sides.

"She hit the ball extremely hard and had great returns," Kleinecke said. "Her serve was nothing special, but it never hurt her. She could do pretty much everything with the ball."

Tami was "very pleasant" off the court, Kleinecke added.

"I can't remember any problems with her. We still keep in touch. She came to a [tennis] reunion here [in February]," Kleinecke said.

Tami, who graduated from Texas A & M in speech communication, runs a foundation in Seattle for Gary Payton, the star guard of the SuperSonics.

Could Tami have played professional tennis?

"If she had decided earlier in her career what she wanted to do, I'd say yes," Kleinecke said. "She had the talent, but as far as the drive, she wanted to be her own person."

Mike had one more crack at producing a world champion.

Jackpot

Andre had two major advantages over his brother and sisters. As the youngest child, he received the benefit of Mike's mistakes with the others and perhaps tried harder to please him. Also, Andre left home at 13 to attend the Nick Bollettieri Tennis Academy. That was no picnic, either, but at least he got away from Mike, who was loving but relentless.

Andre was born at Sunrise Hospital in Las Vegas on Wednesday, April 29, 1970.

A glance at the *Las Vegas Review-Journal* that day shows how much has changed since then. The newspaper sold for ten cents, compared to fifty cents today ($2.50 on Sunday).

Richard Nixon was the president in 1970, and the Vietnam war was spreading to Cambodia. Nixon died in 1994, and the United States is at peace, although scars remain from the war.

Wilt Chamberlain was preparing to lead the Los Angeles Lakers against the New York Knicks in Game 3 of the

National Basketball Association finals in 1970. We now know that Chamberlain scored almost as often off the court as on, and that of the NBA's — What, 150? — teams, only the Vancouver Grizzlies have been eliminated from title contention by April 29.

Tony Perez of the Cincinnati Reds tied what was then a major-league record with his 10th home run in April 1970. Today — with various measures designed to increase offense and boost flagging interest in the game — that's a good week for Ken Griffey Jr.

Listed in the 1970 television highlights in the *Review-Journal* were *The Virginian* with Doug McClure, *Medical Center* with Chad Everett, *The Johnny Cash Show, Hawaii Five-O* with Jack Lord and *The Engelbert Humperdinck Show.*

Playing at Las Vegas theaters were *M*A*S*H*, with Donald Sutherland and Elliott Gould; *Butch Cassidy and the Sundance Kid,* with Paul Newman and Robert Redford; and *Patton* with George C. Scott. (Twenty-one years later, Agassi would become friends with Gould's ex-wife, Barbra Streisand.)

Well, thanks to cable TV and VCRs, maybe not so much has changed after all.

Headliners in Las Vegas in 1970 included Jerry Lewis at Caesars Palace, Mitzi Gaynor at the Riviera, Robert Goulet at the Frontier, Alan King at the Sands and Tom Jones at the International (now the Hilton). Jones, in fact, still performs in Las Vegas. King, a tennis nut, would launch the immensely popular but ill-fated Alan King/ Caesars Palace Tennis Classic in Las Vegas in 1972.

Andre's tennis training began as soon as he got home from the hospital. Mike swung a tennis ball over Andre's crib so Andre could track the ball with his eyes. As soon as Andre could sit in a high chair, Mike stuck a ping-pong paddle in the boy's fist and strung up a balloon to swing at.

When Andre was in a walker, Mike gave him a full-size tennis racket. Betty Agassi had to put all objects out of reach after Andre belted a salt shaker so hard it cracked a glass door. When Andre was 3, Mike was teaching him strokes.

"I put him on a one-handed forehand then," Mike said. "I had made some mistakes teaching his older brother a two-handed stroke at that age."

What did Andre think of all of this?

"He just thought this was the greatest thing in the world," Mike said. "Whatever I said, he did."

Boy, did that change eventually.

Mike said he first saw something special in his son when Andre was 2.

"We were watching a pingpong game at the Frontier Hotel," Mike said. "He followed the ball with his eyes without turning his head. No kids in the world will do that. It was the greatest eye coordination I had ever seen. He always had quick hands. That's all you need in the game of tennis — fast hand-eye coordination."

Said Perry Rogers, Andre's business manager and best friend since childhood: "I think his dad said, 'This'll be the one.' Andre has the best hand speed I've ever seen. Playing golf with him is the best way to see it. He powers through the ball so fast."

Marty Hennessy Sr., the Desert Inn pro, said Andre was 3 the first time he saw him play.

"I was the tennis pro at the Frontier Hotel," Hennessy Sr. recalled. "His father dropped him off at the enclosed backboard there. It was a pretty warm day, and Andre was there about 2½ hours on his own kind of entertaining himself. There was nobody else around. As soon as he hit it one or two or three times against the wall, he picked that ball up and went at it again without saying a peep. That mentality was very interesting for me to see."

At 4, Andre rallied with Jimmy Connors at the old Alan King tournament. Most of Agassi's peers were *making* a racket at that age, not swinging one.

"It happened accidentally," Mike said of the encounter with Connors. "I used to string rackets for Jimmy Connors."

At the time, Connors used the revolutionary Wilson T-2000, which featured an aluminum frame and round head.

"I used to play with that racket," Mike said. "I was one of the few people in town who could string that racket. It was very difficult. Jimmy and his mother brought a few rackets for me to string. Jimmy had seen Andre hit balls, and he said, 'Hey, kid, let's go hit some.' "

Connors, 21 at the time, and Andre rallied for 15 to 20 minutes on a side court and attracted 300 to 400 spectators. Connors won his first Wimbledon singles title a few months later and began a run of 159 consecutive weeks at No. 1, still a record.

"Jimmy was feeding him [balls]," Mike said. "If the ball went too wide, Andre hit it on two or three bounces. After they were through, Andre hit with some 10- and 12-year-old kids."

Connors made a somewhat prophetic statement when he came off the court with Andre.

"He said, 'I'm going to retire when this kid grows up and beats me,' " Mike said. "Andre reminded him of that a couple of times when they played matches. He said, 'Why haven't you retired yet?' "

Andre won both of his professional matches against Connors. Each was in the quarterfinals of the U.S. Open (in 1988 and 1989). Agassi angered the elder statesman after the first victory by saying he expected to win even easier than he did.

Andre has a fantastic memory, anyway, but hitting with Connors at Caesars left a strong impression on him.

"It was on my fourth birthday," Andre said. "It's a part of me I consider very special. You grow up looking at role models and wish you could be half of what they are. It was funny later to get out there and play against him [on the pro tour]."

Another of Andre's early memories is of a crowd of 50-odd awestruck spectators gathering at courtside at the

Tropicana as he hit with tennis Hall of Famer and noted hustler Bobby Riggs.

"I remember being watched," Andre said. "And I remember liking it."

Andre imitated pros as a child while practicing.

"[Andre] would put two balls in his pocket and four in his hand," Mike said. "He'd hit a backhand and say 'Connors,' a forehand and say '[Ilie] Nastase,' an undercut [slice] and say '[Ken] Rosewall,' a volley and say '[Rod] Laver.' "

Andre's favorite player, Mike said, was Bjorn Borg. It was an almost eerie choice in retrospect. Like Borg, Andre would become a Wimbledon champion as a baseliner and a teen heartthrob with shaggy hair. Unlike the stoical Borg, however, Andre would become a showman on the court and frequently lose his temper.

Andre, though, insisted that he's never had any heroes.

"I've always been independent, and I usually find myself looking to who I want to be tomorrow," Andre said. "I'm a perfectionist, so I look at where I want to be in an ideal world — what kind of person and champion I want to be. I've always felt that I can improve on who I am."

When Andre was 5, the Agassis moved into a five-bedroom house in west Las Vegas. When they went to inspect the house, Mike immediately went around to see if there was enough room in the back yard for a tennis court. There was. Betty inspected the house and said all it needed was new carpeting. The Agassis bought the house that night. Mike still had not been inside of it.

That year, Mike built a court with a seven-foot concrete green wall and a 10½-foot fence on top of that for $21,000. He sealed the walls so insects couldn't nest in the small holes in the concrete, sprayed the court once a week for bugs, and made sure there were never cracks in the court.

"Not from craziness, but from love for the game," Mike said.

The court eventually became known as "The Yard" by the countless Las Vegas juniors who received free lessons from Mike.

Andre signed his first autograph at 6 after hitting with Nastase and entered his first tournament at 7, early even for tennis. He played in the 10-and-unders and won his first nine events. Andre rallied with Borg the next year.

"It was just a matter of time," said Mary Rowan, who trained for six years with the Agassi children at their court. "I definitely saw [Andre] becoming one of the best in the world."

Former doubles star David Pate grew up playing Phillip Agassi in Las Vegas and witnessed Andre's stunning development.

"Andre was so good so young, you always knew he was going to be a great player," said Pate, who coaches the popular, wacky Jensen brothers [Luke and Murphy] and owns the tennis concession at Bally's hotel in Las Vegas.

Mike brashly predicted to everyone but the trash collector that Andre would be ranked No. 1 in the world someday.

"Mike has a very unique way of looking at things," Hennessy Sr. said. "I remember him telling me when Andre was about 10 basically the picture you're seeing now. I have to pinch myself to see if I'm in a dream. He was telling me, 'This boy will be the premier tennis player around. Kids will be wearing his shirts and his hats.'

"It's even bigger than what he said. I mean, that's a hard prediction to make. That's an *unbelievable* prediction. Every father kind of dreams that of his own kids, but for him to come out and say that. . . . He's never short on expressing his opinions. The good thing about it is he can back them all up. He backed this up."

Linda Vincent, executive director of the Utah Tennis Association, recalled a conversation with Mike when Andre was 16.

"He told me and my husband, 'My son will be No. 1 in the world one day,' " Vincent said. "We kind of giggled at each other and said, 'Yeah, right.' "

Mary Ann Rivera, who had two tennis-playing sons, said Mike once gave her one of Andre's old warmup jackets. Andre, about 12 at the time, was on tennis manufacturers' "free list" and had more clothes than he could use.

"It was a really good jacket, and it said 'Andre Agassi' on it," said Rivera, the very woman Mike allegedly called a "motherfucker" at the Las Vegas Country Club. "It was for some tournament he won. Mike said to me: "[Imitating a Middle Eastern accent] 'You keep this. He be famous someday. It be worth lot of money.' Of course, I didn't. I don't know who I gave it to after my kids were finished with it, but anyway, I wasn't that smart."

Andre *was* smart, according to his elementary school prinicipal. Andre attended First Good Shepherd Lutheran School in Las Vegas from kindergarten through sixth grade.

"He was an A-B student," said Jim Krafft. "He was an excellent athlete, obviously. He played on our championship soccer team. Math was probably his best subject. He was certainly above average in all his academic areas. His parents were very good about making sure he did his work, just as they were very good about making sure he practiced his tennis. He was very popular. He had an excellent memory."

Mike made sure, though, that Andre's life revolved around tennis.

"Three thousand balls a day, seven days a week," Andre droned.

"Mike was very driven," said Marty Hennessy Jr., who played junior tennis in Las Vegas and now works with Mike at the MGM Grand Hotel/Casino as a bellman. "Everything was always tennis, tennis, tennis. I think that would drive somebody a little nuts, because truthfully, you don't have a childhood that way. You come home from school, and it's off to the court. That's it."

Wendi Stewart said she can't remember a day when Andre didn't play tennis as a child.

"He *always* played," she said.

Andre didn't seem to mind initially. Then again, he didn't have much choice.

"Dad raised me to play," he said. "I never considered doing anything else. As a kid, all you know is what you see around you, and tennis was all I saw. Why would I want to do anything else?"

Rowan said Mike never had to push Andre onto the court.

"I did see [Mike] have to take him *off* the court," Rowan said. "Andre would say, 'Just 20 more, Dad. Just 50 more, Dad.' "

Mike said: "He was hitting with love. I had to force him to stop. I was very afraid he'd get burned out."

To the surprise of more than a few people around town, Andre actually played on another type of court — a basketball court — when he was 10 and 11.

Hans Riehemann convinced Mike to let Andre play on Riehemann's youth basketball team.

"Mike was hesitant at first because he told me that one day Andre was going to be No. 1 in the world, and he did not want him injured playing anything else," said Riehemann, the fitness/tennis coordinator at the Spanish Trail Golf and Country Club in Las Vegas. "I told him I would make sure that he wasn't injured and that I thought he would have a good time playing another sport. I got him on the team, and he was a great guard and a good shooter."

Andre started and averaged 10 to 12 points in the 30-minute games, Riehemann said.

Hennessy Jr. was a teammate of Agassi's.

"Doing a sport he wasn't really used to, he was actually a tremendous athlete," said Hennessy Jr. "He had the utmost respect from everybody on the team. He had one of the best attitudes you could find. He wasn't a ball hog. He was essentially a team player. He would pass the ball whenever needed."

The team — composed of "castoffs," Riehemann said — went 3-12 in the regular season in Andre's first year and 3-14 in his second year. All teams made the playoffs, though, and Andre's squad finished third in the 12-team league each year.

"Either I'm a very bad coach during the regular season, or I know how to prepare the team to peak at the right time," Riehemann said with a laugh.

Playing on the team was a liberating experience for Andre. For one of the few times in his life, he played a sport just for fun. The pressure was off.

"Andre had a ball," Riehemann said. "I think it was a nice change of pace for him from tennis."

There was another benefit, according to Hennessy Jr.

"It got him used to a team attitude and probably helped out with Davis Cup later," Hennessy Jr. said.

There were many millions of tennis balls to hit first, though. Literally.

Mike had 13 ball machines at home. He redesigned them so they would hold 10 times as many balls and set each one for a different shot (topspin, slice, flat, forehand, backhand, volley, serve, return of serve, etc.). He used "only" three machines at once.

"The bottom line is it's not hard to hit the ball," Mike said. "It's hard to hit every type of ball. If a machine gives you only one type of ball, that's all you'll learn. You'll have a one-dimensional game."

The slice machines, Mike said, imparted "by far more backspin than any pro."

The return-of-serve machine propelled balls from a server's point of impact at 110 to 112 mph. Mike put the machine on the baseline, pointed it at a corner of the service box and moved it closer and closer to the net.

"Who can give you 600 to 700 returns of serve on the line?" Mike asked. "Nobody."

Rowan vividly recalled returning off the serve machine.

"You wouldn't even stand in the return position [facing the net]," she said. "You'd stand sideways with the racket back because that puppy was humming."

And you wonder why Andre returns serve so well?

Each machine propelled 20 or 30 balls a minute.

"If a kid is over there [on the other side of the net] for two hours, he has hit well over 3,000 balls," Mike said.

Thirty-two garbage cans full of balls lined the sides of the court. In all, Mike had 30,000 balls at one time. By the end of the day, there would be 10,000 balls on the court. No problem. Mike had a scheme to pick them up as efficiently as possible.

Mike had four giant blowers — the kind used to dry baseball fields after rain — to blow the balls to one side. The place must have been noisier than nearby McCarran International Airport.

Then Mike got out his invention called "the pusher," an eight-foot-long beam of steel on wheels that pushed the balls into one corner. Then Mike brought out "the scoopers." There were several sizes of scoopers so that children of all ages could pick up balls. The biggest was a massive shovel that could hold hundreds of balls. The smallest held about 30 balls.

"If they don't help, they take everything for granted," Mike said.

Mike tolerated no nonsense on the court.

"When you go on a tennis court [for a lesson], I want you to have more respect and be quieter than if you were in a church," he said. "If you talk during a match, you don't hit the ball good. I want nothing between tennis and learning. There's nothing wrong with that. . . . When you put all your life, love and every dime you make into tennis, all the talk is serious. Is that rough? I don't know."

Rowan didn't think so.

"Mike expected 100 percent," she said. "That's all he asked. Everything else was free. He loves children and tennis. He expected 100 percent from Andre, and he got it.

Andre had great love and respect for his dad. He certainly never feared him.

"People try to portray Mike as very intimidating. That was never the case. He could be a very warm, gentle, tender man with Andre as well as the other kids. He's a very physical person. Mike was not afraid to kiss all of us on the forehead when we'd do something well. Sometimes if you didn't, he'd grab the racket out of your hand and show you how to do it.

"I would categorize him as a tough coach but very fair. You always knew where you stood. You never had to guess because he'd tell you. [His concern] was not necessarily executing better. It was primarily geared around effort.

"He can have a difficult temper at times, but I don't think I've ever met a more generous person. He'd hit us two or three thousand balls and then take us out to dinner. He worked the graveyard shift [at Bally's]. He would get home at 7 A.M. and get up by 9 A.M. because all these kids were there for a workout. All his money went into tennis. It [the lessons] was something I never could have afforded."

Rowan, who played at Western High School in Las Vegas, said Mike once advised her to use topspin lobs in an upcoming Southern Nevada final.

"He hit me a thousand topspin lobs and came to my match," she said. "I won, 6-0, 6-0."

Stewart said Mike did intimidate Andre. Even she, however, praised him highly.

Mike criticized Andre harshly and relentlessly, according to Stewart and Bollettieri.

"I mean, it used to drive . . . me . . . nuts. I wanted to lock Mike in his room, because it was always *something*," said Stewart, who trained with the Agassi children at their court when she was 9 and 10. "Like if Andre didn't *play* well, or if he didn't go get a linesman when he should have. I mean, it was *serious*. It was not just [junior] tennis, it was *really* serious."

In 1984, Andre won the National Boys Indoor 16-and-under singles and doubles titles at 14 years old.

"Every time he played a match, he had to report the result to his father, but no matter how well Andre did, he never quite seemed to measure up to Mr. Agassi's expectations," Bollettieri wrote in *My Aces, My Faults*. "If Andre called Las Vegas and said, 'Dad, I won two and two,' meaning 6-2 and 6-2, Mike would say, 'Why wasn't it love and love?' Mike never congratulated Andre and often excoriated him."

Mike's language was laced with profanity, Stewart said.

"I heard him say probably everything there was to say, and we were young kids," she said.

Then, in the next breath, Stewart said Mike "was always sweet to me. I would go play tennis at his house every weekend, and he was always sweet to me."

Of course, Mike wasn't trying to mold Stewart into a champion.

"As hard as Mike was — and he had a *hard* side — he also had this soft side," Stewart said. "He had a big heart, and he loved Andre . . . *loved* him. But he was just so backward about doing anything about it.

"I would spend the night there on Fridays when we were little, and he would take us to the movies. We'd wake up Saturday and hit on the ball machines all day long, and he'd take us out to dinner and the movies. He was *so* nice. He'd buy my ticket, and he didn't have a lot of money. He had this good side. He wasn't evil. It wasn't like he was straight from hell. He had this side that was hell-bent on having a champion."

Even Rita Agassi is baffled by her dad.

"There are people you can talk to about my dad," she said, "and they think he's the sweetest, kindest guy you'd ever meet, and there are people you can talk to about my dad, and they say he's evil, he's this, that and the other thing. I don't know how to describe my dad."

Mike didn't care who was around when he swore.

"It was just his vocabulary," Stewart said. "He would speak that way to everybody. He had a temper. It wasn't 'the tennis court,' it was 'the *fucking* tennis court.' It was always something like that. His favorite was [imitating a Middle Eastern accent], 'Sons of *bitches*,' " Stewart added with a laugh.

Stewart said she never saw Mike hit Andre.

"Andre was very, *very* obedient [to his father]," she said. "I think he was afraid. I mean, we were little kids. . . . Mike would whistle. He had this certain whistle. There were like 10 courts at [the old Cambridge Racket Club]. Andre would be all the way at the other end, and he would hear this whistle. He would get his stuff, and he would run because he knew his dad was waiting. He knew he was going to get an earful if he didn't hightail it."

Did Betty Agassi ever object to Mike's treatment of Andre?

"I never saw it," Stewart said. "She would just kind of shrug it off, like, 'You know your dad. . . . ' Maybe once in a blue moon she would, but she was very, very much in the background and not heard from much. I used to wonder why she didn't, but they just work different. I don't remember her ever saying anything [in defense of Andre] . . . and I wanted somebody to, because it really wasn't my place."

Mike did praise Andre, according to Stewart.

"Oh yeah," she said. "He told us from the time we were kids that Andre was going to be a champion. He loved it when Andre would hit the hell out of the ball. He absolutely loved it. He just said, 'Hit the hell out of the ball, and one day it'll go in.' "

Former junior player Chris Entzel of Las Vegas agreed that Andre was intimidated by his father, but said Andre never resented him.

"Andre was in love with the game," Entzel said. "He took the criticism and used it wisely. . . .

"Mike is a genius when it comes to tennis. He has helped a lot of people with their games."

Andre said he did not have "by any means an abusive childhood; after all, I loved the game for a lot of years. The only thing that took my love away from the game for a few years was being at Nick Bollettieri's academy in Florida. That was way too much for any child to go through.

"But in every area of life, you run into complications and struggles. It's unfair to think that just because I'm so successful at what I do these days that there aren't huge costs involved, so I have talked heavily about the cost. By the same token, I wouldn't trade it for the world. It's been quite a learning experience, and I don't believe in regrets. This has been my journey, and I'm very proud of it."

*   *   *

Andre and Mike carved legendary reputations in the juniors — Andre for his talent and Mike for his perfectionism, meddling and temper.

"When kids played Andre," Rivera said, "we didn't count how many *games* they got, we counted how many *points* they got. They never got games . . . unless he gave them to them. There were a few exceptions, but my kid wasn't one of them."

Matt Rivera, a 26-year-old stockbroker in Las Vegas, said he played Agassi "five or seven times" in the juniors.

"Andre *killed* me in the juniors," said Matt, who won four state high school singles championships and played No. 3 and No. 4 singles at UNLV. "He could beat me whatever he wanted to beat me — love and love, whatever. He did that to just about everyone. He was spectacular, unbelievable."

As Andre's occasional doubles partner, Matt also benefited from the prodigy's talent. They won the Intermountain Sectional boys' 14-and-under title together in Las Vegas.

"He was so good, I could play in the doubles alley and let Andre do all the work," Matt recalled. "[The opponents] were trying to hit to me, but it was pretty tough when I was in the doubles alley. If they hit the ball to him, he was going to hit a winner. It was that easy. He was head and shoulders above everybody. Even then he was one of a kind. From his serve to his groundstrokes, he was on another level that no one in the section or country had seen."

Including Andy Potter, a former junior player from Denver. Potter was winless in three singles matches and three doubles contests against Agassi.

"The closest I came in singles was 6-4, 6-2," said Potter, an assistant tennis pro at the Colorado Athletic Club at Inverness in Englewood, Colo. "His confidence at that age was unbelievable. He had the mental edge on everybody. He knew [how good he was] — the way he walked, the way he talked, everything. He was cocky to an extent, but he had every right to be cocky. Everybody just felt intimidated by his presence. He'd walk around, and there'd be kind of a glow. Everybody was just kind of, 'Whoa.' He was that good."

Future pro player Jeff Tarango of Manhattan Beach, Calif., said he beat Agassi once in four or five junior matches.

"He was definitely unique," said Tarango, who gained international notoriety in 1995 when he accused French chair umpire Bruno Rebeuh of corruption and stormed off the court during a third-round match at Wimbledon. "You just didn't want to get him mad. He was always moody. You'd win the first set 7-5, and if you said, 'C'mon, let's go,' he'd beat you, 6-1, 6-1.

"I remember him playing one guy who was up 4-0. Andre said, 'You're not going to win another game.' I think the guy won three points the rest of the match. And this was a good player."

Agassi also mowed down a couple of pretty fair Southern California juniors named Pete Sampras and Michael Chang.

Sampras, who grew up in the Los Angeles area, was 9 and Agassi 10 when they first squared off at a tournament in the L.A. suburb of Northridge, Calif.

"He toyed with me for about two hours," Sampras recalled.

Sampras added that Agassi "used as many trick shots as I had ever seen. He was kind of a hot dog."

There are amazing similarities between Sampras' junior coach, Dr. Pete Fischer, and Mike Agassi. Both were "mad scientists" with no formal tennis background. Both were blunt perfectionists and taught for free. Unlike Mike, however, Fischer emphasized the long term.

"That might have been the difference between him and Mike Agassi," Sampras said. "Andre's father was more concerned with winning."

Chang and Agassi played about a dozen times in the juniors with Agassi winning every time.

"The most difficult thing about playing Andre when he was younger was the spins," said Chang, who also grew up in the L.A. area, but moved to the Las Vegas suburb of Henderson, Nev., in 1991. "He would play unbelievable spins, really wild. Occasionally, he'd throw in an underhand serve. It would land within two feet of the net [on the other side] and totally spin off to the side. You couldn't do anything."

Chang, meanwhile, gave little indication of future stardom, according to Agassi.

"Believe it or not, he was even smaller then," Agassi said. "He had a little more difficult time covering the court, so his speed was never a problem [for opponents]. His strengths didn't kick in until he was 18."

That is an interesting statement, considering that Chang, who is listed at 5 feet nine inches and 150 pounds, won the French Open at 17.

Agassi did not dominate national junior tournaments, however.

"At the national level, he was a little different," said Potter, who competed in many of the same national tournaments. "Everybody wasn't intimidated by him."

Agassi won four national junior doubles titles (14-and-under Indoors twice, 16-and-under Indoors once and

16s once), but only one singles crown (16-and-under Indoors). He turned pro one week after his 16th birthday.

"He was so talented, so far ahead of everybody, that
he didn't have that killer instinct as far as winning tough
matches," Potter said. "He would always kind of drop off
in the third set. He felt he shouldn't even be going into the
third set with some of these guys.

"He plays his best when he's real loose. If he feels
like he's getting threatened by someone, he kind of tightens
up and starts missing a lot of shots. He was always a make-
or-break player anyway. He hit the ball so much harder
than anyone else."

David Kass said he was 8-0 against Agassi in the juniors, all in national tournaments. But Kass, who attended
the Bollettieri academy with Agassi, peaked at No. 288 in
the pros before retiring in 1994.

"My style was more suited for the juniors and less
for the pros," said Kass, a real-estate developer in Colum-
bus, Ohio. "Andre's was less suited for the juniors and
more for the pros. He was aggressive and went for a lot of
big shots. When you're young and not that big, it's tough to
make them. By the time you get older and bigger and
stronger, it becomes easier to make them.

"He was willing to go for his shots and make a lot of
errors whereas I was just more of a steady player. I would
just get the ball back and frustrate him. He had a lot more
talent than I did, but he would get frustrated a little with
my game.

"His father told me after the last time we played that
the next time they saw my name in the draw near Andre's
at a tournament, they were going to fly home."

Agassi's highest national junior ranking was No. 4
— in the 12-and-unders in 1982 and the 14-and-unders
in 1984.

"He was always underrated," said Mike Agassi.
"He's beaten all the No. 1 [junior] players."

Andre knew he was special and acted that way,
sources said.

Tom Dye, an assistant news editor at the *Las Vegas Review-Journal* and recreational tennis player, recalled an incident when Andre was 11 or 12.

"I was playing doubles at Spanish Oaks two courts down from Andre, who was practicing very intently with someone who was giving him instruction," Dye said. "A couple of balls from our court landed on his court. The Spanish Oaks pro informed us that Andre wanted us thrown out because of the errant tennis balls and because we were making too much noise. The pro was apologetic about Andre's attitude and moved us to another court."

Kellogg said he did not recall the incident.

Even Rogers wanted to "kick [Andre's] ass" initially.

Rogers met Agassi at a junior tournament when they were 12 and 11, respectively. Rogers had the hots for Tami, David Higdon reported in *Tennis*, and figured the fastest way to her heart was through Andre. Rogers had just won the doubles title, but Agassi fell in singles.

"Don't feel bad," Rogers told Agassi, "you didn't play your game."

Agassi sniffed, "Who the hell are you?"

As Agassi stomped off, the insulted Rogers turned to his doubles partner and declared: "I'm the guy who's going to kick his ass, that's who I am."

But the sensitive Agassi has always sought approval because he never got much from his father. After Agassi got wind of Rogers' plot, he called Rogers and invited him to a movie. As Rogers prowled the dark theater in search of his prey, he heard Agassi whisper for him.

"I'm going there to beat him up, and there was this little guy, with his bowl cut," Rogers recalled. "I thought to myself: He's too nice. But what he was, actually, was scared. We talked, and from then on we've been best friends."

*   *   *

Mike insisted that Andre win, many sources said.

"If Andre got a second-place or third-place trophy, it was destroyed," Stewart said. "Second place wasn't good enough. It was first or nothing. There was a lot of heat on a little boy."

Entzel corroborated Stewart's story.

"Mike was really caught up with being No. 1," he said. "He used to make comments like, 'We don't accept second best.' I remember one time Andre lost in the final of a tournament, and his father took the trophy and smashed it all over the ground."

Entzel said he played Andre 40 times in the juniors, winning once.

"When I beat him, I remember his father being furious," Entzel said. "Andre and I were pretty good friends, but Mike said Andre was not going to hang around with me anymore."

Mike reacted strongly to Entzel's charges.

"I worked with that kid [Entzel] free for several years," Mike said. "To say things like that, I wouldn't do that to my enemy."

Entzel's charge of accepting nothing less than No. 1 was "the most ridiculous statement," Mike said. "I want each person to be the best he can be."

The trophy incident wasn't as simple as Entzel described, according to Mike.

"The trophy cost $1.50," Mike said. "Andre said he didn't want it. I said, 'Go give it back or throw it away.' He gave it to me, and I smashed it on the ground."

As for allegedly refusing to let Entzel associate with Andre, Mike said: "I didn't tell him not to talk to my son. He stopped coming over to our house, but he was welcome to."

Mike said he wanted Andre to believe he was the best.

Andre got the message.

"Andre was a very persistent young man," said Hennessy Jr. "He *had* to be the best. His father definitely put that into him. Mike didn't allow him *not* to be the best."

As Rita said, though, winning was expected. If Andre didn't win, Mike went through the roof.

"My father put a lot of pressure on me to not accept losing," Andre said on *60 Minutes* in 1995. "I never felt pressured to win. I felt pressured just to not accept losing — to absolutely believe beyond any shadow of a doubt that you shouldn't have lost and what are you going to do to not accept losing the next time?"

Mike didn't wait until after matches to offer advice.

"Andre's dad was always on the sidelines and shouting back to him: [imitating a Middle Eastern accent] 'Get back to ready position. . . . What are you doing? . . . Blah, blah, blah,' " said Hennessy Jr.

Andre's reaction?

"Andre usually tried to ignore it," Hennessy Jr. said with a laugh. "Because it would be ignored, his father would either get louder or get a little angrier. It definitely drove Andre a little batty. There were a couple of times when we had to have Mr. Agassi taken away from the court.

"I'm very happy Andre has gotten to where he did. For being pushed that hard, instead of going off the deep end, he handled the pressures."

But Hennessy Jr. added: "I don't want to be pinned with too many negatives. His father's a great guy."

The pressure affected Andre on the court, according to former Utah Tennis Association administrator Sterling Patrick.

"There were matches I watched where Andre's behavior would change when his father would come to the courts because he wanted so much to win when his father was watching and to please his father," Patrick said. "He would go from a very sportsmanlike and friendly player to a very intense and very critical player."

Critical of his opponent?

"And of himself and of his surroundings — just more intense," Patrick said. "And closer on his [line] calls — not giving benefit of the doubt necessarily, but not openly cheating either."

Andre was well-behaved most of the time, observers said.

"He knew he was going to win, so he always had that air of confidence," Potter said. "If he was coming close to losing, or felt tight, he'd get a little bit upset."

Hennessy Sr. paused when asked about Andre's behavior.

"How do you explain that?" Hennessy Sr. said. "He would get upset like the other kids, and he showed his emotion a lot like he does today."

How?

"I really don't want to get into too much negativity with the family," Hennessy Sr. said.

Mike, meanwhile, repeatedly had confrontations with administrators and other parents.

One former administrator said, on the condition of anonymity, that Mike "had four or five words he used over and over, usually prefaced by 'mother.' He always made accusations — coaching [players during matches, which is forbidden], petty things, the very things he was probably doing more of than anyone."

Tarango, a former scholar-athlete award winner at Stanford University, recalled his lone victory over Andre in the juniors. He said it came in Southern California when he was 8 and Agassi 7.

"That was quite an experience," Tarango said with a chuckle. "We were so young. I won 7-6 in the third [set], 5-4 in the tiebreaker. I got a linesman after the first set, and one of his girlfriends ended up being a linesman. They took volunteers back then, and she volunteered, but I didn't know she was one of his girlfriends.

"I won the first set, and he won the second set, but he was getting a lot of really good calls," Tarango continued with a laugh. "In the third set, the SCTA [Southern California Tennis Association] actually replaced her. I remember it was 4-3 for him [in the tiebreaker]. I won a real long point, then it was 4 all. I think he got overruled on that point to make it my match.

"He was crying after that. And then he had to endure the drive back to Vegas with his father. We always used to speculate what went on in that van, but we never knew for sure."

How did Mike act during the match?

"Well . . . ummm . . . it was a circus," Tarango said. "It was a definite circus, let's put it that way. My mom was there with me, and the next time we went to a tournament that he was there, my dad came because my mom didn't feel she should be there alone. It was pretty ugly. For parents to handle themselves that way. . . . It kind of epitomizes junior tennis, but at the same time, it was pretty bad."

Tarango would not elaborate, and his parents did not return several calls.

Said ex-Intermountain tournament director Lee Hammell: "The biggest problem in junior tennis is the parents, not the players. Mike was very aggressive, overzealous."

Sampras' father, meanwhile, was as relaxed as Mike was intense. Soterios (Sam) Sampras once said, "Whatever makes Pete happy makes his mother and I happy."

Of course, Sam Sampras had Fischer to apply the pressure for him. But Pete didn't have to live with Fischer.

"The main thing is [Mike] had a fiery temper, and you would not get in his way if he was on fire," a Las Vegas teaching pro said, on the condition of anonymity. "I mean, just *fuming* . . . if somebody was cheating his kid [on a line call] or something [negative] happened out there, he just took it so personally because it was him out there you were playing almost. Those are kids he trained.

"It's just like when I coach kids, [the opponent] is playing me because I've worked with the child. But you can't get involved because that's their scenario. But he would get involved and scream things and had to be restrained sometimes."

Gene Corrigan, an Intermountain president and grievance committee chairman in the 1980s, said he once wrote Mike a letter threatening to ban Andre from a sectional tournament in Colorado if Mike came.

"I really didn't have any authority to do that, but we were trying to get a message to [Mike]," said Corrigan, a lawyer who works for a large accounting firm in Sacramento, Calif. "He's OK, except at those tournaments.

"I had reports that he had hit somebody at one tournament — the parent of another player — and that he tended to intimidate opponents of Andre. There was never any suggestion that Andre was misbehaving.

"I discussed it with Mike's lawyer, and he said, 'How about if I draft an agreement that Mike will behave and you'll let him come to the tournament, and you won't interfere with Andre's playing?' I said, 'Fine.'

"So that's what we did. To the best of my knowledge, Mike was never a problem at any other tournament after that."

Another ex-administrator, requesting anonymity, said he "wrote a letter to Mike complaining of coaching, profanity, physical abuse of a male chaperone and destruction of [Andre's] second-place trophy. There was no response that I remember. I don't think [Andre] ever came back."

Back in Las Vegas, Stewart said Mike "would carry a hammer and hit the railing at Cambridge. It was like this tin railing that would echo all the way down 12 courts. He was just absolutely bizarre."

When asked why Mike carried a hammer, Stewart said: "I have no idea. I guess if somebody was going to mess with him."

Mike said he was protecting his children in his disputes.

"I have never let someone come between my kids and me," he said. "I'm always suspicious of any parents or outsiders coming to my kids. I've watched them like a hawk so they won't be kidnapped. A lot of kids have been sexually abused."

Mike was convinced that the tennis establishment was against his family, and he transmitted that belief to his children. Mike was the ultimate tennis outsider: a middle-class Armenian in a rich-man's sport who lived in the desert and had all these wacky ideas.

"If I wasn't behind Andre, brainwashing him that he was great, that it didn't matter what they did to us, the kid would have quit," Mike said. "What's wrong with American tennis? I could give you 10,000 reasons. They did everything they could to take away his desire."

Said Andre: "They made me want to turn pro to escape them."

Mike said he once told the United States Tennis Association (USTA): "One day you're going to beg me for Andre to play Davis Cup, and I'm going to give you my middle finger. The first time he played, they thanked me. They knew I had problems with the USTA. I said, 'Let's forget about the past.' "

Las Vegan Sandy Tueller, president of the ITA and the Nevada Tennis Association in the early 1980s, said Mike tried to "buck the system" but sympathizes with him in retrospect.

"There's a set format that we have for kids to go through locals and sectionals," said Tueller, now chair-woman of the USTA Junior Competition Committee. "Probably Mike was right on this. Because Andre was so good, he didn't really get any competition on the Intermountain level.

"At the time, the Intermountain was real strict about the kids doing that, so Andre just bypassed the system, moved up an age group, and did very well. Mike made the right decision, I'm sure, for Andre at the time. Since then, we're a lot more flexible about exceptional players not having to abide by the same process."

Mike sometimes won his arguments.

Tennis reported that officials once planned to ban Mike from a regional tournament. A 13-year-old girl had claimed, erroneously said Mike, that he had cursed her at an event. Mike spent $10,000 in attorney fees and other costs, but he won.

At other times, Mike reluctantly succumbed to the system.

"I took Andre to Shreveport, La., for the national 12-and-unders," he said. "The guy running the tournament had a right to give eight wild cards [special invitations to those who wouldn't otherwise qualify for whatever reason]. I took him out to dinner and kissed his ass to put my son in the tournament. He did. Andre lost in the final."

Rita defended her father.

"Armenians have this idea of family," she said. "You protect your family and do what's right. My dad has lived his whole life protecting his family and doing what's right, or at least what he *believed* was right.

"And he did protect us. After my tires were slashed, he altered things to where nobody would be able to get that close to do things like that."

Mike was no more fond of tennis parents than administrators.

"When you're No. 1 in California, and you have a dream, and you lose to somebody in Nevada, I'm putting a mark on your dream," he said. "Tennis parents are phonies. They can't see anybody better than their own child. I love to see somebody beat Andre to see how they did it."

Said Rita: "Other parents were resentful because what my dad did worked. My father never held anyone back. He helped anyone he could. Other people are selfish. They're only interested in their own kids. They totally resented the fact that Andre was good."

Riehemann, the president of the Nevada Tennis Association from 1986 to 1990, had a novel way of dealing with Mike.

"My feeling with Mike — knowing his background, whether it was justified or not — was to deal with him head on," Riehemann said. "I told him where I stood, he told me where he stood, and we got along famously.

"One of the best moves I ever made — which a lot of people questioned at the time — was when I was president of the NTA, I made him chairman of a couple of committees. They said, 'Why would you put this hothead as a chairman of a couple of committees?' I said, 'Hey, he can't do me any harm being the chairman.' If he wasn't the chairman, he'd be attacking the chairman, based upon his reputation.

"So it ended up working out great. He didn't want to be real active because of teaching his kids tennis and his job and everything else, but whenever I needed help, he was always there to help me."

Everyone agrees that Mike has mellowed since Andre's junior days.

"He's changed now," Kellogg said. "He's got what he wanted."

Even Kellogg said he doesn't dislike Mike, who once threatened to "waste" Kellogg.

"He's never really apologized for what he did [over the years], but he has intimated it," Kellogg said. "He told me, 'I grew up fighting in Iran. That's what I learned.' "

*   *   *

The question remains: Why was Mike obsessed with producing a tennis champion? There are several theories:

- The American dream. "My dad was bound and determined to better the lives of his family, no matter what it took," Rita said.
- A love of tennis. "He was a boxer and didn't want his son playing a contact sport," Andre said. "He got fascinated with [tennis] when he was about 25 years old."
- Perfectionism. "Mike is consumed," Rogers said. "Andre is the vehicle through which he satiates his desire to see tennis played the way he thinks it should be."
- Insecurity. Mike almost invariably refers to Andre as "my son" rather than by name. It's as if Mike is

taking credit for Andre's success, which would be largely justified. Observers insisted, though, that Mike was not living vicariously through his children.

"That's just not what Mike's about," said Mary Ann Rivera. "He wanted the best for those kids, not for himself. I don't think it was an ego trip on his part one bit."

Riehemann said: "I know from having been around junior tennis here in town that a lot of parents live their life vicariously through their children. Mike acted a lot different than some of these other parents.

"Mike *drove* his kids, but it was a different way of driving. He knew his kids had athletic ability. Mike knew their strengths and weaknesses. Some of these other parents who had no athletic training in their background whatsoever, they just *assumed* their kids had this ability. Mike actually knew what he had to work with."

Mike said several years ago, however, that he regretted his obsession with producing a tennis champion. All the years of working full-time, staggering out of bed with a few hours of sleep, teaching tennis under a blazing sun, keeping the ball machines humming, driving to California for tournaments and battling tennis administrators and parents took their toll on Mike.

"If I live again, I won't do what I have done," Mike said. "Working with kids and [developing] a Wimbledon champion is more difficult than winning a jackpot or the California Lottery. I would teach kids to learn memory and speed reading. You can have an easy life. People who go this route, I want them to know how difficult it is."

Las Vegas: On A Roll

The question irritated Agassi.

On the eve of the 1995 Davis Cup semifinals between the United States and Sweden, at Caesars Palace, a Swedish reporter asked Agassi what it was like to grow up in Las Vegas.

"I grew up in a hotel, actually," Agassi said snidely, repeating an old wives' tale about Las Vegans.

Turning serious, Agassi added wearily: "I answer this question probably more than any other. Living here is quite different than visiting here. I've been to Caesars maybe once in 10 years. [Las Vegas] is a beautiful place to live. I live out in the west near the base of the mountains. The views are some of the best I've seen. It's a nice, quiet lifestyle."

Because of legalized gambling, Las Vegas might be the most unusual — some would say phoniest — city in the world. How many cities do you know with nine of the 10 biggest hotels in the world? Valet parking at the airport?

More than 6,000 new residents a month? Water sports and snow skiing available within a one-hour drive? A drive-up window at a wedding chapel? No corporate or personal income tax?

But as Agassi's experience indicates, Las Vegas is also one of the most misunderstood cities in the world. To non-residents, it's as mysterious as Mars. They seem to think Las Vegas consists only of the Strip.

One Floridian who had never been to Las Vegas mentioned the galaxy of lights on the Strip and asked a local resident seriously, "You do sleep, don't you?" The implication was that the lights on the Strip shine through the windows in every household and render sleep impossible. Not so. When the resident told her he lives 10 miles from the Strip, she asked warily of Las Vegas, "So it's normal, right?"

In fact, there are two Las Vegases. One is the Strip and nearby casinos. The other is the rest of the city, which is much like anywhere else.

"We operate totally outside the world of the casinos," said Alan Bond, the manager of a mall east of the Strip and father of three young children. "We just think of them as a blob of real estate downtown that we avoid with a passion."

Agassi lives on a golf course in the exclusive Spanish Trail walled development several miles west of the Strip. His three-bedroom, two-story house is comfortable but hardly spectacular. Mike Agassi said Andre is moving to a larger house to accommodate him and Brooke Shields.

Another Spanish Trail resident is Atlanta Braves pitcher Greg Maddux, who won four straight Cy Young Awards from 1992 through 1995. The normally mild-mannered Maddux, whose profile is as low as Agassi's is high, also gets defensive about Las Vegas. When asked why he lives there, he said: "It's my home. I grew up there. I have family and friends there. It's the people I know in the city that make the city for me.

"People think Las Vegas is the Strip — a bunch of lights, a lot of gambling, drinking and prostitutes. It's not like that. We got parks, Little League, churches, theaters, Denny's — all the things other cities have. The Strip is an extra bonus. We have the best entertainment in the world.

"If you want to go to the park and feed the ducks with your kids, you can do that. But if you have insomnia and want to knock out the grocery list at 3 A.M., they'll have a slot machine in the store."

Agassi purchased four lots in the even-more-exclusive Spanish Hills Estates, one mile further west on the outskirts of Las Vegas, in 1992. He built houses for his parents and trainer, Gil Reyes, on two of the lots. A huge health spa occupies the third lot, and an immaculate tennis court with a state-of-the-art lighting system sits on the fourth. Andre trains at the spa and tennis court.

The names of two streets bordering the property were changed to Andre Drive and Agassi Court. Some Las Vegans branded Andre an egomaniac for having the audacity to request the change, but Mike said it was his doing.

"My son doesn't give a damn what the streets are named," Mike said at the time. "But I'm 62 years old, and I'm going to live here the rest of my life. I'm so proud of my son, why not have my streets named after him?"

Minnesota Vikings quarterback Randall Cunningham, who starred at UNLV, lives up the hill in an 11,000-square-foot home. He calls Spanish Hills "the Beverly Hills of Las Vegas."

Agassi said the biggest misconception about him is that he's as flamboyant off the court as on it.

"One of the realities that seems to shock most people as they get closer to me is how simple and, quite honestly, boring my life is," Agassi said. "I go about my day as any normal person goes about his day."

Except that Agassi is probably busier and more intense. Agassi probably gets his drive from his father. But whereas Mike's was focused on tennis, Andre's is divided among his Christianity, his family and friends, tennis, the

Andre Agassi Foundation for underprivileged children and golf.

"There's a lot more to me than just tennis," Agassi said. "If you spent a day with me, that's the least part you'd want to ask me about. My interest in life is personal growth. Faith in God is the strongest part of my life."

World-class tennis players are not known as deep thinkers, but Agassi is introspective and inquisitive.

Agassi "really likes to talk to people, have long discussions about life, friends, responsibility," said Rogers, Agassi's best friend since childhood.

And golf. Although Agassi plays tennis right-handed, he is a left-handed golfer with a plus 2.2 handicap. Agassi out-drove professional golfer Robert Gamez of Las Vegas in Gamez's charity tournament in 1993.

Agassi is a self-taught golfer.

"I took a couple of lessons once," he said. "I'm not very coachable."

Phillip Agassi said Andre "loves golf. He'll talk to you about golf 10 times faster than about tennis."

Agassi was so busy one day last December, he didn't have time for golf, although it's warm enough to play year round in Las Vegas. *USA TODAY* reported that Agassi discussed business deals with Rogers, scheduled tennis exhibitions and considered Davis Cup media requests with Phillip, submitted to an interview over lunch, played Santa Claus at the foundation's Christmas party for 300 local underprivileged children, held a dinner with Shields for the 10-member staff of Agassi Enterprises and worked out from midnight to 2:45 A.M.

The workout, according to *USA TODAY*, included two hours of grueling weight training in his gym followed by 45 minutes of nonstop, high-intensity aerobics on seven state-of-the-art exercise machines side-by-side on a wall he calls "Death Row."

At other times, Agassi sprints 300 yards up the hill behind the complex a dozen times. Each sprint is faster than the one before. Then he races up the hill in a series of shorter sprints: 100 yards, 80, 60, 40.

Reyes never intends to make Agassi throw up in these sessions they call "training camp," but it never fails to happen, according to *USA TODAY*.

Agassi has been known to pop into the Muleteer Restaurant at the Flying J Travel Plaza, a truck stop, at 3 or 4 A.M.

"I don't think he ever comes in by himself," said waitress Jo Ellen White. "He's always with his brother, a group of guys or Brooke."

The Muleteer, one of Agassi's favorite restaurants in Las Vegas, is about as far removed from the tea room at Wimbledon as you can get, which is probably just the way Agassi wants it. The conversation at the Muleteer is unlikely to revolve around topspin lobs. Brands of chewing tobacco maybe.

The dining room smells like one of those deodorizers you buy at the car wash.

But the food is good, the waitress calls you "hon" and Agassi can eat in peace.

Agassi, who has tried to improve his diet with varying degrees of success over the years, favors the "Santa Fe" skillet breakfast, White said. The Santa Fe consists of eggs, cheese and sausage scrambled together. A typical lunch for Agassi, White said, is a grilled cheese sandwich, french fries and a cup of soup.

White described Agassi as "very polite, very nice."

Now Agassi can eat at his own restaurant, though. He is a partner with fellow sports stars Ken Griffey Jr. (baseball), Wayne Gretzky (ice hockey), Shaquille O'Neal (basketball), Monica Seles and Joe Montana (retired from football) in the Official All Star Cafe chain.

An All Star Cafe opened on the Las Vegas Strip in December 1996, joining previous outlets in New York and Cancun, Mexico. All Star Cafes were also set to open this year in Atlanta; Chicago; Orlando, Fla.; Miami; Atlantic City, N.J.; Myrtle Beach, S.C.; and Melbourne, Australia.

Michael Paskevich of the *Las Vegas Review-Journal* called the All Star Cafe on the Strip "part American restaurant, part memorabilia-laden celebrity hangout and part traditional sports bar on steroids."

The restaurant occupies three floors and 36,000 square feet. It operates two kitchens to feed a capacity of 600 — "or 400 if Shaquille shows up with a bunch of his friends," joked Lee Knolton, operations director for the All Star. The bustling restaurant is not the place to go for a romantic dinner, but it is the place to go if you're a sports fan.

The All Star Cafe is designed like a stadium or arena. The circular first floor is known as the "arena level," the second as the "sky box area" and the third as the "outfield." A big-screen scoreboard hangs in the middle, televisions line the walls and banks of stadium-style lighting loom above the second floor.

Customers are called "fans," waiters wear jerseys and the doors of the managers' offices have "coach" and "assistant coach" printed on them. The menu is divided into Top of the Order (appetizers), Field of Greens (salads), Bull Pen (hamburgers), sidelines (side orders), Main Event (entrees) and Home Stretch (desserts). The favorite dish of each partner is listed. Agassi's is the linguine pomodoro (fresh chopped tomatoes, garlic and basil, tossed with linguine and Parmesan cheese for $9.50).

Truck loads of authentic sports memorabilia are displayed throughout the restaurant. Among the items are a Babe Ruth bat and autographed picture; Michael Jordan's autographed jersey from the United States Olympic "Dream Team;" boxing gloves signed by Muhammad Ali; a Jack Nicklaus golf bag; and a jersey, glove and hat from Maddux.

Each of the partners has a blue caged locker on the first floor featuring his or her memorabilia. Agassi's includes the white Nike jacket and tennis shoes he wore when he won Wimbledon in 1992. A glassed-in display on the first floor features his tennis outfits, his shoes, a broken racket and a credential from the 1996 Olympics.

A lounge called the "Agassi room" on the second floor is devoted to his memorabilia. Among the more unusual items is a photograph of Agassi pitching horseshoes with George Bush at the White House in 1990. The former president signed the photograph and wrote, "Andre, go for it!" Also displayed are scores of trophies and plaques, old tennis outfits, other photos, Agassi's old ponytail and an expired passport of his. Agassi's Olympic gold medal and Grand Slam trophies, however, are in his house.

Not long ago, though, Agassi's neighborhood was nothing but dirt and sagebrush.

*   *   *

Southern Paiute Indians had resided in the Las Vegas Valley for hundreds of years when the first Europeans arrived in the 1820s. The settlers found a grassy area created by springs that have since dried up and named the place Las Vegas, Spanish for "the meadows." In 1829, a New Mexican merchant, Antonio Armijo, crossed Southern Nevada on his way to California. His route became known as the Spanish Trail, hence the name of Agassi's residential development. Mormons tried to establish a mission in the Las Vegas Valley in 1855 but abandoned the effort two years later.

Las Vegas was founded when a railroad linking Salt Lake City and Los Angeles via the Las Vegas Valley was completed in 1905. By the late 1920s, Las Vegas had a population of only 5,000. The legalization of gambling and easy divorce and the construction of nearby Hoover Dam, all in the 1930s, set the stage for future growth.

In the 1940s, Nellis Air Force Base was established, and the world's largest magnesium processing plant (for bombs used in World War II) was built. Tourists flocked to the Nevada Test Site, established 60 miles north of Las Vegas in 1950, to witness the testing of atomic weapons. By then, the population of Clark County, which includes Las Vegas, was 48,589.

Resorts began to sprout up on the Strip — the four-mile stretch of Highway 91 (now Las Vegas Boulevard) south of downtown, named after Sunset Strip in Los Angeles — after a crackdown on illegal prostitution and gambling in Los Angeles in 1938. The El Rancho Vegas opened in 1941, the Last Frontier in 1942, the Golden Nugget in 1945, the Flamingo in 1946 and the Thunderbird in 1948. Ben "Bugsy" Siegel, a New York mobster, opened the Flamingo in 1946 but was murdered by his business partners the following year.

El Rancho Vegas used big-name entertainers, such as Milton Berle, Jackie Gleason, Dean Martin and Jerry Lewis, to lure gamblers.

A massive publicity campaign, the growing popularity of the automobile, postwar national prosperity and a population boom in Southern California combined to boost tourism in Las Vegas in the 1950s. The city has continued to boom ever since.

Almost all of the resorts had underworld ties until Howard Hughes went on a casino shopping spree in the 1960s, legitimizing investment in Las Vegas. The eccentric billionaire purchased the Desert Inn, the Sands, the Frontier, the Castaways, the Silver Slipper and the Landmark. Companies such as Hyatt, Hilton, Ramada, Holiday Inn and MGM quickly bought casinos, too.

Hughes stayed in Las Vegas for nine years to the day, living in a suite at the Desert Inn. When he left, the drapes were dry-rotted because he had never opened them.

Kirk Kerkorian, the son of Armenian farmers from Fresno, Calif., built the 1,568-room International Hotel (now the Las Vegas Hilton) in 1969 for an unheard-of $60 million. It was the largest hotel in the world at the time. Many thought Kerkorian was crazy because hotels averaged about 250 rooms back then.

Kerkorian topped the International with the 2,100-room, $106 million MGM (now Bally's) in 1973 and the 5,005-room, $1 billion MGM Grand in 1993. The MGM

Grand is the second-largest hotel in the world, 95 rooms behind Thailand's Ambassador City Jomtlen.

The most powerful man in Las Vegas today is Steve Wynn. An English literature major at Pennsylvania State University who came to Las Vegas as a liquor distributor, Wynn opened the gleaming 3,049-room Mirage in 1989 for $610 million and the 2,900-room Treasure Island in 1993 for $430 million.

To distinguish themselves from each other and attract families, most resorts in Las Vegas have themes: The Mirage (South Seas), Treasure Island (Caribbean pirates), MGM Grand (*The Wizard of Oz*), pyramid-shaped Luxor (Egypt), Excalibur (medieval castle), etc.

Fierce competition — not to mention developers' egos — forces each new resort to be bigger, more extravagant or more imaginative than the last. The Luxor's atrium, the world's largest, could accommodate nine Boeing 747s stacked on top of each other. The Stratosphere's 1,149-foot tower is the tallest structure west of the Mississippi River. On top of the Stratosphere is the world's highest roller coaster. New York-New York, opened in January 1997, is a stunning reproduction of the Manhattan skyline.

The New York Mets stayed at New York-New York when they played three exhibition games in Las Vegas in March 1997. Catcher Todd Hundley said the hotel is amazingly realistic, except for one thing.

"It's too clean," he said. "No rats running around or anything."

By the end of 1997, Las Vegas is expected to have 119,700 hotel rooms. The 3,000-room, $1.5 billion Bellagio ("elegant relaxation" in Italian) is scheduled to open in late 1997. Wynn, the owner, said Bellagio "will be the most wonderful, most exquisite, most lovely hotel anywhere." The 6,000-room, $1.8 billion Sands Venetian Resort, expected to open in January 1999, will be the largest hotel in the world.

To keep pace, established Las Vegas resorts such as Caesars Palace, Circus Circus, Harrah's and the Desert Inn are expanding. New York-New York has been so successful that resort executives announced expansion plans 10 weeks after opening.

Las Vegas attracts 30 million visitors annually, but ranks second behind Orlando, Fla., the home of Disney World, among the nation's most popular travel destinations. Many of Las Vegas' visitors come for conventions, although a few have been known to sample the nightlife, too. The week-long Comdex computer show attracted 210,000 guests in November 1996.

Gross gaming revenues in Las Vegas total more than $5 billion each year, or more than $171 in profit every second.

Resorts will send a corporate jet anywhere in the world to pick up high rollers and will put them up in sprawling penthouse suites that make Versailles look like a slum. All guests have to do to merit such treatment is drop a few million dollars at the baccarat table.

Las Vegas isn't quite as kind to Harry and Gladys from Dubuque, Iowa. J.R. Rose, a manager at the Desert Inn, said he can always tell when a gambler is in trouble.

"Slowly shaking the head, closing the eyes, like they're saying, 'What'll I do? What'll I do?'" Rose said. "I've had 'em tell me, 'I'm gonna go out and kill myself.' And that's when I say, 'Let's go out back and talk.'"

Rose then pulls a spiral-bound New Testament out of his pocket.

"I tell them, 'The Lord sent you over here for a reason. That's only money.' I invite them to the church where I'm an usher. One fellow even stayed in town an extra day just to come by."

Las Vegas is famous not only for gambling, but also as the self-proclaimed "Entertainment Capital of the World."

In what has been called the city's biggest entertainment event ever, the Beatles performed two shows at the Convention Center in 1964. More than 8,400 frenzied fans jammed into the facility, which had a capacity of 7,000, for each performance. Tickets sold for $4 each.

Elvis Presley performed at the International from its opening in 1969 until he died in 1977, packing the 2,000-seat showroom every night.

Barbra Streisand helped open the MGM Grand by performing her first concerts in 22 years on December 31, 1993, and January 1, 1994. The hotel received more than *one million* ticket requests for the concerts in the 15,200-seat arena. Scalpers received $5,000 for tickets with a face value of $500-$1,000. Streisand was paid $20 million for the two performances.

Wayne Newton, who began his career in 1959 at the age of 16 at the Fremont Hotel & Casino in downtown Las Vegas, continues to perform in Las Vegas and Branson, Mo.

The most popular entertainers in Las Vegas, though, are Siegfried & Roy. As of February 1997, the tiger-taming illusionists from Germany had drawn 4.71 million people and grossed $350 million in seven years at The Mirage. They have a five-year contract worth a reported $57.5 million. Tickets to the show cost $89.35 each.

Las Vegas' robust economy has helped make it the fastest-growing metropolitan area in the United States. Other factors are sunny weather, the lack of state income tax and an exodus from expensive, crime-infested Los Angeles.

The population of Clark County skyrocketed to 127,016 in 1960, 463,087 in 1980 and 1 million in 1994. It now stands at 1.2 million, about two-thirds of Nevada's total. The population of Clark County is projected to top 2 million between 2005 and 2010.

Construction is everywhere.

"In Nevada, they say the state bird is the crane," quipped state demographer Dean Judson.

It is almost impossible to drive in town without encountering road work. Clark County's employment profile seems to be:

Gaming/hotels	500,000 employees
Construction	127,993
Other	7
Total	628,000

Actually, gaming and hotels account for 30 percent of all jobs. Construction accounts for about 10 percent, more than twice the national average.

One other thing about Las Vegas. It's hot. Very hot. The average high temperature in July is 106 degrees. It's dry heat, but that was little comfort to Martina Navratilova when she arrived at Caesars Palace in 1992 for the Battle of Champions against Jimmy Connors. Navratilova complained that she had never been so hot in her life. And this was in late September.

*   *   *

Las Vegas was once the home of perhaps the most popular non-Grand Slam tennis tournament in the world.

Caesars Palace offered comedian Alan King a major deal in the early 1970s to headline there, and asked if it could "sweeten the pot" for him. King asked for, and got, a professional tournament. The Alan King/Caesars Palace Tennis Classic, launched in 1972, "became the single biggest attraction in town, the Siegfried & Roy of its day," King said.

It was also criticized.

"Because money seemed to have no meaning whatsoever in Las Vegas, we started with a $50,000 [total] prize, then moved it up to $100,000," King said. "For this we were condemned by *Tennis* magazine: 'Alan King and his Las Vegas mentality will ruin the game.' "

The Alan King Classic didn't last, but tennis has done all right. The tournament moved to Palm Springs, Calif., in 1986. Now known as the *Newsweek* Champions Cup and situated in the Palm Springs suburb of Indian Wells, Calif., it offered $2.05 million in prize money in 1997.

Like Las Vegas itself, the Alan King Classic was glitzy and glamorous.

"Gigantic ice sculptures and baskets filled with bottles of vintage wine covered the tables poolside at Caesars for the annual tournament party that many considered among the most lavish social productions anywhere," wrote Jim Fossum of the *Review-Journal* in a 1995 column. "Roman gladiators with lions and tigers roamed the deck, and tropical birds flew about in an area adjacent to the courts that earlier that day featured the likes of John Newcombe, Rod Laver, Arthur Ashe, Bjorn Borg and Ivan Lendl."

The Alan King Classic treated the players royally. It was the first tournament to provide free hotel rooms, food and drinks — now standard procedure on the circuit. Players were encouraged to bring their wives and children or girlfriends and received complimentary show tickets. There were pro-celebrity tournaments and tournaments for seniors and wives.

"They bent over backward to do everything right," said Connors, who won the Alan King Classic four times (1976, 1977, 1982 and 1983). "That's what Las Vegas is famous for."

Celebrities such as Diana Ross used to drop by the courts. ABC covered the tournament, unheard of for a non-Grand Slam event. Even Howard Cosell — "not much of a tennis aficianado," according to King — came to town for the broadcast.

You know those tiresome check presentation ceremonies after each final in other cities? That wouldn't do in Las Vegas. Connors received a bowl filled with $60,000 in poker chips from bare-chested gladiators in 1982. He gleefully dug his hands into $62,500 in silver dollars the following year.

"It was what I wanted it to be — more than a tennis tournament," King said. "It had a carnival atmosphere."

It was also rich in tennis history.

Borg won the Alan King Classic in 1979 and 1980 but was forced to play in the qualifying in 1982. Borg refused to play in the required 10 tournaments that year because he took the first three months of the year off, and the governing Men's International Professional Tennis Council declined to make an exception for the five-time Wimbledon champion and six-time French Open winner. Playing indif-

ferently in Las Vegas, Borg lost in the second round of qualifying to fellow veteran Dick Stockton.

Borg announced his retirement nine months later at
26 years old. He divorced his first wife, had a child out of
wedlock, failed in several business ventures, was rushed to
a hospital in Milan, Italy, in 1989 to have his stomach
pumped for what was either an overdose of sleeping pills
or (Borg's version) food poisoning aggravated by medica-
tion, and tried unsuccessfully to return to tennis in 1991 and
1992.

A mop-topped 14-year-old named Andre Agassi
played in the qualifying of the last Alan King Classic in
1985. Agassi drew a bye in the first round and lost to Hank
Pfister, a hard-serving veteran, 6-3, 6-3, in the second
round. Phillip Agassi also played in the qualifying, losing
to veteran Steve Meister 7-5, 3-6, 6-3 in the first round.

In the first round of the main draw that year, Paul
Annacone defeated Brad Gilbert 6-3, 6-3 in a matchup of
unseeded Americans. Today, Annacone coaches Pete Sampras, and Gilbert tutors Andre Agassi.

Cliff Perlman's sale of Caesars Palace led to the
demise of the Alan King tournament, King said.

"I had an obligation and a loyalty to Cliff Perlman,"
King said. "He was going to buy the Dunes, and the tour-
nament belonged to me. I was going to move it to the
Dunes, but the deal fell apart."

Charlie Pasarell, a friend of King's and a former
player, was running the Pilot Pen Classic in La Quinta,
Calif., near Palm Springs.

"He came to me," King said. "I became a partner in
building the Grand Champions resort (at Indian Wells). I
took my tournament and Charlie's and combined them."

The *Newsweek* Champions Cup and the Lipton International at Key Biscayne, Fla., the following week, are the
two most popular non-Grand Slam tournaments in the
United States, possibly in the world. Still, King longs for the
old days in Las Vegas.

"Those were the happiest years of my life," he said in 1995. "I still have players come up to me and talk about it. It was very innovative for its time."

Caesars has held two notable tennis events since the Alan King classic left: the hokey 1992 Battle of Champions between Connors and Navratilova and the prestigious 1995 Davis Cup semifinals between the United States and Sweden.

The match between Connors and Navratilova — who lead all players with 109 and 167 titles, respectively, in the Open era (since 1968) — was nicknamed the "Geezers at Caesars." Connors was 40 years old and ranked 62nd at the time; Navratilova was 35 and ranked fourth. Connors was allowed only one serve and forced to cover half of each doubles alley in addition to the singles court.

Mike Agassi's comments before the match turned out to be more interesting than the contest itself. Outspoken as always, Mike called the match "a joke, an embarrassment for the game of tennis."

Mike predicted that Connors, if he played his hardest, would win 6-0, 6-0.

"It's not going to be any match unless Connors takes a dive on some points," Mike said. "The only way it would be a good match is if Navratilova and Seles played Connors — two against one. To put a lady who's already over the hill against a 40-year-old with the body of an 18- or 19-year-old . . . Connors hits the ball twice as well as he did when he was 23 to 30, but he's a step slower. People who pay money to see something like that must be out of their minds."

Tickets were priced at $75, $50, $30 and $20. The match was also available on live pay-per-view television at $24.95.

The handicaps wouldn't help Navratilova much, according to Mike. Connors, he said, had too much power.

"Yeah, they're giving [Navratilova] half of the doubles alleys, but she's not going to touch the ball to return it," Mike said. "Even if she had the whole alleys, she'd have no chance. The big [male] pros' second serve is better than their first because it's a spin serve. A girl has to jump to return it, and Jimmy will put it away."

Connors, hitting softly in the first set, defeated Navratilova 7-5, 6-2 in a dull, tentative match before a sell-out crowd of 13,832 and a pay-per-view audience of about 100,000. Connors received $1.15 million and Navratilova $500,000.

"Jimmy will do anything for money," Mike said.

Andre Agassi played a key role in the Davis Cup, the venerable men's international team competition, coming to Las Vegas. Because the U.S. had played in Sweden the year before (losing 3-2 in the semifinals), it was the Americans' turn to choose the site. Les Snyder, then the president of the USTA, asked the American players where they'd like to play. Agassi didn't hesitate to speak up.

"I really felt Las Vegas could be a great place for the Davis Cup, because I thought we could fill up [the stadium] and the crowd would be enthusiastic. They haven't had championship tennis here since 1985, and I felt they would treat it like an event."

Agassi was right. Near-capacity crowds of 11,500 to 12,500 watched the U.S. overwhelm Sweden, the defending champion, 4-1 in an anticlimactic series at Caesars' make-shift outdoor stadium.

It marked the only time that four players who have been ranked No. 1 in singles have competed in one Davis Cup series. Agassi was No. 1 at the time. Second-ranked Sampras and No. 20 Stefan Edberg and No. 50 Mats Wilander of Sweden had all been on top.

Agassi, then 25, and Sampras, 24, were in their prime entering the 1995 Davis Cup semifinals. They had met two weeks earlier in the U.S. Open final, with Sampras winning in four sets. In contrast, Edberg, 29, and Wilander, 31, were rapidly approaching retirement.

Edberg played doubles only against the U.S. because of a lingering cold, and Wilander replaced Magnus Larsson, who was out with a broken foot after reaching the top 10 in singles earlier in the year. Sweden's other singles player, 21-year-old Thomas Enqvist, was ranked eighth in the world but had never played in the pressure-packed Davis Cup.

Edberg teamed with Jonas Bjorkman in doubles against Todd Martin and Jonathan Stark. Bjorkman's regular partner, countryman Jan Apell, was recovering from surgery for a torn rotator cuff. Injuries would not strike the U.S. until the competition started.

The teams combined business with pleasure in the days preceding the competition. The U.S. team took in the Sigfried & Roy show at The Mirage, and Agassi held a private party for both teams at a water amusement park on the Strip.

Sampras defeated Enqvist in four sets in the opening match. Agassi overcame an early case of the jitters to beat Wilander, a seven-time Grand Slam singles champion, 7-6 (7-5), 6-2, 6-2 and give the U.S. a 2-0 first-day lead. It was Agassi's 13th straight Davis Cup singles victory.

Afterward, Agassi admitted that playing in his hometown was somewhat of a distraction.

"I tried to stay focused inside the lines," he said. "I did well with that, except when I was on one side of the court. I would toss the ball and see [a sign saying] 'Caesars Palace' off in the distance. That was the only reminder when I was out there.

"I felt so close to everybody, but in other ways, it felt very strange. I had to force myself to think about tennis and not that blue sky that I've seen since I was a kid.

"It's also strange knowing some of the ball kids. I was about to call them by name. It was quite a different experience for me. It was nice to raise my level to the standard that I set for myself and get a chance for my hometown to see me play that way."

The U.S. suffered its customary loss in doubles on the second day as Bjorkman and Edberg topped Martin and Stark in straight sets. That cut the Americans' lead to 2-1 in the best-of-five-match competition and set the stage for

Agassi to clinch the series in his hometown against Enqvist in the first match of the last day.

Agassi, however, withdrew 90 minutes before his match Sunday with a pulled chest muscle. He said he suffered the injury early in the third set of his victory over Wilander.

The 6-foot-6 Martin, ranked 19th in singles after reaching No. 5 in 1994, blasted 27 aces and defeated Enqvist 7-5, 7-5, 7-6 (7-2) to put the U.S. in the final against Russia. Afterward, Martin joyously flung his racket into the flag-waving crowd of 11,503, and Tom Gullikson, the U.S. non-playing captain, jumped into Martin's arms like a kid greeting his father at home after a long day at work.

"Playing the type of match I did in the situation that was presented to me was certainly my highest moment in tennis," said Martin, the runner-up in the 1994 Australian Open to Sampras. "I just hope there's another chance to equal it."

Agassi watched the match from the stands with a bandage around his chest and no shirt. Shields sat next to him.

The lingering injury prevented Agassi from playing in the Davis Cup final at Moscow in December, but the U.S. still defeated Russia 3-2 indoors on clay for the title. Sampras had a hand in all three U.S. victories despite playing on his worst surface and collapsing after his five-set victory over Andrei Chesnokov on the first day. Sampras won both of his singles matches and teamed with Martin to win the doubles.

The only other significant professional tennis events in Las Vegas since the King tournament have been at the MGM Grand Garden.

Agassi defeated Connors 6-4, 7-6 (7-1) in a March 1994 exhibition before 10,144 fans in the arena, which seats 11,400 for tennis. Agassi, 23 at the time, had not played in Las Vegas since the Alan King qualifying in 1985. Connors was 41. Agassi undoubtedly would have won much more easily in a tournament with ranking points at stake.

Agassi also beat Southern Nevada rival Michael Chang 6-3, 6-3 in a March 1995 exhibition before 9,290 fans at the MGM Grand.

A 35-and-over tournament featuring Connors, Borg and Guillermo Vilas flopped at the MGM Grand in May 1994. Curtains reduced the seating capacity to 4,500, and the event didn't come close to filling that. Connors' semifinal victory over Borg drew the biggest crowd of the week, around 2,500.

Organizers later said they made the mistake of holding the tournament indoors at a resort rather than outdoors at an intimate club. The 35-and-over circuit has not returned to Las Vegas since then.

Las Vegas, in fact, hasn't had a professional tennis event since the 1995 Davis Cup semifinals.

Will the men's circuit ever return to the city? A familiar refrain is that casinos aren't interested in holding an annual tournament because tennis fans supposedly aren't big gamblers.

"I don't buy that," said Lornie Kuhle, the tennis director at the MGM Grand and Connors' former hitting partner and traveling companion. "I think tennis would be great for Las Vegas. It's prestigious, high class. It's a good image for the town. But somebody's got to step up to bat."

Like Agassi? During the Davis Cup semifinals, he said he'd like to "make an impact to get a tour event here."

It won't be easy.

"Every year the ATP [Association of Tennis Professionals] turns down a dozen [proposed] events," Pasarell said. "People are throwing money beyond belief."

Agassi has not only money but clout. It might have to wait until he retires from tennis, but don't be surprised to see the Andre Agassi Classic or the Nike Classic in Las Vegas with Phillip Agassi as the tournament director one day. Andre formed a foundation to benefit underprivileged children in Las Vegas. He might give tennis in his hometown a similar boost.

Leaving Las Vegas

5

By the time Agassi was 13, he had begun to rebel against his strict regimen.

"If I didn't leave Las Vegas, either my dad was going to pop me or I was going to pop him, and I was probably going to quit tennis," Andre said.

Futhermore, nobody in Las Vegas could compete with Andre on the court.

Then Mike saw a *60 Minutes* segment on the Nick Bollettieri Tennis Academy in Bradenton, Fla., on January 1, 1984. The report was called "Tennis Boot Camp."

Shortly after the program aired, Mike called Bollettieri and told him about Andre.

"I taught him to hit and to hit and to hit," Mike said. "Now I can't do anything more. He doesn't listen to me. He doesn't want to play. And Las Vegas isn't the place for him. If he comes to you, I know he can make it."

Mike said that, although he wasn't rich, he was willing to pay the monthly fee of close to $1,500, which did not include tuition, of several thousand dollars a year, at one of the two local private schools.

"Whatever it takes, I'm going to do it," Mike said. "I want him to be a champion."

Bollettieri, vaguely aware of Andre's success on the West Coast, offered to accept Andre for $800 a month. Mike agreed and sent Bollettieri a check for $1,600 to cover the first two months.

Andre left Cashman Junior High School in Las Vegas midway through the eighth grade. "Me and school never got along," Andre said.

The night before Andre left Las Vegas for Florida, he and Perry Rogers rented a chauffeured limousine and cruised the Strip for hours, reminiscing.

"It was like he was a condemned guy," Rogers said.

Bollettieri paid more attention to rising stars Aaron Krickstein and Carling Bassett at first. But Agassi was too talented to ignore for long.

After the second month, Bollettieri refunded Mike's money and put Andre on a full scholarship.

Agassi also stood out for his bad attitude, according to Bollettieri.

"I had never met a kid quite like Andre," Bollettieri wrote in his 1996 autobiography, *My Aces, My Faults*. "Rules were made for him to break. Adults were made for him to test. Schedules were made for him to ignore. He didn't dress like anyone else. He didn't look like anyone else. He didn't practice like anyone else. He didn't even play matches like anyone else."

Efforts to interview Bollettieri were unsuccessful.

Agassi dyed his hair different colors and wore makeup long before Dennis Rodman did.

Agassi once showed up for a match in Pensacola, Fla., wearing jeans, high tops and heavy makeup. Curry Kirkpatrick, writing in *Sports Illustrated*, called Agassi "a nifty combination of Alice Marble and Alice Cooper."

"That was pure rebellion," Rogers said. "He was letting a few people know he was not happy. I don't want to make it sound like some huge sob story because Andre had a lot of advantages, but there wasn't a lot of stability. He was 3,000 miles from home, his girlfriend and his best friend. That makes you pretty unhappy. His childhood truly was taken away from him [at the academy] in certain respects."

Wendi Stewart said Agassi told her that he drank heavily at the academy. Rogers also said Agassi was almost kicked out of the academy at least once for getting drunk.

"He was screaming for attention," Stewart said.

Agassi told *The Los Angeles Times* that he drank his first beer at 12, and remembers getting drunk for the first time at 13. He said it wasn't a problem at the time.

"But let me put it this way," Agassi said. "If you said, 'Let's get drunk tonight,' I probably wouldn't have complained. That's kind of the way I was. I was more or less a rebel. If you said I shouldn't do it, I did it."

Agassi said in *The Times* that his drinking increased "a lot" when he was 14 and 15 (coinciding with his stay at the academy) and that he began experimenting with marijuana. But after Agassi turned pro at 16, Christianity replaced the bad habits, he said.

Stewart confirmed that Agassi straightened himself out, saying, "The whole first two years we went out [1990 to 1991, when Agassi was 20 and 21], he never had a drink . . . nothing."

There has been no sign of a problem since then.

Agassi acknowledged past alcohol problems and marijuana use in *Tennis* (France).

". . . I don't hide that I was at one time on the edge of a cliff as far as drugs and alcohol are concerned," Agassi said. "I was really headed downhill. But I was able to catch myself, and now that's all in the past. However, I haven't forgotten. I consider myself lucky to have pulled myself out of it, as opposed to many others.

"That's why I want now to get involved in works of charity designed to help drug users, alcoholics and children who are left to themselves in the streets. I feel really useful to society by doing that."

Agassi, in fact, formed a foundation in 1994 to benefit underprivileged children in Las Vegas and has donated or raised millions of dollars for it since then.

Agassi did get caught skipping classes and practices in Bradenton, Bollettieri wrote. The teenager received the standard punishment of doing chores such as pulling weeds around Bollettieri's house, mowing the lawn, trimming the hedges, washing dishes and polishing his cars.

Bollettieri wrote that Agassi was kicked off of a junior team sponsored by Nike for selling the tennis shoes and warmup suits the company was giving him. Agassi, however, paid for Rogers to fly to a national tournament in Florida. Agassi had enlisted Bollettieri's help in getting Rogers, a junior player, into the tournament.

Agassi attended Bradenton Academy, one of two private schools in the area, in the mornings, but wasn't particularly interested.

Agassi, Bollettieri concluded, was "a ticking time bomb, waiting to explode. With so many kids, you could read their future, see exactly where they were heading. Not Andre. He could skyrocket. He could tumble. He could dominate. He could self-destruct. The thin line between triumph and disaster was never thinner, and the potential for both was enormous.

"He drove me crazy. I was used to intimidating kids. I was harsher then than I am now. I was also louder. And less flexible. Everything had to be my way. Andre flouted my rules, defied my discipline, violated the spirit of the NBTA and of Bradenton Academy. Dr. Murray Gerber, who ran the private school, threatened to kick Andre out almost every time his hair changed color. I pleaded for Andre. 'Hey, Doc,' I'd say, 'I know you've got those rules, but you've got to give me a little leeway here.' Dr. Gerber was, reluctantly, understanding."

Jim Courier, who roomed with Agassi at the academy, said Agassi "was a bit of a punk, in trouble at the academy, never much of a student. If Andre had continued where he was heading, he would have gone down the toilet."

Agassi was afraid he wasn't going to succeed, that all of this would be for nothing. He had his chance to leave the academy in his second year there, when he was 15. Bollettieri decided to expel him. If he had, Agassi "might be dealing blackjack in Las Vegas today," Bollettieri wrote.

Then Agassi, who admitted that he "hated growing up in Florida, 3,000 miles from home," did something strange. He convinced Bollettieri to let him stay at the academy.

The day after Agassi's meeting with Bollettieri, the coach found a huge teddy bear in his office. Rogers said he had won it at Busch Gardens in Tampa, Fla. It was too large to take on the plane back to Las Vegas, so he gave it to Agassi, who left it for Bollettieri's young daughter.

Late in 1985, after Andre had been at the academy for more than a year, Phillip came to Bradenton to live with him. Tami also came to Florida to train at the academy on a scholarship and attend Bradenton Academy. "She took school more seriously than Andre did," Bollettieri wrote.

By 1985, Agassi, Courier, David Wheaton and Mark Knowles were living at the academy. Agassi and Courier eventually rose to No. 1 in the world, and Wheaton was ranked as high as No. 12. Knowles reached No. 3 in doubles. Monica Seles arrived at the academy early in 1986.

Bollettieri coached Agassi until resigning abruptly in 1993.

*   *   *

The middle of three children, Bollettieri grew up playing football, baseball and basketball in middle-class North Pelham, N.Y., north of the Bronx. Tennis was for rich kids, and there were no Italian-American tennis players to serve as role models.

Bollettieri's grandparents emigrated from Italy, but his parents were born in the United States. Bollettieri's father worked his way through nearby Fordham University and became a pharmacist. His mother was a housewife.

In the foreword of the 1984 book *Nick Bollettieri's Junior Tennis,* Barry McDermott wrote that "Bollettieri came up the hard way, which is often the best way. It probably is easier to ace John McEnroe than it is to fool Nick. He knows people. . . ."

Bollettieri's father wanted Nick to get a good Catholic education and pointed him toward Spring Hill College, a Jesuit school in Mobile, Ala. A classmate of Nick's father at Fordham taught at Spring Hill.

Bollettieri enrolled at Spring Hill in 1949 and played four years of intramural football, basketball, volleyball and baseball. He played one round of golf as a freshman, but did so badly that he threw his clubs away and never played again at the college.

As a senior, Bollettieri had a light academic schedule, so he decided to go out for the tennis team. A wealthy uncle had introduced him to the game. Bollettieri somehow made the team and worked his way up to No. 5 singles.

After graduating from Spring Hill in 1953, Bollettieri finished his ROTC training at Fort Story, Va., and became a paratrooper. He married Phyllis Johnson, the first of his five wives, before he was sent to Japan, where he supplemented his lieutenant's wages by jumping out of airplanes, playing poker and gin rummy and teaching tennis.

"I told people I knew a lot more about tennis than I really did," he said.

The Bollettieris returned from Japan in 1955 and had a son. Nick fulfilled his army obligation in 1956, and took his father's advice and enrolled in law school. Nick chose the University of Miami because it had a good law program and the weather was sunny. With a family, though, Nick needed a job.

One of Bollettieri's uncles was the assistant water commissioner in North Miami Beach. He helped Nick get a job as a tennis pro at a public facility, Victory Park, for $100 a week plus $1.50 per half-hour lesson. Bollettieri still didn't know much about tennis.

"I faked it," he wrote in *My Aces, My Faults*. "I used to send Phyllis to watch the other pros in the area work. She would take notes and then tell me what they were teaching, and I would copy them."

The restless Bollettieri had found his calling. He decided he wanted to be a tennis coach rather than a lawyer.

"I wanted to be Fred Perry, not Perry Mason," he wrote.

When Bollettieri told his father he wanted to be the No. 1 tennis coach in the world, his father didn't argue. He just said, "If anyone can do it, son, you can."

Bollettieri began teaching 9-year-old Brian Gottfried at Victory Park in 1961. Gottfried eventually won three Grand Slam doubles titles with Raul Ramirez of Mexico, and was ranked No. 3 in the world in singles in 1977.

Bollettieri moved on to the Sahara Hotel in Miami Beach. It was too hot to play tennis in the summer, so he headed north to be the resident pro at the municipal courts in Springfield, Ohio. That's where Bollettieri got his big break.

Springfield was the site of the Western Juniors, a warm-up tournament for the nationals in Kalamazoo, Mich. Bollettieri coordinated the tournament, which attracted the best young players in the country, and met Dora Pasarell of Puerto Rico there. Pasarell's son, Charles, was one of the top juniors in the world. Charlie later played professionally, and is now the tournament director of the immensely successful *Newsweek* Champions Cup and State Farm Evert Cup in Indian Wells, Calif.

Dora Pasarell was close to Lawrence Rockefeller and his wife. Mr. Rockefeller and his family owned and operated the famous Dorado Beach Hotel in Puerto Rico, and Mrs. Pasarell helped Bollettieri become the head pro there. Bollettieri stayed at Dorado Beach for 17 years. There, he got to know Vince Lombardi; Art Nielsen Jr., of the television ratings family; and Louis Marx Jr., the chairman of the company that distributes Swiss Army knives and watches in the United States. All were instrumental in boosting Bollettieri's career.

In 1967, Lombardi and Nielsen recommended Bollettieri for a job running the summer tennis camp at the Wayland Academy in Beaver Dam, Wisc. Bollettieri got the position and operated the Nick Bollettieri Tennis Camp in Beaver Dam for 25 years.

Bollettieri left Dorado Beach when there was a management shakeup in 1976. Mike DePalmer Sr., the tennis pro at the Bradenton Country Club, helped Bollettieri become the head pro at the Colony Beach Resort on Longboat Key near Sarasota, Fla. DePalmer's daughter had attended the Beaver Dam camp.

DePalmer suggested that Bollettieri give adult clinics two or three nights a week at the Bradenton Country Club. They proved popular, and Bollettieri started weekend clinics for juniors at the Colony. If youngsters wanted to stay at the Colony for the weekend, Bollettieri got them a bargain rate.

In the summer of 1978, Bollettieri told several families at Beaver Dam that he was opening a tennis boarding school in Sarasota. He signed up 20 children, but had no boarding facilities. Half of the kids lived at Bollettieri's house, and half stayed with the other pros.

Bollettieri's first prominent live-in student was Anne White of West Virginia. She reached No. 19 in the world in 1981 and created an uproar by wearing a form-fitting bodysuit in her first-round match at Wimbledon in 1985.

DePalmer and Bollettieri bought a small club in West Bradenton with seven courts. They named it the DePalmer Bollettieri Tennis Club, and DePalmer resigned from the Bradenton Country Club to run it. They still held classes at the Colony, but ran tournaments at the DePalmer Bollettieri Tennis Club.

For housing, the coaches then bought a run-down motel in Bradenton with $50,000 from Marx. Among those checking into the motel was Paul Annacone, who eventually reached No. 12 in the world, won the 1985 Australian Open doubles title with South African Christo Van Rensburg and became Pete Sampras' coach.

Shortly after DePalmer and Bollettieri bought the motel, they got another break when ABC-TV's *20-20* ran a segment on the tennis program.

"The demand was suddenly so great we had to start working longer days," Bollettieri wrote in *My Aces, My Faults*. "Instead of working 15 hours daily, we worked 17 or 18. During the school year, we worked nine straight months. My pros got a day off only if there was a major emergency. Their loyalty, their belief in what we were doing, was incredible."

The academy began cranking out future top-10 players: Kathleen Horvath, Carling Bassett, Lisa Bonder, Jimmy Arias and Aaron Krickstein.

Bollettieri received loans of $1 million from Marx and $1 million from the bank to buy an old tomato farm, on 34th Avenue and 55th Street in Bradenton, in order to build the Nick Bollettieri Tennis Academy. Construction began in early 1981, and the academy opened that November.

Financial mismanagement put the academy on the brink of bankruptcy in the mid-1980s. Bollettieri sold it to the International Management Group (IMG), a huge sports marketing company, for $7 million. IMG, however, kept Bollettieri in charge of every area except finances.

Bollettieri attributes his success to "getting to know people, their needs and what they're capable of doing, rather than putting them in a mold."

Trim and perpetually tanned, the raspy-voiced Bollettieri looks much younger than his age of 66. Formerly a yeller and screamer, he said he has mellowed.

"I used to demand 110 percent all the time, but nobody is capable of that," he said. "I try to get a person to operate at 70-80 percent and then put it into overdrive."

* * *

Almost 200 tennis players from around the world attend the academy, located 30 miles south of Tampa, Fla., on the state's west coast. Most of them are boarding students, and about 20 percent receive full or partial scholarships. There are 75 courts (four indoors), 40 condominiums housing up to eight students each, junior and adult dining halls, fitness and rehabilitation centers, a language center, a pro shop, an Olympic-size swimming pool and a junior recreation center.

Tuition is $21,700 per nine-month school year for boarding students. The facility, now called the Bollettieri Tennis and Sports Academy, also offers golf, soccer and baseball programs.

Junior tennis players attend either the nearby Bradenton Academy or St. Stephens School.

Mark Knowles, a Bahamian who roomed with Agassi at the academy from 1983 to 1985, described a typical day there.

"You got up around 6 A.M., went to breakfast and got on the bus to go to school maybe around 7," Knowles said. "School went from about 8 to 12:30 straight — like a minute in between classes. That was pretty hard-core because you didn't have a free moment to relax. At 12:30, you got on the bus, went back to the academy and had lunch.

"From 1:30 to 4:30, you practiced for three straight hours just beating balls and playing a couple of sets. Then you'd go to the weight room or the track for about an hour. You'd go back to the room, shower and eat dinner. Then you had study hall from 7 to 9 to get your homework done. You had free time from 9 to 10 to hang out with other students, hang out by the pool, play video games, whatever. Lights out was at 10:30.

"That was pretty much the regimen six days a week. Sunday was the only day we were allowed to sleep in and kind of relax a little. Tennis was optional [on Sundays]. There were times you opted to play, but sometimes we'd play football or soccer — something different to kind of change it up — or go to the mall and see a movie."

All of the taboos kids get away with at public high schools are strictly forbidden at the academy: use of drugs or alcohol, smoking and chewing tobacco, sex, leaving campus without permission, stealing, using profanity, etc. Students are not even allowed to enter someone else's condominium or to chew gum on campus.

The academy was "brutally tough," Knowles said. "As of today, there's no place that matches it in discipline. In hindsight, it was a great place. When we were going there, it was really strict. There were times when we thought Nick was brutal, but in the end he was just doing it for us. To be successful in any profession, you need to be disciplined. It also gave you determination. . . .

"I'm probably one of the biggest fans of Nick. He's a phenomenal motivator. What he does is whether it's criticism or not, at the end of the conversation, he makes you feel good about yourself. To this day, when I see him, he's so uplifting and has a great zest for life, and I think that rubs off on people around him."

Wheaton is another big Bollettieri fan.

"He's a very positive individual," Wheaton said. "You never hear anything negative come out of his mouth. He'd get you on the court, tell you something to do on your forehand, and say, 'Good, better, better.'

"I wouldn't say he's the best technical coach in the world, but a lot of other coaches don't have the positive approach he does. He's a great person. I'm indebted to Nick."

Wheaton, 6 feet 4 inches, is a serve-and-volleyer from Lake Minnetonka, Minn., which is not usually mentioned in discussions of tennis hotbeds.

"I was hurting in Minnesota — I had no one to play with," Wheaton said. "Nick gave me a full scholarship when I didn't really deserve it. He believed in me."

The knock on Bollettieri was that his players had one-dimensional games — rocket forehands and little else — and they didn't reach their potential. Exhibits A and B were prodigies Arias and Krickstein. Both cracked the top 10, but neither won a Grand Slam title.

There was some truth to the criticism, the players said.

"If we had worked on my net game and sacrificed when I was 16, 17, it might have helped me [later]," Krickstein said. "But I was winning."

Arias admitted: ". . . We made mistakes, Nick made mistakes. But Andre can learn from them. . . ."

He did. Bollettieri and Agassi worked more on the other parts of Agassi's game — his serve, backhand and even volley — and it showed.

At 15, Agassi qualified for a USTA satellite circuit in the summer of 1985. His best showing in the five tournaments was an appearance in the semifinals on clay at Monroe, La., losing to 14th seed and eventual champion Luke Jensen.

Andre and Phillip played doubles together at St. Joseph, Mo., losing in the first round. Andre finished the circuit with four coveted singles ranking points, tying for 11th place. That gave him a world ranking of No. 618.

Agassi qualified to play in his first Grand Prix tournament, the $405,000 Pilot Pen Classic at La Quinta, Calif., in February 1986. He beat John Austin, Tracy's brother, in the first round, before falling to third-ranked Mats Wilander 6-1, 6-1 in the second round.

Still 15, Agassi played another USTA satellite circuit in the spring of 1986, finishing third with 19 singles ranking points. He trailed only 22-year-old Jonny Levine of Phoenix with 34 points and 27-year-old Jay Lapidus of Palm Beach Gardens, Fla., with 27 points.

Agassi reached two finals on the circuit, losing to ninth-seeded Levine 6-1, 6-0 in the first tournament at Kissimmee, Fla., and to fifth-seeded Lapidus by the same score in the circuit-culminating masters tournament at Mt. Pleasant, S.C.

Agassi turned pro in the middle of the masters tournament — on May 1, 1986, two days past his 16th birthday. He was a sophomore in high school.

Breakthrough

Fans at the $10,000 Nevada State Open in Reno in May 1986 got a glimpse of what was to come on the international circuit. Agassi amazed fans at the Lakeridge Tennis Club with his explosive shotmaking, amused them with his baggy tennis shorts and two-tone punk haircut and alienated them with his petulance. Any one of the three would have made Agassi stand out. Together, they made him a phenomenon.

Tired after the five-week USTA satellite circuit, Agassi played in Reno the following week only as a favor to Phillip.

"I thought I was going to have a couple weeks of rest after five tough weeks, but my brother said he wanted me to come up here and play doubles with him," Andre said. "I just made the best of it. . . ."

Ironically, Andre won the singles title in Reno, but lost early in doubles. Even in singles, though, Agassi struggled against far inferior competition, surviving four straight three-set matches before the final. In addition to his fatigue, the thin air at Reno's 4,498-foot altitude favored serve-and-volleyers, not baseliners like Agassi.

Agassi showed his frustration throughout the tournament. He smashed a couple of balls against the fence, sarcastically criticized his opponent's game, suggestively put his racket between his legs and muttered "shut up" when fans applauded points for his opponent. None of this would have been tolerated at the Bollettieri academy, but Agassi was never penalized in Reno.

"I don't blame him [for his behavior]," said Scott Lipton, Agassi's quarterfinal victim. "It's society. There's pressure from the very beginning. McEnroe and Connors get away with it, and the kids see they can, too."

Lipton, a 26-year-old former touring pro at the time, called for an umpire in the quarterfinals after accusing Agassi of cheating him out of a point. Players called their own lines in the tournament. The umpire sat at courtside for the rest of the match, and there were no further incidents.

The semifinal between Agassi and Matt Wooldridge was a study in contrasts. Agassi, seeded third, was a volatile 16-year-old baseliner. Wooldridge, the top seed and defending champion from Santa Clara, Calif., (just north of San Jose), was a serene 29-year-old serve-and-volleyer.

It didn't take long for sparks to fly. In the seventh game of the first set, Agassi hit a forehand long. Wooldridge, a teaching professional, hesitated for a split second before calling the ball out. "Nice late call," Agassi yelled.

Agassi's bad-boy reputation was well-known at Lakeridge by then, and Wooldridge obviously had decided he wasn't going to put up with any shenanigans from the kid. "Shut up," Wooldridge uncharacteristically snapped.

Wooldridge, who had been the director of tennis at Lakeridge from 1980 to 1984, won the first set 6-3 and led 3-1 in the second set.

"He was getting more and more upset and being kind of a baby about it . . ." Wooldridge said. "He was saying derogatory things about my game out of frustration in front of my 'home' crowd."

Wooldridge hesitated when asked if he remembered what Agassi said.

"Um, no, not, I mean . . . not really," Wooldridge said. "I, I do, but it, it wasn't really important. It doesn't need to be stated, put it that way."

When pressed further, Wooldridge said: "Um, you know, he was just, um, referring to how I hit the ball as, uh, you know, weak or wimpy or whatever the words would be. Actually, the words were a lot more [explicit] than that, but I'd rather not say."

Profanity?

"Yeah."

Faggot?

"No, it had more profanity than that."

Referring to the female anatomy?

"No comment."

Wooldridge said he told Agassi to "shut up and play tennis. Unfortunately, that's kind of what happened. . . . I should have allowed him to continue on his way."

Agassi won 3-6, 6-3, 6-3 and beat 10th-seeded Doug Stone, a touring pro from Berkeley, Calif., ranked No. 483, 6-3, 6-2 later that day for the title. There were no incidents in the final, which lasted only 50 minutes. But then, just about everything went Agassi's way.

"He hits the ball real hard," Stone, a Bjorn Borg look-alike with short hair, said after the match. "When he's on, you don't feel there's a whole lot you can do."

Wooldridge said in retrospect that he didn't envision Agassi becoming one of the top players in the world eventually.

"Nooo, no, uh-uh," Wooldridge said. "All of us who played tennis at the time didn't foresee that at all."

Agassi was too inconsistent to be headed for stardom, according to Wooldridge.

"I was impressed with how hard he actually could hit the ball," he said. "But for a set and a half, I saw the ball going out all the time. Then for the next set and a half, I saw the ball always going in. . . . In the years to come, I became very impressed with how much he had improved."

Wooldridge said he has no hard feelings toward Agassi over their skirmish in Reno.

"Absolutely not. That was at the end of my playing career and the beginning of his. I don't think that was a milestone in anybody's career," Wooldridge said.

After taking a much-needed break, Agassi reached the final of a $50,000 tournament at Schenectady, N.Y., in July 1986, losing to crafty veteran Ramesh Krishnan of India, 6-2, 6-3.

Agassi first gained national attention the following month in the $315,000 Volvo International at Stratton Mountain, Vt. He beat 12th-ranked Tim Mayotte in the second round before losing to John McEnroe 6-3, 6-3 in the quarterfinals. McEnroe, a three-time Wimbledon and four-time U.S. Open champion, was returning after a 6½ month sabbatical from tennis.

During the loss to McEnroe, Agassi blasted a forehand return of serve for a winner. McEnroe could only stand and watch helplessly.

"No one's ever hit that hard against me," McEnroe said later.

Agassi jumped from No. 211 to No. 105 in the world rankings, becoming the youngest player at 16 years, three months to rank that high since Krickstein was ranked No. 97 at 16 years, two months in October 1983.

Agassi made his first appearance in a Grand Slam tournament later that month, losing to Jeremy Bates of Great Britain in four sets in the first round of the U.S. Open.

Although Agassi failed to advance past the second round in his last six tournaments of 1986, he finished the year ranked No. 91. Agassi, who earned $24,938 for half a year's work, made the biggest jump from the previous year of anyone in the top 100.

*   *   *

Agassi began 1987 with three straight first-round losses, extending his slump to nine consecutive tournaments without advancing past the second round.

"When I beat Mayotte last year I thought I should be number 12 in the world," said Agassi, who graduated from high school by correspondence. "I thought I should beat most of the players, and I paid for that. It's not that easy. I'm smarter now. I'll take it a match at a time."

Agassi ended his slump by reaching the quarterfinals of the Japan Open in April 1987, losing to Andres Gomez. Three years later, Agassi suffered a loss to the Ecuadorian in the final of the French Open that he said will always haunt him.

The week after the Japan Open, Agassi reached the first Grand Prix final of his career, but fell to fellow American Jim Grabb 6-1, 4-6, 6-2 at Seoul, South Korea. The runner-up trophy sits in "the Agassi room" on the second floor of the Official All Star Cafe on the Strip in Las Vegas. Agassi had beaten Grabb, a former Stanford All-American, 6-3, 6-3 in the semifinals at Schenectady in 1986.

After Seoul, Agassi played the European clay-court circuit for the first time and struggled. He lost in the second round at Rome, the quarterfinals at Florence, Italy and the second round of the French Open.

When Agassi set foot on the red clay in Rome, he looked at Phillip and Bollettieri and proclaimed, "This isn't for me. I can't play it."

Agassi was raised on hard courts. Clay, a type of dirt, slows the ball down when it bounces, making it difficult to serve-and-volley effectively or hit passing shots. The surface suits Agassi because he's a baseliner, but it also hurts him because it reduces his power.

Agassi's first trip to Wimbledon's grass courts one month later was even more of a jolt. Grass is as fast a surface as clay is slow. The only two shots that really matter on grass in men's tennis are the serve and return of serve.

Some would add the volley to that list, but grass is so slick that a strong server will have easy volleys. The 5-foot-11 Agassi's serve is good but not overpowering. His return of serve, however, is considered the best in history.

Ranked 61st in the world, Agassi lost to French veteran Henri Leconte 6-2, 6-1, 6-2 in the first round at Wimbledon. Leconte reached No. 5 in the singles world rankings in 1986 and No. 5 in doubles in 1985.

"[Agassi] did not fall in love with the grass or the ambiance," Bollettieri wrote in *My Aces, My Faults.* " 'That's it for me,' Andre said. 'I don't have to play this kind of tournament. This is bullshit. This isn't tennis.' "

Agassi skipped Wimbledon for the next three years.

He didn't fare much better in his next tournament, losing to Francesco Cancellotti of Italy 6-2, 6-2 on clay in the first round of the $293,400 U.S. Pro Championships at Boston. Many observers, including Bollettieri, said Agassi tanked (intentionally lost) the match. Agassi said he suffered an "emotional letdown," but did not tank.

The first of many crises in Agassi's career occurred at the $293,400 Sovran Bank/D.C. National Tennis Classic in Washington, D.C. in July 1987. After losing to 106th-ranked Patrick Kuhnen 6-4, 4-6, 6-0 in the first round to fall to 90th in the world, Agassi was ready to quit tennis. It was his third first-round loss in his last four tournaments.

Afterward, Agassi threw away his rackets and told his brother, Phillip, and agent, Bill Shelton, that he was never going to play tennis again. Bollettieri, however, lifted Agassi's spirits by saying the teenager had all the ingredients to become a star.

Agassi's resolve was tested again that summer in an exhibition against Michael Chang, 15, at Winston-Salem, N.C. Agassi had dominated Chang in the juniors, but Chang was hanging in this time. No way did Agassi want to lose to a younger player, even if it was an exhibition. Agassi persevered and won 7-6, 6-4. That match got him back on track.

Agassi went from Winston-Salem back to Stratton Mountain, where he beat reigning Wimbledon champion Pat Cash 7-6, 7-6 in the second round en route to the semifinals.

"I thought I had a shot at beating him," Agassi said. "I like playing serve-and-volleyers. The best part of my game is return-of-serve and passing shots."

Cash said afterward: "He basically hits the ball as hard as he can every time. He hits the ball a million miles an hour."

Jimmy Arias thought he could hit a forehand pretty well until he saw Agassi.

"He hits the ball harder than anyone else — by far," Arias said. "It's not even close. It's like a slap shot. It's the kind of shot, if I'm mad about something and I smash the ball over the fence . . . that's his regular stroke. It's unbelievable."

People would talk about golfer Tiger Woods in similar awestruck terms in 1996 and 1997. Agassi and Woods were both groomed for stardom from birth and have comparable talent. The big difference is Woods' confidence.

Agassi, 17, lost to Ivan Lendl 6-2, 5-7, 6-3 in a memorable semifinal at Stratton Mountain. Taking a set off the No. 1 player in the world in the nationally televised match boosted Agassi's confidence.

Lendl was typically glib afterward in his assessment of Agassi.

"He sure is a kid," Lendl said. "It's amazing how long your hair can grow at 17. But, yes, if he plays the way he does right now, he could be top 20."

Leconte beat Agassi again in the first round of the 1987 U.S. Open on hard courts, but it was much closer this time: 6-4, 7-6, 4-6, 6-3.

Agassi reached the semifinals at Basle, Switzerland, in October and won his first Grand Prix title in November 1987 at Itaparica, Brazil. He blitzed Brad Gilbert, his future coach, 6-1, 6-3 in the quarterfinals at Itaparica, and defeated Brazilian Luiz Mattar 7-6, 6-2 in the final.

Agassi was so popular, even then, with his blistering groundstrokes and long, frosted hair that half of the Brazilian crowd rooted for him.

"Usually, all of the crowd is for me [in Brazil]," Mattar said, "but they were applauding him for good shots."

Agassi earned $90,000 to give him $205,555 for the year, and ended 1987 with a world ranking of No. 25.

*   *   *

Agassi continued his meteoric rise and became a born-again Christian in 1988. He won six singles titles, reached the semifinals of the French Open and U.S. Open, soared to No. 3 and earned $822,062. Agassi also unintentionally offended many fellow pros with impertinent remarks and actions.

In his first tournament of 1988, Agassi beat Mikael Pernfors of Sweden to win the $415,000 U.S. National Indoor Championships at Memphis, Tenn., for his first Grand Prix title in the U.S.

Agassi's behavior had improved drastically since the Nevada State Open less than two years before. He couldn't have been more charming in Memphis.

Agassi applauded good shots by Pernfors in the final. When Pernfors muttered something in Swedish, Agassi joked aloud, "I feel the same way." When Pernfors dropped his racket, so did Agassi.

After Agassi won the match, he hugged his father, mother and brother and a handicapped person sitting in a wheelchair at courtside. Then Agassi retrieved his racket and gave it to the disabled person.

Tennis psychologist Jim Loehr wrote in the June 1988 issue of *World Tennis* that Agassi's emotional turnaround was the greatest he had seen. Agassi said in the story there were two reasons for his turnaround — his born-again Christianity and Bollettieri's confidence in him.

"Two years ago I was competitive but could only accept winning," Agassi said at the time. "Winning was everything. If I wasn't winning, I couldn't handle it. I was very self-centered. I've come to understand that my problems on the court were really problems in me off the court."

Agassi stopped playing for his father and Bollettieri in an effort to pay them back for all of their sacrifices.

"I had to go through some really bad times before I could start taking responsibility for myself," Agassi said. "Now I'm playing for myself, and that's a big difference. Playing for someone else makes you very lonely. . . .

"Suddenly, I realized I could still be competitive and say 'nice shot.' And it's not a facade. . . . The thought of losing doesn't bother me now. It only bothers me if I haven't given 100 percent effort. So the pressure is off. If I lose, I lose. I now know that if I stay positive and keep on working, my talent will eventually come out."

It did, but losing would continue to bother Agassi a great deal.

Agassi was introduced to religion by his father and attended First Good Shepherd Lutheran School in Las Vegas.

"He was always raised with a belief in God and Christianity, I know, from his father," Wendi Stewart said. "He was always aware of it."

In the winter of 1987, he received guidance from Fritz Glauss, the pro tour's traveling minister.

"He earned my trust," Agassi said. "I was facing a lot of questions in my life. I knew there had to be more important things than tennis, money and fame. I thought I'd give the Bible a chance."

David Wheaton and his mother, Mary Jane, also played a role in Agassi's conversion.

"Mrs. Wheaton asked Andre, 'Do you know where you're going when you die?' " Perry Rogers said. "Andre said he didn't begin to know. There was no crisis. It was a very thoughtful process."

Agassi and Chang, also a devout Christian, attended Bible class together in the Vermont woods in the summer of 1988.

"In the juniors Andre had a bad attitude," Chang said. "This is a whole new guy. Studying the Bible, learning about the Lord, stuff like that, has really calmed him down."

Temporarily.

Meanwhile, Agassi showed signs in 1988 of becoming the superstar Americans had longed for since Jimmy Connors and McEnroe dominated the late 1970s and early 1980s. Once they passed their prime, however, nobody took their places. From the 1985 Australian Open through the 1989 Australian Open, foreign players won all 16 Grand Slam men's singles titles. Czechoslovakia's Lendl won six, Mats Wilander four, Stefan Edberg of Sweden three, Germany's Boris Becker two and Australia's Cash one.

Agassi appeared to be America's best bet to break the streak. Jim Courier and Pete Sampras turned 18 and 17, respectively, in 1988 and were obscure. Chang was only 16.

The Las Vegan played even with Wilander for four sets in the semifinals of the 1988 French Open before wilting and losing the decisive fifth set 6-0. Wilander went on to win the sixth of his seven Grand Slam singles titles.

Agassi lost to Lendl in four sets in the semifinals of the U.S. Open, his only other Grand Slam tournament of the year. He skipped the Australian Open and Wimbledon from 1988 through 1990.

Among Agassi's six titles in 1988 was the Volvo International at Stratton Mountain. He defeated Paul Annacone in the final in a matchup of alumni from the Bollettieri academy.

Agassi qualified for his first Nabisco Grand Prix Masters (now the ATP Tour World Championship), featuring the top eight singles players of the year. He finished 1-2 in round-robin play to drop out of contention.

Agassi also debuted in the Davis Cup in 1988. He won all three of his singles matches, in the American Zone semifinals at Peru and the final at Argentina. That put the U.S. back in the World Group, consisting of the top 16 nations, to contend for the Davis Cup title in 1989.

It's no coincidence that Agassi won more as he tamed his power.

"When I started off playing tournaments, I tried to hit the ball as hard as I could all the time," he said. "When I played well, I won. When I didn't, I lost. I've learned to be more consistent and play with the talent I've been given."

Wherever he played, Agassi charmed crowds with his flowing locks, exotic good looks, denim shorts and dynamic game. Agassi was a showman in true Las Vegas style, applauding opponents' winners, bowing to the crowd after victories and tossing his shirt to the crowd.

Agassi was becoming the biggest draw in tennis since Borg was a teenage heartthrob. At a Davis Cup match in Peru, the crowd gave him two standing ovations. In Paris, the crowd stormed Court 2 after he won his second-round match. When he played in Seoul, girls skipped class to watch him play.

"Seeing Agassi play in person is a little bit like attending a Beatles concert during the 1960s," wrote Brian Hewitt of *The Los Angeles Times*. ". . . Agassi's fans squeal. And they shriek. . . ."

Sales of Agassi's denim shorts tripled since he began wearing them in March 1988, according to *Tennis*. Nike had a first print run of 25,000 Agassi posters, five times the amount for its other star athletes. Agassi received 2,000 letters a week at the Association of Tennis Professionals office in Texas, forcing staffers to give him his own mailbox. One batch included three separate letters from women that included pictures of them nude.

"I've never seen anything like it," Lori Stukes, a tour press liaison, said of Agassi's skyrocketing popularity. "At the French Open last May, Agassi had by far more requests for interviews than any other player. It was the same at the U.S. Open. It all started when he won Memphis, and it just kept escalating from there. He could spend *all* his time doing interviews."

Agassi, however, was starting to annoy many players with what they considered showboating and disrespect.

In the process of routing Martin Jaite of Argentina in the Davis Cup, Agassi showed him up by catching one of Jaite's serves to give him a game in the third set.

After beating Connors 6-2, 7-6, 6-1 in the quarterfinals of the 1988 U.S. Open, Agassi announced that he had told Rogers he expected to win "three, three and three." Although Connors ended up winning only nine games, he had pushed Agassi at times. "I didn't know Jimmy would have that much in him," Agassi said.

Connors — 36 at the time, twice as old as Agassi — rolled his eyes when told of Agassi's comments.

"That's a bad mistake," Connors said. "I'll remember that. I'll play him again. Hell, I've followed guys to the end of the earth."

Connors added, though: "Now I don't think I'll follow *him*. I'm not begging for respect. It's a war zone out there. I enjoy playing guys who could be my children. Maybe he's one of them. I spent a lot of time in Vegas."

Two more incidents occurred two weeks later in back-to-back matches at Los Angeles.

Mark Woodforde, 22 at the time, was arguing with the umpire over a line call in the middle of his 2-6, 7-5, 6-3 loss to Agassi in the quarterfinals. Agassi, 18, loudly reprimanded Woodforde for challenging the umpire's authority. That just isn't done.

When Agassi tanked a set in his 6-4, 0-6, 6-4 victory over McEnroe in the semifinals, McEnroe blew up, calling Agassi's ploy "insulting, immature, a cop-out." Agassi had pulled the stunt before. It was his way of creating more of a challenge.

Agassi also led some to question his intelligence when he asked in Peru, "What's an Inca?"

Agassi eventually toned down his act.

Meanwhile, many felt Agassi's entourage was giving him bad advice. Shelton was becoming notorious for refusing to grant interview requests with Agassi.

Agassi acknowledged that the people around him "all made decisions that probably hurt me. They didn't call the shots; I just decided that I'd entrust them with certain things, and I wouldn't do it any differently today.

"Also, all of them will be with me to the end, because I have a natural instinct to stand by my loved ones. In a way, it's my downfall in relationships. I'm the last one to get out of the trench once we're in it. I won't bail out, and I hope I never lose that quality. It shouldn't be easy to hurt people, or to take their lives lightly."

Shelton later quit by mutual agreement, and Bollettieri quit on his own, wounding Agassi emotionally.

None of the controversies, though, could overshadow Agassi's breakthrough year.

Image Is Everything

Agassi slumped in 1989 after his impressive 1988. He won only one title, in a minor tournament at Orlando, Fla., and fell to No. 7 in the year-end rankings. His prize money plummeted to $478,901. Agassi did, however, pass $1 million in career earnings in only his 43rd tournament, faster than any player before him.

Agassi, burned out after his lucrative year, admitted that he "didn't care about playing at all [in 1989]. Ninety-five percent of the time I didn't really feel like being out there."

There was one controversy and setback after another in 1989.

Agassi switched from the Prince racket that took him so close to the top to a Belgian-made Donnay racket, receiving a five-year, $6 million contract.

As usual, Agassi skipped the Australian Open. His first competition of the year was the first round of the Davis Cup against Paraguay at Fort Myers, Fla. In the United States' 5-0 victory, Agassi ridiculed Paraguayan fans by putting his thumbs in his ears and wiggling his fingers. When someone mentioned the bloody coup that had just occurred in Paraguay, Agassi, probably trying to be funny, said, "I don't even know how to spell 'coup.' "

Writer Curry Kirkpatrick exposed Agassi's warts in the March 13, 1989, issue of *Sports Illustrated*. It was the first critical national press Agassi had received.

"The press and a lot of people started to voice doubts about me and were very critical in a vindictive way," Agassi said. "It affected me. I was shellshocked. They first built me up as a role model, then they attacked me and made me out as the bad guy.

"For a while, I wondered whether tennis was worth it. I had to dig deep. I just decided to be my own person, and if people don't like it, then just let it go."

Two weeks after the *Sports Illustrated* story appeared, Agassi lost to Carl-Uwe Steeb of what was then West Germany 6-4, 7-5, 6-0 in the first round of the Lipton International Players Championships at Key Biscayne, Fla. Afterward, Agassi disrespectfully said he had never heard of Steeb. All Steeb had done was upset Mats Wilander in West Germany's 4-1 triumph over Sweden in the Davis Cup final the previous December.

Agassi reached his first final of the year in the Italian Open on clay in May. He held a match point against Alberto Mancini of Argentina in the fourth set before losing 6-3, 4-6, 2-6, 7-6 (7-2), 6-1. It would have been Agassi's biggest title.

The French Open later that month was notable for two reasons: Agassi and Jim Courier, both coached by Nick Bollettieri, met in the third round, and Michael Chang shocked the tennis world by winning the tournament.

Rather than sit in a neutral corner for the Agassi-Courier match, Bollettieri joined Phillip Agassi and Bill Shelton and rooted for Andre. "I realized that Nick didn't want me to win," Courier said later, "and it kind of hurt me."

With extra motivation, Courier defeated Agassi, 7-6, 4-6, 6-3, 6-2.

Chang stunned top-ranked Ivan Lendl 4-6, 4-6, 6-3, 6-3, 6-3 in the round of 16 in one of the most memorable matches of the Open era. Chang overcame cramps, at one point serving underhand, to win in four hours and 37 minutes. He left the court in tears and collapsed in the training room.

In the final, Chang came from two sets to one down to beat Stefan Edberg. Three months past his 17th birthday, Chang became the youngest male to win a Grand Slam singles title, a distinction he still holds. He also became the first American to win the French Open since Tony Trabert in 1955, and ended foreign domination of Grand Slam tournaments.

So it turned out that Chang was America's newest superstar, not Agassi. But Agassi didn't seem to mind.

"It's almost a sense of relief," he said. "People stop talking to me and picking on me. For the first time, I get questions about other players instead of other players getting questions about me."

One question Agassi couldn't avoid was why he skipped Wimbledon for the second straight year. He squirmed when the subject arose at the ANA Cup, a four-man, $500,000 special event in Yokohama, Japan.

"I wanted to take some time off," Agassi said. "It doesn't mean as much to me as other players. As far as Grand Slams are concerned, it falls third [after the U.S. Open and the French Open]. It's a good time to go home and work on my strength for the rest of the year."

Agassi, meanwhile, suffered the first losses of his Davis Cup career, after seven straight victories, as West Germany defeated the U.S. 3-2 in the semifinals indoors at Munich, West Germany.

His first match was a classic. Agassi, ranked sixth, won the first two sets against Boris Becker, ranked second, in tiebreakers. Agassi served for the match at 5-4 in the third set, but Becker broke back and won the set before a midnight curfew caused the match to be suspended until the next morning. Becker, who had just won his third Wimbledon title, prevailed in five sets.

Steeb, ranked 28th, upset Agassi the next day 4-6, 6-4, 6-4, 6-2 to clinch the series for Germany.

"The first match against Becker, I played about as well as I could," Agassi said. "I almost won a couple of times in the third set. After we lost the doubles, the way I played in the next match left a lot to be desired."

John Feinstein wrote in *Hard Courts*, his 1991 book about the men's and women's professional tennis tours, that Agassi gave up against Steeb. On each changeover, U.S. non-playing captain Tom Gorman pleaded with Agassi to fight back.

"It's too tough," Agassi kept saying. "Just too tough."

Feinstein blasted Agassi in the book.

"Tanking — giving up, quitting, just going through the motions — when playing in a tournament is a rotten thing to do," Feinstein wrote. "At least when Agassi did it in tournaments, he was representing only himself. In the Davis Cup, he was representing his country. To tank was unthinkable.

"And yet, Agassi had done it. In one short year he had gone from being the delight of the tennis tour to its mystery player. He had become the most blatant tank artist in the game and didn't seem the least bit bothered by it. When the media began to criticize Agassi for his half-hearted efforts, he responded by turning down virtually all interview requests, saying that he had been treated unfairly. . . ."

There was some question whether Gorman would ever use Agassi again after the showing against Steeb.

"It shook me up, no doubt about it," Gorman said later that year. "I just couldn't figure out a way to get through to Andre. If he's going to play for me again, he and I are going to have to communicate a lot better. I don't think I could go through a match like the Steeb match again."

Agassi returned to the Davis Cup team the following year under controversial circumstances.

After the fiasco against Steeb, Agassi returned to his sanctuary, the Volvo International at Stratton Mountain. This time, Agassi lost to David Wheaton 1-6, 7-6, 6-1 in the round of 16. When Agassi came off the court, he pointed at Bollettieri and demanded, "Fire Fritz [Glauss]," a reference to Agassi's spiritual adviser.

For the second straight year, Agassi beat Jimmy Connors in the quarterfinals of the U.S. Open. Agassi trailed Connors, 37, two sets to one before winning in five sets for the first time in his career. Agassi had been 0-4 in five-set matches, most likely a reflection of inadequate conditioning and reliance on his talent.

Agassi played in his second straight Grand Prix Masters, but was eliminated with an 0-3 record in round-robin play. Becker improved his career record against Agassi to 3-0 with a 6-1, 6-3 victory. However, Becker would not beat Agassi again for almost six years.

*   *   *

Agassi bounced back in 1990, but the year was still a disappointment. He reached the first two Grand Slam finals of his career, led the U.S. to its first Davis Cup title since 1982, won the inaugural ATP Tour World Championship and three other tournaments and improved to No. 4 in the year-end rankings. He beat Becker three times and Edberg twice, dispelling the notion that he couldn't beat the top players.

But Agassi, 20, lost the two matches that mattered most — the French Open final to a player supposedly too old (30-year-old Andres Gomez) and the U.S. Open final to a player supposedly too young (19-year-old Pete Sampras).

"I'll take those to my grave," Agassi said.

As usual, the year was laced with controversy.

Agassi's preparation for the French Open, which began in late May, was meager. Since beating Edberg to win the Lipton in March, Agassi had played in only one tournament and a couple of exhibitions. He reached the third round of the German Open in Hamburg three weeks before the French Open.

Agassi, ranked fifth in the world, arrived in Paris 24 hours before his first match — unthinkable for anyone else.

No sooner had Agassi landed at Charles de Gaulle Airport than he reportedly got into an argument.

"He was met there by a [tournament] chauffeur in a Peugeot 605, a new luxury model," Alexander Wolff wrote in *Sports Illustrated*. "Agassi, a lover of automobiles, insisted on driving into town himself. The chauffeur was equally insistent that this was not possible. By the driver's account, Agassi threw a tantrum, calming only after a phone call to the tournament office established that the auto insurance policy ruled out his getting behind the wheel."

Agassi's temper continued to flare when he struggled to beat Canadian Martin Wostenholme, ranked 122nd, 4-6, 7-6, 6-0, 6-1 in the first round.

Agassi drew a warning from umpire Sultan Gangji in the first set for throwing his racket and stepping on it in anger over a line call. After losing his serve early in the second set, Agassi called Gangji "a little shit," according to Feinstein, but Gangji claimed later he hadn't heard the remark.

After a close line call later in the match, Agassi yelled at Gangji, "You get out of that damn chair right now and come check this mark!" Gangji ignored him.

Agassi was fined $2,000 for racket abuse after the match, rather than the usual $500.

Later in the week, Agassi feuded with Philippe Chatrier, the president of the International Tennis Federation and the French Tennis Federation, over the player's colorful tennis attire. Agassi wore his usual black denim shorts over fluorescent pink stretch pants. His shirt and headband were black, pink and white. When Chatrier objected to the outfit, Agassi called him a "bozo."

Meanwhile, the third-seeded Agassi avenged his loss to Courier the year before by beating him in the round of 16, eliminated defending champion Chang and ousted Jonas Svensson of Sweden to reach his first Grand Slam final.

Gomez, the fourth seed and one of only six players in the 128-man singles draw 30 years old or older, was also playing in his first Grand Slam final. He had reached No. 5 in 1984 but now was near retirement. Gomez had even considered serving as a commentator on Ecuadorian television for the 1990 French Open, rather than playing, until he heard that Lendl, his nemesis, was skipping the tournament to practice on grass for Wimbledon.

Gomez, knowing this was his last chance to win a Grand Slam title, outplayed Agassi, 6-3, 2-6, 6-4, 6-4.

"I've never had a problem getting beat," Agassi said. "I've always had a problem losing."

Agassi admitted that he got beat in the final.

Mike Agassi, however, said Andre was overconfident.

"When he won in the semifinals, he thought he had won the tournament," Mike said. "He thought Gomez was nothing, and then he lost."

Agassi skipped Wimbledon again and returned to Las Vegas with Gil Reyes, the former conditioning coach at the University of Nevada Las Vegas, to work on his strength. In fact, Agassi had grown an inch to 5 feet 11 inches and added about a dozen pounds of muscle.

Agassi won the title at Washington, D.C., but then struggled during the summer.

When Agassi arrived in Cincinnati for the ATP Championship, he told the volunteer driver he needed security so he wouldn't be mobbed at the rural airport, which was empty. The driver looked curiously at Agassi and said: "Andre, it's 11:30 at night. We're in Kentucky. Unless you've appeared on *Hee Haw* lately, no one here is going to mob you."

At Cincinnati, Agassi was fined $1,850 for twice using the word "fuck" during a three-set loss to Richard Fromberg of Australia in the round of 16. For the year, Agassi had been fined in four of his eight ATP tournaments and once for racket abuse at the French Open for a total penalty of $5,650.

After the loss to Fromberg, Agassi complained that it was impossible to get motivated to play "guys like this every week." Fromberg was ranked 32nd in the world.

Agassi lost 6-4, 6-0 to Peter Lundgren of Sweden in the quarterfinals at Indianapolis the following week.

"Any rumors that Agassi had quit tanking were clearly exaggerated," Feinstein wrote.

The U.S. Open was similar to the French Open for Agassi. There was more talk about his clothes, even worse behavior on the court and a one-sided loss in the final.

Agassi showed up for his first-round match against Grant Connell of Canada in a new outfit accented by chartreuse rather than fluorescent pink. His shirt was cut short in the front to reveal his stomach whenever he hit a forehand. Agassi's entire first-round postmatch press conference was devoted to questions about the outfit.

In a second-round victory over Petr Korda, Agassi was warned by chair umpire Wayne McKewen for saying "fuck." Agassi then called McKewen a "sonofabitch," but the umpire didn't hear it. If he had, Agassi would have been assessed a point penalty, putting him one misstep from a default.

On the next changeover, Agassi spit in McKewen's direction. The saliva landed on McKewen's leg and foot. When supervisor Ken Farrar and referee Keith Johnson were summoned, Agassi insisted it was an accident and offered McKewen a towel. Farrar and Johnson could have ruled that the incident constituted gross misconduct, which would have resulted in immediate default. Instead, they believed Agassi and decided not to penalize him. But after viewing a tape of the incident the next day, Farrar fined Agassi $3,000.

"It's clear from the tape that he spit in McKewen's direction," Farrar said. "I wouldn't say he spit on him, but he definitely spit at him. There's a difference, but it isn't a big difference. If he spit on him, you would default him immediately. For spitting at him, he should definitely have been given a point penalty."

Agassi later apologized to Farrar and insisted he wouldn't cause any more trouble. But in his next news conference, Agassi accused McKewen of incompetence and bias.

"When Farrar heard these comments, he was furious," Feinstein wrote. "Twice, he had believed Agassi — on the court and then on the phone — and twice Agassi had been proved deceitful."

Agassi defeated Becker in a four-set semifinal to advance to the final against Sampras. Lendl announced he was rooting for Sampras.

"I'm sad anyone can cherish Agassi," said the clean-cut Lendl. "The kids see him as a rebel with his earring, hair and no-shave look."

Agassi was nervous entering the final, and Sampras never gave him a chance in a 6-4, 6-3, 6-2 victory. Sampras befuddled Agassi with 120-mph serves, firing 13 aces and 12 service winners. Agassi never forced a deuce game on Sampras' serve in the first two sets.

"The better man won today," Agassi admitted, adding that he wanted to take Sampras back to Las Vegas with him.

"Anything he touched turned to gold," Agassi said. "I'd like to turn him loose in the casinos."

Agassi wasn't ready to confer greatness on Sampras, though.

"Hey, let's not get carried away here," Agassi said. "The guy's still got a lot of tennis to play before we start assuming too much about him. He still has a lot to prove."

So did Agassi. His just-released camera commercial, featuring the slogan "Image is Everything," would haunt him for years.

Agassi beat Sampras 6-4, 6-2 two months later en route to the ATP Tour World Championship title at Frankfurt, West Germany. Agassi was highly motivated, and Sampras was suffering from shin splints.

"I was out to prove that the Open was just one day in New York," Agassi said.

Agassi went on to beat Becker in the semifinals and Edberg in the final. Agassi's weight training was paying off — literally. He earned $950,000 for the ATP title.

"A year ago, I would not have been able to lift 135 pounds one or two times," he said. "Before coming here, I lifted 245 pounds three times."

After winning the ATP championship, Agassi helped the U.S. beat Australia in the Davis Cup final.

Even the United States' march to the Davis Cup title was plagued by turmoil.

Agassi, wrote Feinstein, withdrew from the team that was going to Czechoslovakia for the quarterfinals because Gorman objected to Agassi's entourage. Gorman considered them a distraction to the rest of the team.

"Agassi immediately called for Gorman's replacement; he said Gorman was a follower, not a leader, and said the *players* should pick their captain," Feinstein wrote.

Aaron Krickstein replaced Agassi and won both of his singles matches to lead the U.S. over the Czechs 4-1 at Prague.

USTA president David Markin, however, decided that Agassi would play against Austria in the semifinals and could bring anyone he wanted. Agassi would also play in the final if the U.S. beat the Austrians.

Chang reluctantly agreed to play for the U.S. against Austria. He and Agassi would play singles, and Rick Leach and Jim Pugh would play doubles.

They faced a formidable challenge against Thomas Muster and Horst Skoff in singles and Muster and Alexander Antonitsch in doubles. The matches would be held on clay in one corner of a soccer stadium with about 17,000 seats. Muster had never lost a Davis Cup match on clay.

Muster and the flaky Skoff weren't on speaking terms, but Muster said that didn't matter.

"This isn't soccer," he said. "We all have a job to do. We don't have to like each other to do it."

Muster knocked off Chang in four sets, but Agassi followed with a straight-set victory over Skoff to tie the series 1-1 after the first day. During the second match, Gorman periodically relayed notes from Agassi's entourage to Agassi. Davis Cup rules allow communication only between a player and his coach.

"The entourage situation was completely overrated," Gorman said. "Yes, we have put a stop to the passing of notes down. That happened in Austria."

Leach and Pugh won the doubles in four sets on the second day to give the U.S. a 2-1 lead heading into the final day. That night, the Austrians threw a lavish dinner for the two teams at the Hoffberg Palace, but Feinstein wrote that neither Agassi nor Chang appeared.

Muster beat Agassi 6-2, 6-2, 7-6 Sunday to even the series 2-2. That left it up to Chang, who thrives on pressure. But Skoff, blasting forehands, won the first two sets 6-3, 7-6. After Chang won the third set 6-4, darkness forced the match to be suspended until Monday. No American since Don Budge in 1938 had come back from two sets down in the deciding match of a Davis Cup.

Chang called his older brother and coach Carl on Sunday night. Carl, who had watched the match on television, advised Michael to hit every shot to Skoff's backhand. Michael followed the advice and won the last two sets, 6-4, 6-3.

The final between longtime rivals, the U.S. and Australia, was practically a foregone conclusion. Australia did not have the firepower to match the U.S., particularly on the clay court at the dreary Suncoast Dome in St. Petersburg, Fla. Agassi edged Fromberg 6-4 in the fifth set in the first match, and Chang beat Darren Cahill in straight sets for a 2-0 lead.

Agassi said after his match that he had been so sick all week he couldn't even roll over in bed.

"I just won it on sheer guts," Agassi said repeatedly.

Fromberg shook his head when he heard that and said, "Just rubbish. I didn't see him sick during the match."

Leach and Pugh clinched the Cup for the U.S. on Saturday with a four-set victory over Pat Cash and John Fitzgerald.

In a meaningless match Sunday, Agassi and Cahill were tied at one set apiece when Agassi quit with what he said was a pulled stomach muscle. Again, the Aussies were skeptical.

"He didn't look injured to me," Cahill said. "Andre is a great player, but what comes out of his mouth is of little significance. I wouldn't want him on [our] team. We have a tradition; we go down fighting."

Agassi has won 15 straight Davis Cup singles matches since then, one short of the American record set by the legendary Bill Tilden.

Agassi became embroiled in another controversy late that night at a pancake house. Reporter Barry Lorge overheard Andre and Phillip ripping Gorman and saying they had to find a doctor who would certify that Agassi was too hurt to play in the inaugural Grand Slam Cup in 10 days. Lorge mentioned the conversation in a column. Three doctors later swore that Agassi was hurt, and Agassi claimed that Lorge had misunderstood the conversation. Agassi also denied he had criticized Gorman.

Agassi had signed up in October to play in the Grand Slam Cup. He announced two weeks later that he was withdrawing, saying it detracted from the ATP Tour World Championship. Just before the ITF planned to announce that Agassi would be suspended for the 1991 French Open, Agassi relented and said he would play. Then came Agassi's injury in the Davis Cup and another withdrawal. The ITF fined Agassi $25,000, but he avoided suspension because the doctors had sworn he was injured.

Agassi's image was also damaged. Feinstein reported that Agassi hadn't done a one-on-one interview with a print journalist for almost two years. Then Bob Kain of International Management Group (IMG) launched a PR campaign. Suddenly Agassi was available to the media. He even picked up reporters at the airport.

*   *   *

Very little went right for Agassi in 1991. He lost his third straight Grand Slam final, fell in the first round of the U.S. Open, won only two titles (against relatively weak competition in Orlando, Fla., and Washington, D.C.) and dropped to No. 10 in the year-end rankings. Agassi did, however, return to Wimbledon after a three-year absence and reached the quarterfinals.

Agassi checked into the opulent Georges V Hotel in Paris with his entourage — Phillip, Bollettieri, hitting partner Fritz Nau, Shelton and Reyes — for the French Open. Rather than eat at one of the nearby gourmet restaurants, though, they dined at McDonald's or brought tacos to their room.

For the tournament, Agassi wore purple stretch pants under his denim shorts and a white and purple shirt. He had little trouble reaching the semifinals, in which he beat Becker for the fourth straight time and advanced to the final against his former roommate at the Bollettieri academy, Courier.

Agassi was a solid favorite to beat Courier in the first all-American men's final in the French Open since 1954, when Tony Trabert beat Art (Tappy) Larsen. Agassi was 4-2 in the pros against Courier, who was appearing in his first Grand Slam final.

The first set went to Agassi 6-2. He had a break point to lead 4-1 in the second set but squandered it. Then rain interrupted the match. During the short delay, Courier's coach, Jose Higueras, advised Courier to move 10 feet behind the baseline to work his way into rallies with the hard-hitting Agassi.

It worked. Courier won the second set 6-4, but Agassi recovered to capture the third set 6-2. For the first time, Agassi was within one set of a Grand Slam title. But he lost 12 of the first 13 points of the fourth set, which Courier won 6-1.

At 4-4 in the fifth set, Agassi succumbed to the pressure and lost his serve. Courier held his for the match. Agassi was 0-3 in Grand Slam finals.

"The pessimistic side of me questions if I'll ever win one," a devastated Agassi said afterward, with his voice breaking and eyes tearing.

Agassi finally returned to Wimbledon later that month.

"We had bullshitted the media," Bollettieri wrote in *My Aces, My Faults* about Agassi's absence from the world's most prestigious tennis tournament. "We had said Andre wasn't ready for the grass courts, he wasn't strong enough, he wasn't mature enough. But the truth was that, after being eliminated in the first round in 1987, he simply decided he didn't like the surface or the atmosphere. I should have argued with him, emphasizing the significance of Wimbledon, but instead, I just went along.

"Now Andre was stronger and more mature — and, most important, confident enough to believe he could do well on any surface. He dressed in Wimbledon white, charmed the press by saying all the right things about the tradition and magnitude of the tournament, and as soon as he got out on the grass courts, he realized that the surface actually played to his strength, rewarded him for moving in and hitting the ball on the rise as it skidded off the grass."

Agassi had added 26 pounds of muscle in a year and a half with rigorous weight training. He addressed rumors of steroid use in *Tennis* (France).

"I can understand that certain people were surprised at my having added muscle so quickly — 26 pounds total — that they had trouble admitting that it was only due to training," Agassi said. "That is the case, however, I assure you. I've worked out in a totally natural way, I never took steroids, and I can tell you that if I had wanted to, I'd have to find a trainer other than Gil Reyes.

"I decided to do this to counter the power of others. I had never had a real problem giving my game a certain power. But in 1988 and 1989, Boris Becker had beaten me three times. I felt that in terms of pure tennis, we were about equal, but he dominated me in athletic power. That's why I wanted to get stronger. . . ."

Agassi was listed at 5 feet 11 inches and 155 pounds at 20 years old in the 1990 ATP Tour media guide and 5 feet 11 inches, 175 pounds the next year. Becker, 2½ years older than Agassi, was listed at 6 feet 3 inches, 187 pounds in 1990 and 1991.

After losing to Becker in their first three meetings (1988 to 1989), Agassi won the next eight (1990 to 1995).

Wendi Stewart, who traveled full time with Agassi on the circuit as his girlfriend, from 1990 through 1992, also said the rumors were unfounded.

"When I started traveling with him, his legs were skinnier than mine," she admitted. "But I saw him working his ass off in the weight room and drinking protein shakes to gain weight."

There is no evidence that Agassi has ever used steroids.

Meanwhile, Agassi was showing at Wimbledon in 1991 that he could indeed play on grass. He beat Richard Krajicek of the Netherlands in a third-round matchup of future Wimbledon champions before losing to hard-serving Wheaton in the quarterfinals.

As the eighth seed and a returning finalist in the U.S. Open, Agassi lost listlessly to unseeded Krickstein 7-5, 7-6, 6-2 in the first round.

One night later, Connors, a 39-year-old wild card, clawed his way to a 4-6, 6-7, 6-4, 6-2, 6-4 victory over Patrick McEnroe in four hours and 20 minutes. Connors had trailed 0-3 and 0-40 in the third set.

The irony of the two matches was not lost on Kirkpatrick of *Sports Illustrated*.

"Old versus young. Substance versus style. Never were the contrasts between how much Connors means to the game and how little Agassi cares about it so obvious as they were in New York . . ." Kirkpatrick wrote in a column.

It wasn't that Agassi didn't care about tennis. It was that he cared so much. Agassi was still agonizing over the French Open loss to Courier. Agassi's father taught him that to lose any match was a crisis. How was Andre going to feel after losing his third Grand Slam final after leading two sets to one?

"Wimbledon was my last hurrah for the year," Agassi said. "I felt fried mentally. I think after Wimbledon, the French Open took its toll on me. I almost felt like it wasn't worth getting to another final to feel that amount of pain."

Agassi considered quitting again.

Christianity had helped Agassi, but it wasn't a panacea. A lifetime of expectations was preventing him from winning the big one. What to do now?

Move away from home. Get away from his father. After all, Andre was 21. Mike was still pushing, still meddling, but Andre was no longer listening. Two months after the U.S. Open loss, Agassi moved into a house of his own. It was only a few miles away, but it was an important step.

There was one more piece of business to take care of in 1991 — the Davis Cup final at Lyon, France. Agassi and Stewart dined on cheeseburgers on the flight to France, *Sports Illustrated* reported. Agassi had called ahead to order a special meal.

As if that wasn't bad enough for a world-class athlete, Agassi filled up on Reese's peanut butter cups and Snicker's candy bars in Lyon.

Sampras was making his Davis Cup debut under the most difficult circumstances — in a final on the road. Even he was not quite ready for such a challenge. Admittedly overwhelmed by the occasion, Sampras lost both of his singles matches as the two-man team of Henri Leconte and Guy Forget (pronounced "ghee for-ZHAY") defeated the U.S., 3-1.

France rejoiced over its first Davis Cup title since 1932. The Davis Cup is much more popular outside of the U.S. than in it because other countries have fewer major sports and star athletes. When one of them wins an international title, especially against the mighty U.S., it's a big deal.

Agassi, rising to the occasion, gave the U.S. its only point against France with an opening four-set victory over Forget. Agassi's troubles were far from over, though.

Beating The Odds

8

Agassi passed up the Australian Open for the sixth straight year in January 1992. This time, he admitted that he made a mistake.

"I was getting away from the burned-out, latter part of the year," said Agassi, who still had never played in the year's first Grand Slam tournament. "I had no motivation, no desire to dig down and fight. I just wanted to get away. I thought that was the right play."

But Agassi fell behind players who competed in the Australian.

"It makes you tournament tough," Perry Rogers said.

Injuries prevented Agassi from playing in the Australian Open for three more years. He has still competed in it only twice.

Agassi began 1992 by winning both of his Davis Cup singles matches in the United States' 5-0 victory over Argentina in the first round at the beautiful Mauna Lani Racquet Club on the big island of Hawaii. One of the victories, however, was a meaningless two-set triumph after the outcome had been decided.

Then Agassi struggled again, failing to reach the quarterfinals in his first six tournaments of the year. He dropped out of the top 10 in January for the first time since May 1988 and hit a season-low of No. 17 on April 13. It was the worst slump of his seven-year career.

Agassi and Wendi Stewart traveled 32 hours door to door from Hawaii to the $565,000 Muratti Time Indoor in Milan, Italy. This was one year before Agassi bought a jet. Under the circumstances, it was hardly surprising when Jakob Hlasek of Switzerland routed Agassi 6-2, 6-1 in the first round.

The next week, Agassi fell in the second round of the $656,000 Donnay Indoor Championship at Brussels to Alexander Volkov of Russia 7-6, 6-3. Donnay was the manufacturer of Agassi's racket.

"He played so bad that time," said Volkov, then ranked 31st in the world. "He couldn't move. He was out of confidence, out of shape. He didn't move like he wanted to play."

The losses mounted. Maybe Agassi wasn't as good as he thought he was.

"I've always been such a confidence player," he said. "I've always believed in myself. But now, I'm stepping onto the court with questions."

Meanwhile, the money continued to pour in from sponsors and tournaments eager for his participation. Three times in early 1992 he received tournament guarantees of $300,000 just to play, *Sports Illustrated* reported. Whatever prize money he won was additional. Mind you, he still had not won a Grand Slam title.

"Most people have to work really hard and win some big matches, and then they get money and popularity," Agassi said. "For me it has been the reverse of everybody else. The exact opposite."

Agassi tried everything to snap out of his slump. He experimented with his string tension, footwork, training regimen and diet. Nothing worked.

Once again, though, Agassi got motivated for the Davis Cup. He won both of his singles matches in straight sets as the U.S. defeated Czechoslovakia 3-2 in the quarterfinals at Fort Myers, Fla. Agassi beat Karel Novacek in the deciding match 7-6, 6-0, 6-0 to increase his Davis Cup winning streak to seven.

Agassi uttered one of his more memorable lines after the rout.

"You can never beat anyone too badly or go too far for a Taco Bell," he said.

But Agassi's troubles resumed on the regular tour.

After Agassi lost to 77th-ranked Franco Davin of Argentina 6-4, 7-6 in the quarterfinals on clay at Tampa, Fla., he left the tournament grounds near tears.

Agassi took a week off, did away with all the experiments and decided that what was really bothering him was the loss to Jim Courier in the 1991 French Open final.

"It felt so unfair," he said. "It made me doubt, it hurt my confidence, it made me second-guess myself. And it wasn't until last week that I said, 'I'm done with that.' "

Agassi reverted to his old habits — light on preparation and heavy on junk food. He put in only two 45-minute practice sessions with Nick Bollettieri in Las Vegas for the AT&T Challenge on clay in Atlanta. He then took a red-eye flight that arrived in Atlanta at 7 A.M. on the day of his first match, slept until 2 P.M., hit a few balls and beat Mikael Pernfors 7-5, 6-2 that night.

Agassi won the tournament, beating Pete Sampras 7-5, 6-4 in the final. Clay is Sampras' worst surface, and most of the world's top clay-courters were playing in Madrid or Munich that week, but Agassi had made progress.

Then a strange transformation took place in Agassi during the French Open.

"When I got to Paris, I felt a lot of pressure," he said. "I stepped on the court, and it was as if it wasn't even a

Grand Slam tournament. I was doing something that I love again, and I don't think I've felt that since I was 18 years old. Once I had that feeling, I knew I wouldn't let it go again. It was too important to me."

What happened, Rogers said, was that Agassi decided to play for himself rather than try to prove to the media that he could win the big one.

"It's a lot of pressure for a 22-year-old to say, 'I've got to win a Grand Slam title,' " Rogers said.

Agassi whipped Sampras 7-6, 6-2, 6-1 in the quarterfinals and met Courier in the French Open for the fourth straight year. Courier, ranked No. 1 and the defending champion, crushed Agassi 6-3, 6-2, 6-2, but it was a good tournament for Agassi overall.

With Wimbledon two weeks away, Agassi returned to the U.S. and practiced once for 45 minutes on a *hard court* in Florida before flying to London. When an English reporter asked Agassi how he had prepared for Wimbledon, he said he had been practicing on grass for 10 days, Bollettieri wrote in *My Aces, My Faults*.

"I didn't believe we had the slightest chance at Wimbledon," Bollettieri added. "After one day of practice! After all that bullshit about 10 days on grass! Besides, Andre was seeded 12th, and no 12th seed had ever won the tournament."

Agassi, shunning his usual colorful attire to conform to Wimbledon's predominantly white rule, wore an all-white Nike outfit and a white baseball cap with a Nike logo on the front. He kept two trademarks — stretch pants under his tennis shorts and his shirt cut high in the front. His scraggly bleached hair cascaded from under the cap. An earring dangled from his left ear. He wore a necklace, a ring on the little finger of his right hand and a watch on his left wrist.

In the first round, Agassi faced Andrei Chesnokov, a Russian clay-courter who had ranked among the top 10 in the world the previous year. Agassi lost the first set 7-5, receiving a warning from the umpire for saying "fuck," but won the next three sets.

While Agassi was quietly advancing through the draw in the first week, Russian Andrei Olhovskiy was stunning top-ranked Courier in the third round, and Richard Krajicek was insulting women.

Krajicek stated that "80 percent of the top 100 women are lazy, fat pigs" who shouldn't be allowed on Centre Court. The 11th-seeded Dutchman later amended his self-described "stupid statement."

"What I meant to say, actually, is only 75 percent," he said. "A lot of women are overweight."

Martina Navratilova was not amused.

"I'm going to beat him up," she said.

Agassi's first big test was against Boris Becker in the quarterfinals. This was their first meeting on grass, Becker's best surface because of his booming serve. He had appeared in six of the previous seven Wimbledon finals, winning three.

But Agassi had beaten Becker five straight times.

"When Andre sees my face, his game goes up 20 levels," Becker said.

Also, this was the second week of Wimbledon, when the grass courts turn brown and dry from all the pounding and begin to play like clay courts or slow hard courts. Of course, that never hurt Becker in his title years of 1985, 1986 and 1989.

Agassi prevailed, 4-6, 6-2, 6-2, 4-6, 6-3.

"I have not seen anybody on grass playing that kind of tennis from the back," Becker marveled. "I was serving good. I was playing good. He hit some shots that were not in the book."

Agassi's opponent in the semifinals was John McEnroe, another three-time Wimbledon champion (1981, 1983 and 1984). McEnroe, 33, was unseeded and playing in his last Wimbledon.

McEnroe had publicly blasted Agassi in 1988 for showing up other players, but now they were friends and

Davis Cup teammates. They played doubles together in the 1992 French Open, reaching the quarterfinals, and practiced together regularly in London. McEnroe gave Agassi tips on grass-court play.

"Mac told me I didn't have to serve and volley to win with my game," Agassi said. "He shortened my stroke, showed me how on the grass every point counts and the importance of staying in points. I don't know why, but I really like the guy."

McEnroe, meanwhile, was wary.

"These young guys always say how honored they are to play me, when what they really want to do is kick my ass," he said.

That's exactly what happened as Agassi won, 6-4, 6-2, 6-3. Agassi stepped into McEnroe's tricky left-handed serve and hammered the returns for winners.

"The only guy that I had ever seen who returned that well was Jimmy Connors, and now it seems to me like [Agassi] has taken it to another level," McEnroe said. "It's just incredible the shots he's capable of hitting on grass. I felt like I was hitting some solid approaches, good volleys, and he just would hit some great shots."

In the other semifinal, eighth-seeded Goran Ivanisevic blasted 36 aces in a 6-7, 7-6, 6-4, 6-2 victory over Sampras.

The final would match the best server in the game, Ivanisevic, against the best returner, Agassi.

For the fourth time, Agassi faced an opponent making his first appearance in a Grand Slam final. For the first time, however, Agassi was considered the underdog. Ivanisevic, a 6-foot-4-inch Croatian, was seeded higher and playing on his best surface. Agassi was playing on his supposedly worst surface.

Agassi said later he wasn't concerned about his previous Grand Slam losses.

"Interesting enough, you would think being the fourth Grand Slam final I would go into it almost with the same snowball mentality: 'I hope I don't lose the fourth one,' " Agassi told reporters after the match. "But I felt extremely relaxed and poised out there. I never felt tension. I just felt ability. I felt myself, like, overflowing with this desire to want to go out there and hit shots."

Maybe Agassi's reaction wasn't so strange. He has always tended to win when expected to lose and lose when expected to win. The pressure is off of him in the first case and on him in the second.

Ivanisevic, meanwhile, had political as well as personal inspiration. Croatia was enmeshed in Yugoslavia's civil war.

"At the beginning [of the war], it was tough," he said. "I could not call my family because the lines were cut. I couldn't concentrate, and I couldn't sleep. Then I realized that I was just destroying myself, and I said I would not play for myself but for the whole of Croatia, for the people who are fighting there. And I then got something incredible running through my body. I was playing to destroy the other guy for Croatia."

Agassi and Ivanisevic had met twice, Ivanisevic winning in straight sets both times. But winning at Sydney and Tokyo is one thing. Winning at Wimbledon is another.

Agassi had one advantage over Ivanisevic. The 20-year-old "Ragin' Croatian" was even more of a tennis head case than Agassi. And Agassi knew it.

Goran Prpic, Ivanisevic's good friend and former Davis Cup teammate, said in 1991 of his pal: "Goran is . . . I don't want to say wild . . . just, uh, crazy. But in a good way. He doesn't think about anything. He doesn't know what it means to be concentrated. He is looking always too much around. He needs to work on his head. He is top 10 in the rankings, but he is not top 10 in his head."

A few months after Prpic's statement, Ivanisevic suffered one of the greatest upsets in tennis history. Seeded 10th at Wimbledon in 1991, he fell to England's Nick Brown, ranked No. 591, in the second round.

Jimmy Arias, meanwhile, said of his friend Agassi in early 1992: ". . . His psyche is more fragile than anyone thinks. If I jokingly said, 'You can't hit a forehand for — ,' he'd freak out."

Agassi figured that Ivanisevic would crack first in the Wimbledon final.

"I kept telling myself Goran was capable of giving me a couple of free points," Agassi said. "If I could get him down to one final game, I liked my chances."

Both players held serve throughout the first set, sending it to a tiebreaker. Agassi had a break point at 7-6, but Ivanisevic saved it with a second-serve ace up the middle. Ivanisevic finally took the set, 10-8 in the tiebreaker. The Croatian fired 11 aces in the set.

Agassi took the second set 6-4 and the third by the same score. As in the French Open the year before, he was within one set of a Grand Slam championship.

Ivanisevic, though, breezed through the fourth set in 17 minutes. He won it 6-1, dropping only 10 points.

"I studied Andre, searched for that scared look on his face," wrote Bollettieri, who was watching from the guest box with Stewart. "I didn't see it. His head was up. He wasn't panicking."

Agassi explained afterward: "It wasn't like I didn't expect aces and love games. I enjoyed watching Goran's serves myself."

The players stayed on serve through the first nine games of the fifth set, Agassi saving a break point at 3-3 with a volley, of all things.

Ivanisevic stepped up to serve with Agassi leading, 5-4. Ivanisevic had to hold, or the match would be over and his dream shattered.

As Agassi had hoped, Ivanisevic felt suffocating pressure. He double-faulted twice (only his sixth and seventh double faults of the match) to fall behind 0-30, but two service winners brought him back to 30-30. Agassi reached championship point with a forehand passing shot off a weak volley.

Ivanisevic netted his first serve.

"Was little bit rushing," Ivanisevic said afterward in his delightful Slavic accent. "I throw ball too high. Was looking for ball. Was thinking too much. I don't know where to serve it. I lose motion. I miss."

Second serve.

"After you've been through what I have — I didn't hear the fat lady humming," Agassi said. "But now my eyes lit up."

Ivanisevic served to Agassi's backhand, and Agassi slugged the ball to Ivanisevic's chest. Jammed, Ivanisevic pushed a backhand volley into the top of the net. Agassi had prevailed, 6-7 (8-10), 6-4, 6-4, 1-6, 6-4.

"He did it with thundering returns, when he could get his racket on Ivanisevic's 123-mph serves," wrote Steve Wilstein of *The Associated Press*. "He did it with risky, leaping forehands and two-fisted backhands that kissed the lines and corners for 38 winners.

"He did it at a moment when his peers and fans were giving up on him, considering him much more image than substance, a junk-food addict and advertising pitchman who was squandering his natural talents."

Agassi, already running along the baseline to return Ivanisevic's volley, slid on his knees and raised his arms in triumph while looking up at the guest box. His racket twirled out of his hand.

He eventually flopped onto his stomach and sobbed with his hands covering his eyes and his legs spread. Agassi lay on Wimbledon's hallowed grass for seven seconds of ecstasy.

". . . You work so hard and spend your whole life trying to accomplish these things," Agassi said later. "When you do, you just can't believe it. I was saying [while lying on the grass], 'I can't believe it. I can't believe it.'

"I really didn't realize at that moment what had happened, but I sure felt what had happened. The emotion was just too much for me. As each day goes by, that only becomes stronger."

Agassi finally rose from the grass, covered his eyes again and held his head in disbelief. He briefly waved to the crowd and walked toward the net. Ivanisevic had stepped over the net, and the two embraced.

Ivanisevic, towering over Agassi, talked to his opponent with one arm over Agassi's shoulders and one hand patting Agassi on his chest. It was a warm gesture at the most disappointing moment of Ivanisevic's life.

"I told him, 'Listen, man, you deserve it. You played great, all these two weeks,' " said Ivanisevic, who blasted 37 aces in the final and 206 aces in the tournament. "Nobody expected he was going to win Wimbledon."

Indeed, if Agassi couldn't win a title on the baseliner-friendly surfaces at the French and U.S. Opens, how was he going to do it on grass?

"It is quite an irony," admitted Agassi, the first American Wimbledon champion since McEnroe in 1984. "I really have had my chances to fulfill a lot of my dreams, and I have not come through them in the past. To do it here is more than I could ever ask for."

Agassi's joy, though, was tinged with regret at having skipped Wimbledon from 1988 through 1990.

"I am really kind of sad," the new champion said. "This tournament has offered me and my life so much. It is a shame that I didn't respect it a little earlier."

When you're taught, however, that losing is the end of the world, are you going to play when you feel you don't have a chance? Absolutely not.

After only 13 lifetime matches on grass, Agassi not only reached tennis' pinnacle, but — and this is no exaggeration — justified his existence. By no choice of his own, his life had been devoted to winning tennis matches. The Wimbledon title meant that it hadn't been for nothing. The pressure was off after 22 years.

For about a day.

There were reports that Bollettieri had orchestrated Agassi's dramatic celebration from the guest box by signaling him to remain kneeling the way Bjorn Borg had. Agassi vehemently denied the charge.

"If I find myself having to defend that, I'll leave the game," Agassi said. "That's what sports is all about right there. I won't defend that. I won't put myself in a position where I have to tell people how real that was. People who don't believe that was real can go on believing what they want. I can't control that. But that moment was too special to me. . . . It's an insult. It hurts me to have to defend that."

Pancho Gonzalez, the Hall of Famer and Agassi's former brother-in-law, watched the match on television from his home in Las Vegas. He said he wasn't as surprised as most by Agassi's title.

"I played [Rod] Laver and [Ken] Rosewall on grass," Gonzalez said of the diminutive Australian legends. "Both had such quick hands that they were very good on grass. Andre's even quicker. You have to have speed afoot and quick hands."

Gonzalez admitted, however, that Agassi's baseline game is unorthodox on grass.

"It's not easy to watch him play," Gonzalez said. "He's giving the net-rusher the advantage on grass. But he had the confidence to handle it."

Agassi's parents also watched the match on television from their Las Vegas home. Forty years after Mike emigrated from his native Iran to Chicago, where he would shovel snow off the courts for four hours in order to play, he had achieved his goal of producing a world champion.

"He made us cry like babies," Mike said. "He just wanted it more than the other guy. He was willing to stay there as long as it took. He couldn't accept defeat. He had to win. How many more chances are you going to get? I give him a lot of credit."

Publicly, but not privately. As soon as Andre and Stewart returned home from Wimbledon, they called Mike.

"The first thing out of his mouth wasn't 'Congratulations,' " Stewart said. "It was, 'Why did you lose the fourth set?' Literally."

Andre held a news conference at The Mirage in Las Vegas and reflected on his career.

"I went through stages where I doubted myself, but I don't think I ever will again," Agassi said.

The following week, Agassi drew a bye in the first round at Washington, D.C., and lost 7-5, 6-4 to Kevin Curren in the second round. Curren had reached the Wimbledon final in 1985 when Becker won his first title there at 17, but now Curren was 34 — ancient by tennis standards.

"I don't think it helped to be playing here after being intoxicated for five days in a row after Wimbledon," Agassi said afterward.

When asked for details, Agassi said, "I'd get arrested if I told you."

People were already suggesting Wimbledon was a fluke, but Agassi bounced back the next week to win the Canadian Open at Toronto. He beat Ivan Lendl for the first time 3-6, 6-2, 6-0 in the final and was the runner-up in doubles with McEnroe. Agassi reached the quarterfinals of the U.S. Open before losing to Courier in four sets. Courier was ousted in the semifinals, but ended the year at No. 1.

Agassi won three more Davis Cup singles matches, extending his streak to 10, to lead the U.S. to its second Davis Cup title in three years. The Americans beat Sweden 4-1 in the semifinals at Minneapolis and Switzerland 3-1 in the final at Fort Worth, Texas.

Agassi had snapped out of his early-year slump rather nicely — with Wimbledon and Davis Cup championships.

Surgery

9

Physically and emotionally, 1993 was perhaps the most difficult year of Agassi's life. He battled career-threatening tendinitis in his right wrist, gained eight pounds, plummeted from No. 9 to No. 24 in the rankings and was dumped by his coach and his girlfriend. Also, there was the obligatory Davis Cup fiasco — actually two of them. In the end, though, everything worked out better than Agassi ever could have imagined. He wound up with a new wrist, new coach, new outlook and future wife.

Agassi intended to play in the Australian Open for the first time, but withdrew with bronchitis. He recovered to win two tournaments in February, at San Francisco and Scottsdale, Ariz.

At both tournaments, Agassi shuttled to and from Las Vegas between matches on his 10-seat Lockheed JetStar so he could sleep in his own bed. (When he bought and customized a 727 in 1996, he could sleep in his own bed *on* the plane.)

Agassi bought the four-engine JetStar from then-Los Angeles Kings owner Bruce McNall (who began serving a 70-month prison term in Lompoc, Calif., in March 1997 for his role in a scheme to bilk banks, a securities firm and the Kings of more than $236 million).

"It makes the negatives of what I do a lot easier," Agassi said of the jet. "I have to travel around a lot. You have to deal with people who are constantly pulling at you."

Doubles specialist Luke Jensen, later an ESPN tennis commentator, accompanied Agassi on the jet from Las Vegas to Scottsdale.

"I call it the 'A Train,'" said the ebullient Jensen, who had practiced with Agassi in Las Vegas for three days before the tournament. "It was great. I've never been treated so well in my life. It's a whole new world. A limo is waiting for you, [porters] take care of your bags, you're already checked in [at the hotel]. . . . It's not normal for a tennis player."

At midnight on the eve of the tournament at Scottsdale, a suburb of Phoenix, a party of seven had boarded Agassi's jet at McCarran International Airport in Las Vegas bound for Tucson, Ariz., and Scottsdale.

Painted on the tail was a large "A" with a tennis ball streaking through it. The identification numbers and letters painted on one engine, N792AA, signified the month and year of Agassi's Wimbledon title (July 1992) and his initials (AA).

On board were two pilots, Agassi, Jensen, Fritz Nau, Perry Rogers and Rich McKee, a friend of Agassi's.

They dined on Agassi's usual nutritious fare: Taco Bell, candy and Mountain Dew ("We call it our whiskey," Jensen said). They also relaxed on the couch and listened to music (Jensen didn't remember what kind) on the stereo system. There was a VCR on board, but Jensen said the flights weren't long enough to watch anything.

The trip to Tucson, where Rogers was a second-year law student at the University of Arizona, lasted a little less than an hour. Rogers, just your typical starving student, hopped into a waiting taxi. After about 10 minutes on the ground, the plane departed for the 20-minute flight to Scottsdale and arrived at 2:30 A.M. (Arizona is one hour later than Nevada in the winter).

Thanks to the plane, flying became one of the most enjoyable aspects of Agassi's career, rather than one of the worst.

"He told me it's so much fun that even if the technology existed to beam himself somewhere, he'd rather fly there in his plane," said Jensen, nicknamed "Dual Hand Luke" because he's ambidextrous. "He can cruise with his buddies. It's his way to get away."

Above all, though, the jet was practical.

"It will probably add five or 10 years to his career because it's so convenient," Jensen said. "As far as I'm concerned, being a tennis player is not on-court. It's dealing with the dead days and all the hassles. It's easy to go out and practice, but the traveling days and delays in the airport really get to you.

"Andre once told me he flew from [Nick Bollettieri's] place in Bradenton [Fla.] to Vegas in 3½ hours, door to door. You can spend 3½ hours changing planes in Atlanta."

Jensen, who lived in Ludington, Mich., at the time, addressed the problem in his own way. He moved to Atlanta. He would still have to change planes during his travels, but never in Atlanta.

Agassi spent time with Jenna Jenkins, a blind high school student in Scottsdale, on Tuesday night during the tournament. Agassi signed her program and posed for numerous photographs with her. Jenkins was in tears afterward. Agassi is very accommodating with handicapped people and children in general.

Agassi, seeded second, outlasted unseeded Marcos Ondruska 6-2, 3-6, 6-3 in the Scottsdale final. That gave Agassi a 12-1 record in 1993, the best start of his career until then. (He won his first 15 matches in 1995.)

It was downhill from there.

Agassi, Jim Courier, Pete Sampras and Michael Chang — all ranked in the top 10 — declined to make the trek to Melbourne, Australia, in March for the first round of the Davis Cup. Playing singles instead were No. 30 Brad Gilbert and No. 48 David Wheaton.

Sure enough, the U.S. lost to Australia 4-1 on grass. That not only knocked the Americans out of the 1993 competition but meant they had to qualify in the fall to contend in 1994. It was the first time in 10 years that the defending champion had lost in the first round.

The media immediately denounced the U.S. stars as selfish, unpatriotic and greedy. Rogers defended his friend, saying that playing in Australia would have hurt Agassi's preparation for the French Open on clay in late May and Wimbledon on grass in late June.

"The schedule is horrible," Rogers said. "You can't expect anyone to fly halfway around the world. . . .

"This is the beginning of their year. He's just coming off [the Lipton Championships on hard courts at Key Biscayne, Fla.] and just going into the clay-court season [in Europe]. This is the time of year you have to be ready.

"Remember, everyone else is fresh. Now, you're really behind the 8-ball [if you go to Australia]."

Pat DuPre, then the tennis director at Caesars Palace and a former professional player, sympathized with Agassi.

"[Australia] is a brutal trip," said DuPre, who reached a career high of No. 12 in the world in 1979. "I made it many times, and there's not a harder one on the tour. It takes a week or two to recover.

"I can't fault the guy for not going. It's unfortunate, but it's not the first time it's ever happened to our team."

Agassi said his refusal to play in Australia had nothing to do with the recent renewal of Tom Gorman's contract as captain. Agassi and other players favored John McEnroe.

"It doesn't bother me," Agassi said. "That's the next step in my opinion, but Tom has been a great captain."

After reaching the quarterfinals on clay at Barcelona in April, Agassi was sidelined for two months with tendinitis, forcing him to miss the French Open.

Agassi's doctor, Richard Westbrook of El Paso, Texas, diagnosed the injury as dorsal capsulitis.

"The wrist joint is irritated by overuse," Westbrook said. "There are probably some microtears in the joint capsule that don't have time to repair. The lining of the joint produces extra fluid, which makes the wrist hurt."

Surgery was a remote possibility, Westbrook added.

With Wimbledon two weeks away and Agassi desperate to defend his title, he submitted to a painful cortisone injection in Seattle to reduce inflammation. Agassi left for a tune-up tournament on grass at Halle, Germany, still uncertain if he'd be able to play at Wimbledon.

Agassi lost to his old "friend" Carl-Uwe Steeb 5-7, 6-2, 6-1 in the first round at Halle and complained of a sore elbow, probably caused by compensating for his ailing right wrist.

Wimbledon tradition calls for the defending champion to play the first match of the tournament on Monday. As of Sunday night, there was speculation Agassi would have to withdraw.

But Agassi showed up. This time, his shirt was tucked in, perhaps to conceal a few extra pounds.

With his right wrist wrapped and a shortened service motion to reduce pain in the wrist, Agassi beat Bernd Karbacher of Germany 7-5, 6-4, 6-0 in the first round. Agassi fell behind 4-1 and 5-2 in the first set, but Karbacher was suffering from bronchitis himself and struggling to catch his breath. Karbacher began to spray his shots, and Agassi took control.

Agassi did provide a lighthearted moment though. Before beating Joao Cunha-Silva of Portugal 5-7, 6-3, 6-2, 6-0 in the second round, Agassi got something off of his chest. Literally.

"At the end of the second set, Agassi pulled off his shirt, exposing a newly shorn midsection almost as smooth as Cher's," wrote Steve Wilstein of *The Associated Press*. "The women in the crowd whooped loudly, and Agassi hammed it up by raising his arms and turning around to model for them."

When asked afterward why he had removed his body hair, Agassi deadpanned, "It makes me a little more aerodynamic."

After dispatching hard servers Patrick Rafter of Australia in the third round and Richard Krajicek in the round of 16, Agassi faced top-ranked Sampras in the quarterfinals.

Cheered on by Barbra Streisand, his new friend, and still plagued by his sore wrist, Agassi put up one of the most courageous fights of his career before losing 6-2, 6-2, 3-6, 3-6, 6-4 in 90-degree heat.

"I'm not sure of the reason for the slow start," Agassi said, "but I felt like I was just a hair off."

The media howled at Agassi's unintended reference to his hairless chest.

"Let me rephrase that," he said. "I felt like I was about an inch away from really hitting offensive shots. But I don't know if it was my feet or if it was just nerves.

"I wanted to return here and defend my championship like a champion. I was borderline embarrassed [after the first two sets]. It kept going through my mind: It's not going to end this way, it's not going to end this way."

It didn't.

Agassi's wrist hurt more than anyone realized at Wimbledon, his conditioning coach said.

"He willed himself through the pain," Gil Reyes said. "It was there. He was definitely uncomfortable, some days more than others. . . . He had trouble holding a suitcase and shaking people's hands."

At Wimbledon, Agassi and Bollettieri had a talk. Agassi said that Rogers, who had become his business manager, was going to cut expenses and perhaps drop people from the team.

"I felt uneasy," Bollettieri wrote in *My Aces, My Faults.* "I wondered if Andre might be hinting that he was going to drop me. Not that that would've saved him much money."

Bollettieri contended that Agassi had not compensated him adequately. According to the coach, he and the academy had spent at least $1 million on Agassi's development and received less than $400,000, plus extensive publicity, in return.

Agassi responded: "Some people just look out for themselves, and Nick is that kind of guy. It was just devastating to me when Nick suddenly changed his priorities. Nick somehow feels like I owe him for the years, and I feel like friends aren't supposed to owe friends anything. He's talking to me about material things, and I'm talking to him about the heart. It doesn't seem like he understands me, and I certainly don't understand him. It saddened me. It sucks away at your hope in life."

Bollettieri was also unhappy that Agassi was consulting others about his game — McEnroe, Hall of Famer Pancho Segura and former pro Brian Teacher — and felt Agassi lacked dedication.

One week after Wimbledon, Bollettieri abruptly resigned as Agassi's coach after 10 years.

"I wanted to be sure that I was the one who said goodbye, not Andre," Bollettieri wrote.

Bollettieri notified Agassi by letter.

"I thought it would be easier to express my feelings that way," Bollettieri said, later admitting it was a mistake.

Bollettieri told a newspaperman about his decision before Agassi received the letter. The coach asked the reporter not to print anything before Agassi got the letter, but the reporter felt he couldn't wait.

Agassi called Bollettieri after hearing the news.

"It was emotional," Bollettieri recalled. "It was not easy for either of us. When [Monica] Seles departed, it didn't bother me. It's the chance you take as a coach. It's life. Andre was different. He was like my son. This one was difficult."

Already hurt physically, Agassi was wounded emotionally.

"I'm very disappointed with Nick and how he handled it. . . . I felt a strong sense of abandonment," Agassi said. "It hurt me personally more than professionally. There wasn't much more we could achieve together."

After Bollettieri quit, Agassi turned to Segura, 72, on a trial basis over the summer. Segura, known as a shrewd strategist, focused on Agassi's mental approach.

"He's very gifted," Segura said. "I mean, Courier has a great forehand, and Sampras has a great serve. But this guy has the three shots you need: a serve, a forehand, a backhand, plus mobility. That's a big plus. And he has control of his shots.

"But because of this, his concentration wanders. The game came so easy to him when he was young. And concentration and focus are important, more today than in the old days, because the difference between No. 1 and No. 60 is just a point here and a point there."

Still suffering from tendinitis, Agassi lost in the first round of the U.S. Open to Thomas Enqvist, 19, in five sets. Agassi then decided not to retain Segura.

"I started feeling too much like an intellectual on the court," Agassi explained. "Anyone who knows me knows my best weapon is instinct."

Despite his injury, Agassi agreed to play for the U.S. against The Bahamas in September at Charlotte, N.C., in the relegation round of the Davis Cup. The winner would return to the World Group for 1994, and the loser would drop to the American Zone.

Although a nation of only 260,000 people, The Bahamas had two world-class players in Mark Knowles and Roger Smith. That's all it takes to form a good Davis Cup team. Knowles and Smith were certainly beatable, but not to be taken lightly.

Agassi routed Smith 6-2, 6-2, 6-3 in the opening match September 24, and the U.S. went on to blank The Bahamas, 5-0. With the outcome already decided, Knowles was scheduled to play Agassi on the last day, but withdrew for medical reasons. Agassi refused to play Knowles' replacement, teaching pro John Farrington, and Richey Reneberg beat Farrington 6-1, 6-4.

"I was boycotting something I don't agree with," Agassi said. "There's no reason when a [series] is over to have to risk injury and losing. There was nothing to gain. If I just sit there and go along, I don't think they'll address it."

Agassi recalled his meaningless match against Darren Cahill in the 1990 Davis Cup final against Australia.

"I detached a rib from a cartilage and got off to a horrible start in 1991," Agassi said.

Agassi insisted that Davis Cup matches should end after the outcome has been decided.

"You don't see them playing Game 7 of the World Series if it's over after Game 6," he said.

Agassi not only boycotted the match, he buzzed the stadium in his plane afterward.

"And to thank me for all that, for being the only [top] player to go down there and play for the Davis Cup — the reality is we play for the USTA — they sent me an invoice for the two hotel rooms I had [but didn't use]," Agassi said. "It's like, I love you, too."

The ITF suspended Agassi from the first round of the 1994 Davis Cup and fined the USTA a whopping $1,500. The suspension meant that Agassi couldn't fly halfway around the world to play India in poverty-stricken New Delhi.

Agassi didn't know it at the time, but his victory over Smith at Charlotte would be his last match for five months. He went to UCLA Medical Center for his second cortisone shot in his wrist on October 12, and Dr. Roy Meals, chief of hand surgery at UCLA, advised him not to play tennis for at least four weeks.

"If this doesn't do it," Reyes said, "the next step is surgery."

Agassi withdrew from his last three tournaments of the year — at Vienna, Stockholm and Paris (Indoors) in consecutive weeks.

"He was determined to use the last three tournaments to get his tennis game back in the groove and prepare for 1994," Reyes said. "He was really training hard and looking forward to these tournaments. This is quite a setback."

In contrast to Meals, Westbrook told Agassi to try hitting the ball to test the cortisone treatment.

"If the cortisone is going to work, you should know in three or four days," Westbrook said on October 17. "Resting for four weeks puts us almost to the end of November. If [the wrist] flares up, we're into December. Then it fouls up the 1994 season."

After hitting with Nau for 30 minutes at Spanish Trail in Las Vegas, a downcast Agassi said his wrist was "not good" and only "a miracle" would prevent surgery.

On December 2, Agassi and Jimmy Connors appeared at a news conference in Las Vegas to announce that their exhibition at the MGM Grand Garden had been postponed from December 18 to March 25, 1994. Agassi hadn't played in his hometown in nine years, since he was 14 and lost to Hank Pfister in the qualifying event for the Alan King tournament.

"I was very excited when I committed to this event two weeks ago, and I upped my practice schedule," Agassi said. "I found myself performing really hard on my wrist. . . . I've been put on a very strict program as to how I can get back into tennis.

"I don't feel I'll be at my best for the night of the 18th. If I push the wrist, I'll risk missing more time next year, and that's not good for any of us."

Agassi still hoped to avoid surgery and to play in the Australian Open for the first time in January.

"Surgery is against every expert's opinion," Agassi said. "You risk never getting the movement in your wrist back again. I'll get half a dozen cortisone shots a year before I'll have surgery."

Connors, 41, could sympathize with Agassi better than anyone. He had reconstructive surgery for tendinitis in his left (playing) wrist in 1990. Connors missed a year on the tour, and his world ranking plummeted from No. 14 to No. 936.

Most observers considered Connors' career over at 38, but he returned in 1991 to reach the semifinals of the U.S. Open and skyrocket to No. 48 in the rankings.

In a way, Agassi's injury was a blessing in disguise. It gave him a much-needed rest, not only physically but mentally.

"It has taken me a lot of time and energy to overcome [the injury] emotionally," he said in early December. "But by the same token, it has allowed me a platform to deal with issues of where I am in my career. I find myself saying, 'Gosh, it's been so long, I really love tennis.'

"What I've accomplished the last few months off the court has been so much better for me than if I stayed on the court. . . . I'm in as healthy a place as I've ever been, which will result in my performance and more importantly in my happiness. That's what will bring people out."

Phillip agreed, saying, "This is his first time off since he was 16, and it's done a world of good for him."

Andre changed his mind about surgery after Connors and Dr. Richard Scheinberg, who had operated on Connors, convinced him that the procedure would end the pain.

Agassi, accompanied by Reyes, flew to Scheinberg's clinic in Santa Barbara, Calif., and underwent a 75-minute operation on December 20. They flew home that night.

". . . It was about the scariest thing I've ever done, but the fear before was actually worse than the surgery itself," Agassi said.

Agassi's operation revealed more damage than either he or the surgeon had anticipated, according to *The New York Times*. Scheinberg removed a mass of scar tissue from the top of Agassi's wrist and made some structural changes to the sheath that encases the tendons in order to increase the player's range of motion.

"It was a fairly extensive operation, totally different than Jimmy's," Scheinberg said. "But it was basically a case of either have the surgery or give up the game, because the problem was not going to go away."

The toll of hitting millions of balls as a youngster and Agassi's unorthodox style finally caught up with him, according to Scheinberg.

"The pain was coming on his forehand, where he takes a short backswing and puts a lot of torque and pressure on the wrist," Scheinberg said. "Each time he'd drop his wrist to hit the ball, he'd get a pain that radiated down to his fingers."

Eventually, Agassi was hesitant to hit his trademark shot.

"It caused handicaps mentally and emotionally as well as hurting my game," he said, "because every time I hit the forehand and it didn't hurt, I was wondering when the pain was going to start. And when it hurt, I was wondering how bad it was going to get."

While rehabilitating his wrist, Agassi underwent psychotherapy in Las Vegas for eight months, *Sports Illustrated* later reported. He realized that pushing was Mike's way of showing love.

"I came to terms with my tennis and my childhood and my dad, and it just released me," Agassi said. "When you finally get a little objectivity, you don't take it so personally."

Agassi said in 1996 that his relationship with his father had improved.

"Once tennis was out of the equation, my dad has been an incredible father to me. Tennis has always been part of the equation. As I got older, I've expressed a desire to have tennis not be so important between us, and I think that's been resolved for a few years now," Agassi said.

Agassi's recuperation from wrist surgery knocked him out of the Australian Open again for 1994. During his layoff, he decided to dedicate himself to tennis. Finally.

"I sat there with the wrist healing and feeling like my career might be over, and I became very serious," Agassi said. "I wished I had tapped into my potential more. I wished I had played my best tennis all the time. I wished I had done everything I could to be the best tennis player possible. I wished I had maximized my talent, and I knew I hadn't. And I decided if I recovered that I'd do all those things."

Phillip was worried.

"I honestly didn't think he would ever really come all the way back," he said. "But he just decided he was either going to step up to bat or sit his ass on the bench."

Brad

Agassi was ready to return to the tour in late February 1994 in the $313,750 Arizona Men's Tennis Championships at Scottsdale, Ariz.

Agassi drove to Scottsdale in his customized 1992 Chevrolet Suburban with two friends, Rich McKee and Allen Bunker. Cynthia Bunker, Allen's sister and Agassi's hairdresser, had been killed in a car accident three weeks earlier.

The Suburban was all black with tinted windows, four-wheel drive and dirt tires. It had a racing motor with more than 500 horsepower, two color televisions (one in the dashboard between the driver's seat and the passenger's seat) equipped with VCRs, a state-of-the-art sound system, a 10-disc CD changer and a built-in ice chest.

"You rent three or four movies, fill the ice chest up, and you've got a serious cruising vehicle," McKee said cheerfully.

Agassi and McKee took turns driving, and the three watched *Aliens* during the four-hour trip.

McKee said he didn't know how much the souped-up vehicle cost. Agassi also had a Bentley, Porsche 928, Porsche 930, Ford Bronco, Jeep Cherokee and Hummer, according to McKee.

Agassi and Brad Gilbert went out to dinner Sunday night before the tournament, and Agassi gave Gilbert's five-year-old son Zachary a ride in the Suburban. Gilbert had no idea at the time, but he would become Agassi's coach three weeks later.

Josh Ripple, then the Scottsdale tournament director, and even Agassi's rivals, rejoiced over the flamboyant star's return.

Ripple crowed that Agassi "sells more tickets than any active player in tennis. I wouldn't give him up for seven or eight of the top 10 players."

Gilbert added: "Tennis needs Agassi to be in the top 10. He has flair, personality. He brings out the best in [Pete] Sampras and [Jim] Courier. It's nice to have a top-10 player who's colorful."

Agassi came into the Scottsdale tournament ranked No. 32, his lowest since November 1987, and could not have had a kinder draw. His first-round opponent, qualifier Mark Keil (pronounced "Kyle") of Tampa, Fla., was ranked 48th in doubles but No. 814 in singles, which he rarely played. Keil had, however, defeated a somewhat more illustrious Tampa resident named Sampras on grass at Queen's in London in 1991. Keil had never played Agassi in singles, but Keil and Dave Randall crushed Agassi and Scott Davis 6-1, 6-0 in doubles in the first round at Memphis, Tenn., in 1993.

"I have nothing to lose," said the 26-year-old Keil, whose parents escaped from East Germany in 1960. "I'll just go and play and see what happens."

Agassi, seeded fifth, said he wouldn't be nervous.

"I'm so far past that stage at this point," he said. "I'm just excited as hell to get out there and do what I love doing."

Agassi demolished Keil 6-1, 6-2 in 57 minutes in front of a crowd of 5,758, including Brooke Shields, on a cool, breezy night in the desert.

Agassi, who had switched to a Head racket after Donnay went out of business, said he was somewhat surprised by how he played.

"In one sense no and one sense yes," he said. "I've never hit so many balls and been so prepared. But when you haven't played in four or five months, it does feel strange."

Agassi played with a wristband on his right wrist and wrapped the area with ice after the match.

"There is a little pain when I warm up, but it goes away quicker everyday," he said. "Then it's completely gone."

Agassi's joy was obvious during the match against Keil. Agassi smiled frequently, skipped after hitting passing shots, shrieked in mock horror after missing shots and eagerly hopped back into position to receive serve.

"When I was away, I realized how much I appreciate my ability," Agassi said. "You do take it for granted. It's not just motivating. It's career-changing."

Joining Shields in the stands for Agassi's second-round match against Libor Nemecek, another qualifier, from the Czech Republic, was saxophonist Kenny G, whom Agassi later described as "a dear friend." The musician's wife, Lyndie Benson, had set up Agassi and Shields. Sitting elsewhere in the stands was Barry Bonds of the San Francisco Giants, whose spring training camp is in Scottsdale.

Agassi defeated the 231st-ranked Nemecek (not to be confused with "nemesis") 6-4, 6-3 in one hour and eight minutes. Agassi trailed Nemecek, one of the smallest players on the ATP Tour at 5 feet 6 inches and 125 pounds, 2-4 in the first set before winning the next six games. After Agassi hit a scorching passing shot on an important point in the first set, he yelled at the top of his lungs, "I LOVE THIS GAME!!!"

Agassi's first test figured to come against Gilbert, ranked 27th at age 32, in the quarterfinals. But the third-seeded Gilbert threw up before the match and lost 6-1, 6-2 in one hour.

It took Agassi only one more hour to beat unseeded Karsten Braasch of Germany 6-1, 6-4 in the semifinals.

The left-handed Braasch is one of the more unusual characters on the mèn's tour. With his curly hair and glasses, he looks more like a philosophy major at Heidelberg University than a professional tennis player. He serves like a Heidelberg student, too, bending almost completely over before tossing the ball. It's effective, though. Braasch smokes and drinks beer and goes to every pro basketball game he can in the U.S. — all of which can be hazardous to one's health.

Agassi rolled past Luiz Mattar, ranked 78th and unseeded, 6-4, 6-3 in the final for his 20th career singles title. Agassi had beaten Mattar at Itaparica, Brazil, in 1987 for his first tour singles title.

Unknown to the crowd and even reporters, Agassi didn't get to bed until 6 A.M. the day of the Scottsdale final because a small fire broke out in McKee's nearby suite just past midnight. No one was injured, and damage was minor. The fire was caused by a spark from the fireplace, said a hotel spokeswoman. Agassi awoke at 10 A.M., and the final began at 1 P.M.

Agassi never lost more than four games in a set during the tournament. But the only seeded player he met, Gilbert, was sick.

Agassi said it never crossed his mind that he could win the tournament so easily.

"It was a long road for me coming back," he said. "I have to reassess my plan. I'm ahead of schedule."

Agassi rarely discusses his private life, but he made an exception after beating Mattar. In an emotional speech to the near-capacity crowd of 7,197, Agassi dedicated his title to Cynthia Bunker.

Her death, Agassi said, "really made me realize in so many ways how thankful we need to be for everyday we're here. It made me realize how much we take for granted and how easy it is to lose perspective about what really matters in life."

Agassi fell in the second round at Indian Wells, Calif., the following week to 99th-ranked Fabrice Santoro of France 6-4, 7-6 (7-3). But the loss hardly came as a shock to Agassi.

"In my mind, it was a matter of time before the odds started getting [to be] too much against me," said Agassi, who as a lifelong Las Vegan presumably knows all about odds. "I felt like I toughed it out as much as I could out there, but it just wasn't in me.

"I've got to take a little time off and give my wrist a chance to feel fresh again and give my body and mind a few days [off], then come back at it strong. I feel like I've made some big steps forward."

With Gilbert's help, there were more to come.

Agassi decided he needed a coach, and Gilbert was on his short list. Agassi invited Gilbert to dinner the night before the Lipton Championships at Key Biscayne, Fla., in March 1994.

"I thought we were just going to eat, but then Andre started asking me a bunch of different questions, about his tennis and where his game was going," Gilbert said. "He asked if I thought I could help him, and I said, 'Yes, I think I really can.' "

Agassi was awed by Gilbert's knowledge.

"He had my game diced up like you can't believe," Agassi said. "He knew what I did when I was 18, what I stopped doing when I was 19, what changed in 1990, when I was 20. I mean, every year, he knew what happened and why my game never got better," Agassi said.

Gilbert explained.

"I just told him that I thought he wasn't maximizing his potential, and it wasn't anything to do with his strokes," he said. "He wasn't playing *inside* the court anymore. He was back on his heels behind the baseline. He wasn't competing day in and day out as good as he should have because he wasn't preparing. He played one-dimensional tennis. And he wasn't strategizing.

"See, I think that Nick [Bollettieri] always felt like if you go out and play good tennis, you're going to beat somebody. I feel like there's five days a year you're going to get up, and you're going to beat anybody. There's five days a year that you're not going to beat anybody. All the rest are what make a tennis player."

Gilbert, who had long had a reputation as a thinking-man's player, and Agassi seemed to be a perfect fit.

"Brad's made a career out of winning matches he was supposed to lose," Agassi said. "And I've done just the opposite."

Also, Gilbert is a good talker and Agassi a good listener.

"Brad's got a good heart," Sampras said, "but I couldn't take all that talking, discussing every angle, every shot. Whenever we used to practice together, I'd say, 'Brad, would you just shut the [expletive] up for 30 minutes?' "

Agassi and Gilbert began working together, without a contract, the day after they went out to dinner in Key Biscayne.

*   *   *

Gilbert grew up in a tennis-playing family in the comfortable Oakland, Calif., suburb of Piedmont. His older sister, Dana, upset then-No. 12 Virginia Ruzici to win the 1978 U.S. Clay Court title while still a freshman at UCLA. She played professionally before becoming a teaching pro. Brad's older brother, Barry Jr., played on the South Carolina tennis team.

Like Agassi, Gilbert grew up with a domineering father who pressured him to win. Both Agassi and Gilbert were cocky as juniors and grew up outside the tennis establishment, Gilbert because he was Jewish and Agassi because he had a middle-class background and Armenian heritage.

There was one major difference between Agassi and Gilbert, though. Agassi was groomed from birth to become the No. 1 player in the world. There was never such a lofty goal for Gilbert. Not even close.

"You have to be kidding," Brad's father, Barry Sr., said with a laugh. "We'd hoped that maybe he'd get a college scholarship. We never dreamed he'd be a pro."

Brad was known more for his bad behavior on the court than his ability in the juniors.

"[Brad] was a little bully, a little Napoleon," said his mother, Elaine. "I used to watch when he was 6, 7, 8 and 9, and I was embarrassed. He had tantrums, antics. He was little and scrappy, and his reputation was tall and long — and well deserved."

Peter Herb, the executive director of the Northern California section of the USTA for the past 32 years, described Brad as "volatile" in the juniors.

"There always used to be turmoil at Brad's matches," Herb said, "either arguments player-to-player or requests for an official, but I can't remember any specific [on-court] incidents."

Herb said Gilbert was suspended once for breaking a basketball backboard, with several other uninvited boys, at a tournament host's residence.

Gilbert declined to be interviewed for this book when he was approached at the 1997 *Newsweek* Champions Cup at Indian Wells, Calif.

"They [the Agassi camp] told me not to talk to you," Gilbert said. "They're doing their own thing."

Gilbert would not elaborate.

A shoulder injury sidelined Brad for the season when he was 16. He halfheartedly returned to the juniors, but played well enough to earn a No. 31 national ranking in 1979 and a scholarship to Arizona State. He lasted only one semester before the coach at the time, Myron McNamara, sent him home.

McNamara told the *Arizona Republic* that he didn't like Gilbert's "work ethic and on-court behavior." Gilbert, in turn, insisted he got a "bad" deal from a "bad" coach.

Gilbert enrolled at Foothill College in Los Altos, Calif., near San Francisco and played under coach Tom Chivington.

"When Brad came to me at Foothill College from ASU in 1980, it took me a while to figure him out," Chivington said. "The first time I saw him hitting on a court, I made a mental note: 'No forehand. No backhand. No volley. Weak serve.' I also made note of something else: 'Wins matches.' "

Foothill was the turning point in Gilbert's career.

"I went there thinking it was my last effort," Gilbert said. "I thought, if it doesn't work then I don't have to worry about tennis anymore. The coach turned out to be unbelievable. . . . He put a lot of faith in me and said, 'You can do this for yourself.' He was the first one ever who said, 'You go out there and play for yourself and nobody else.' "

Agassi could certainly appreciate that.

Gilbert grew from 5 feet 8 inches to 6 feet 1 inch, and his game blossomed. He transferred to Division I Pepperdine and reached the singles final of the 1982 NCAA Championships before losing to Mike Leach.

During his 12-year professional career, Gilbert won 20 singles titles, a bronze medal in singles at the 1988 Olympics at Seoul and $5.5 million in prize money.

In 1989, Gilbert became the first player in three years to win three titles in three weeks. The last four victories of his 17-match winning streak came against, in order, Sampras, Michael Chang, Boris Becker and Stefan Edberg. Gilbert achieved a career-high singles ranking of No. 4 on January 1, 1990.

Almost one-fifth of Gilbert's career prize money, $1 million, came in the 1990 Grand Slam Cup in Munich. And Gilbert didn't even win it. He was the runner-up to Sampras, who earned an unfathomable $2 million. Ironically, Gilbert replaced Agassi in the tournament after the entry-withdrawal-entry-withdrawal controversy.

For all of his success, Gilbert never advanced past the quarterfinals of a Grand Slam tournament. He reached the quarters twice, at the U.S. Open in 1987 and Wimbledon in 1990.

Gilbert excelled with grit, intelligence and quickness rather than flashy strokes.

"I'm a real fighter," he said. "I never give up."

Television commentator Mary Carillo said: "He's sort of the ultimate club player. He won't give you any pace. All of a sudden he hits the ball a little bit harder than you can handle, or he angles it away a little bit farther than you thought he could. You think you're dictating to him, and all of a sudden you realize, I'm not dictating anything; I'm being had."

That's what happened to John McEnroe in the 1985 Masters, and he could hardly bear it. Gilbert defeated McEnroe 5-7, 6-4, 6-1 in the first round of the year-end tournament, then featuring the top 16 players in the world, at New York. During a changeover, McEnroe snarled: "Gilbert, you don't deserve to be on the same court with me! You are the worst. *The* [expletive] *worst!*"

Afterward, the 27-year-old McEnroe announced that he was taking a sabbatical from tennis.

"When I start losing to players like him, I've got to reconsider what I'm doing even playing this game," said McEnroe, who had lost only one set to Gilbert in seven previous matches.

Gilbert reveled in McEnroe's frustration, but the euphoria was brief. Anders Jarryd of Sweden eliminated Gilbert in the quarterfinals, 6-1, 6-2.

ATP Tour executive Weller Evans has known Gilbert since 1981, when Gilbert came on the pro tour while attending Pepperdine.

"He has certainly matured since then," Evans said. "When he first came on the tour, the more established players looked at him as cocky, brash, rather annoying on the court, and maybe too talkative off the court.

"One of my first experiences with Brad was [at a tournament] in Manila. He wanted the supervisor removed from the event. I told him the supervisor was the final on-site authority. He's the last one to go, including the player."

How was Gilbert annoying?

"Questioning a lot of calls, arguing with the umpire, histrionics," Evans said.

Gilbert became less obnoxious and more entertaining as he matured, Evans added with a smile.

"He kept up a running monologue during matches," said Evans, whose career has paralleled Gilbert's. "It was very entertaining to sit at courtside as he would basically describe the match from his perspective after each point.

"He alternated between talking to himself and directing comments at somebody he felt a connection with in the crowd, like Tom Chivington or me, which put me in an awkward position. He would berate himself about a second serve that registered 50 mph on the speed gun. He would say things like, 'How'd he hit that backhand pass? He hasn't hit one since 1983.' Once in Taipei, a shot took him wide in a match he was losing, and he took his name off the scoreboard."

And Gilbert today?

"He's a terrific dad and a very responsible husband," Evans said. "When I think of Brad in addition to the exuberance he usually demonstrates — he and I have a love of sports in common — one of his greatest qualities is loyalty. If he develops a friendship with you, there's nothing he wouldn't do for you."

Herb echoed Evans.

"Bradley the man is a totally different person than Bradley the boy," Herb said. "He was very immature as a boy. He matured very quickly probably when he came under the influence of Tom Chivington at [Foothill] JC here in Northern California and turned into a real gentleman. I'm very fond of Brad. He's very charming and polite."

Given Gilbert's loquaciousness and encyclopedic knowledge of sports — he grew up as a fanatical fan of the pro teams in the San Francisco Bay Area — it should come as no surprise that he has listed his ambition as becoming the host of a sports talk show. For now, Gilbert stays busy coaching Agassi.

In his 1993 book *Winning Ugly*, Gilbert explained how he beat better players and how recreational players can do the same.

"I don't overpower people," Gilbert wrote. "I don't have any flashy shots. I win because I have the ability to implement my basic game strategy successfully; maximize my strengths and minimize my weaknesses. That means I consistently get in a position where I'm hitting a shot I like rather than one I don't.

"At the same time, I want to maximize my opponent's weaknesses and minimize their strengths. I want them to be hitting shots they don't like from positions they don't want. I'll lose if I go strength to strength. I'm good, however, at working my strengths against my opponent's weaknesses."

Gilbert's philosophy can be distilled into the advice he received from his coach at Pepperdine, Allen Fox: "Always be asking yourself during a match who's doing what to whom."

Gilbert analyzed several top players in the book, including Agassi.

"I've never seen a guy his size get so much stick on the ball," Gilbert wrote. "It's really unbelievable. He's just got serious heat. Because of it, he puts immediate fear into you because you know he can just rack the ball and control play. When he's on his game, he just moves you back and forth at will. It's no fun to play Andre when he's 'on.' "

The last time Gilbert and Agassi met was at Scottsdale in 1994. Agassi's victory evened their head-to-head record at 4-4.

*   *   *

In his new coaching role, Gilbert immediately told Agassi not to dwell on his three losses in Grand Slam finals.

"First of all, I told him those suckers are gone," Gilbert said. "There's nothing you can do to get them back."

Then Gilbert went to work on Agassi's game.

"We concentrated on two major areas," Gilbert said. "The first was to get Andre to take advantage of his strong groundstrokes. Few people in tennis have ever hit the ball as hard and as deep as Andre Agassi. When you do that as consistently as he does, you create many opportunities to finish off the point with a relatively easy volley. But Andre's tendency had been to stay back too much and not seize his opportunities.

"He was like a boxer who constantly landed good punches but didn't move in for that final knockout punch. And once he let his opponent off the ropes, he'd become frustrated and go for a bigger punch than necessary.

" 'You've got to close off the court,' I told him. 'Open up the court with your forehand and backhand, then move in like a piranha for those volleys.'

"The second was to make Andre smarter about his serve. He had to learn to consider it part of his repertoire. Typically, he'd just walk up to the baseline and hit the ball without even thinking of what he was doing. Winging it this way is like a baseball pitcher winding up but not deciding whether to go with the slider or the fastball until just before the ball leaves his hands."

Agassi got off to a good start under Gilbert, defeating Becker and Edberg, two former No. 1 players, at Key Biscayne en route to the final against the top-ranked Sampras.

Then Sampras came down with food poisoning and was unable to play at the scheduled time. Agassi, refusing to accept a forfeit, gave Sampras an extra hour to recover. Sampras took advantage of the reprieve and won, 5-7, 6-3, 6-3.

"It's not about winning the tournament," Agassi explained. "It's about taking pride in what you do, and you don't deserve to win the tournament unless you beat the best players who are playing the best that they can.

"If I couldn't go out there and beat Pete healthy, I don't deserve to win the tournament."

Agassi struggled throughout the spring and early summer. After Yevgeny Kafelnikov beat him 1-6, 6-3, 6-4 in the first round at Monte Carlo on clay, the promising Russian commented on Agassi's popularity.

"It's difficult [to play him], because Agassi is like Jesus wherever he goes," said Kafelnikov, 20.

Agassi suffered five-set losses in the French Open and at Wimbledon. He fell to Thomas Muster in the second round at Paris and to Todd Martin in the fourth round in England.

Then came another turning point in Agassi's career.

Express Yourself

Motivation can be a problem for anyone, not just Agassi, in the tournament at Washington, D.C., each July. It is the first event after Wimbledon for many top players, and the humidity is brutal.

In this setting, Washington has been a microcosm of Agassi's career. He has been brilliant there, winning the title three times (1990, 1991 and 1995). He has been listless there, losing in the second round in 1992 after winning Wimbledon and wilting against Patrick Rafter 6-7, 6-0, 6-2 in the third round in 1996. And he has had emotional crises there.

The first was in 1987, when Agassi was ready to quit the sport at 17 after losing to Patrick Kuhnen in the first round. The second was in 1994.

Agassi had just lost to journeyman Brett Steven of New Zealand, 6-4 in the third set, in the third round at Washington. As Agassi walked to his car around midnight, there were about 100 people waiting for autographs. Although Agassi was distraught, he patiently signed for everyone.

". . . To me, that's the sign of a warm heart," Brad Gilbert said. "Good things happen to people with warm hearts."

All Agassi needed was a boost to his fragile confidence. He got it from Nick Bollettieri after the 1987 loss to Kuhnen at Washington. This time, he got it from Gilbert.

"I was really hanging my head low, discouraged, feeling like the year was going to be a total disaster," Agassi said, "and Brad said, 'Andre, keep believing, because I promise you good things are going to happen. It'll change. You'll see better days. Because I know the game. You're going to be OK.' Just that belief, I think, was the biggest thing."

Agassi won the Canadian Open at Toronto on hard courts the following week. He saved two match points to beat David Wheaton 3-6, 6-1, 7-6 in the third round and rallied to defeat Sergi Bruguera, the two-time defending French Open champion, 4-6, 7-6, 6-1 in the quarterfinals.

In his last tournament before the U.S. Open, Agassi lost to Jan Siemerink of the Netherlands 6-3, 3-6, 6-3 in the second round of the $915,000 Volvo International in New Haven, Conn. The ATP Tour, panicking over a *Sports Illustrated* cover story that May entitled "Is Tennis Dying?," experimented at New Haven with rock-and-roll music over the loudspeakers during the changeovers in an effort to add excitement. Agassi went nuts.

"To turn the tournament into a concert like that is an absolute joke," he said. "If any other tournament does this, I would quit before I would go out there. If the game doesn't hold its own, then it's over."

Given Agassi's rebellious image, ATP officials and tournament organizers were puzzled by his reaction.

"I would have thought he would've played off it greatly," said tournament chairman Jim Westhall. "It's strictly Andre Agassi. I was a bit surprised."

Ironically, this was the former Stratton Mountain, Vt., tournament, where Agassi accomplished several milestones early in his career. The Volvo International moved from remote Stratton Mountain to New Haven in 1990.

To no one's surprise — considering the thumbs-down by the game's biggest draw — the ATP Tour promptly dropped the rock-and-roll experiment.

Agassi, meanwhile, was optimistic entering the U.S. Open.

"Physically I'm 100 percent, and mentally I'm as strong as ever," he said. "My game is coming around like never before. I couldn't be happier with where I am."

Nor could Gilbert, who predicted that Agassi would win the U.S. Open. Not only that, Gilbert promised to shave his body, as Agassi had at Wimbledon in 1993, if Agassi won the title.

Gilbert's statement was bold, considering that the 20th-ranked Agassi was unseeded. No unseeded player had won the U.S. Open since Fred Stolle in 1966. No unseeded player had ever beaten five seeds to win the U.S. Open, either.

But Agassi — wearing black socks, shorts and cap and a white, blue and black shirt — accomplished both feats. After victories over qualifier Robert Eriksson in the first round and Guy Forget in the second round, Agassi knocked off, in order, 12th-seeded Wayne Ferreira, No. 6 Michael Chang, No. 13 Thomas Muster, No. 9 Todd Martin and No. 4 Michael Stich.

One seed Agassi didn't have to beat was No. 1 Pete Sampras. Suffering from (ironically) tendinitis in his left ankle, Sampras arrived at the U.S. Open out of shape and lost to Jaime Yzaga of Peru in the fourth round.

Agassi completed his run with a 6-1, 7-6 (7-5), 7-5 victory over Stich in the final.

"It's quite amazing what I pulled off," Agassi said. "I can't believe it. It's been an incredible two weeks for me."

Actually, it was typical Agassi — winning when the public didn't expect him to (1994 U.S. Open and 1992 Wimbledon) and not winning when he was expected to (1990 and 1991 French Opens and 1990 U.S. Open). But he proved that Wimbledon wasn't a fluke.

Agassi was brilliant against Stich, committing only 14 errors to the German's 48, as Brooke Shields watched breathlessly.

"Right after the Open, [Agassi] called me 'The Believer,'" Gilbert said. "And I told him it was time to start thinking about the next big title."

And yes, Gilbert kept his promise about shaving his body.

"It was not a pretty sight," he said.

Agassi wasn't finished yet, winning two of his next three tournaments. From the U.S. Open through the Paris Indoors, he won 19 of 20 matches, including nine victories over top-10 players.

During his hot streak, Agassi crushed Mark Woodforde 6-0, 6-0 in the second round at Vienna. Granted, Woodforde is known more as one of the top doubles players in history, but he's no slouch in singles. He was ranked No. 37 in singles at the time and had career victories over Ivan Lendl, John McEnroe, Goran Ivanisevic and Chang. Yet Agassi demolished Woodforde.

"I was hitting the ball extremely well and solidly in the warmup," said Woodforde, who has been shut out in singles two other times in his 14-year professional career (by Sergi Bruguera on clay in Barcelona, Bruguera's hometown, in 1991, and by Steven on grass at Newport, R.I., in 1997). "I thought I had a good chance of winning, but within two games, I knew he had me covered in every area. It's not often that you have that feeling where you know you're going to be in trouble to win a game. But he was just so motivated. I think he probably had something to prove to himself and to Brad Gilbert about trying to get his ranking up to show the tennis world that he was still a force. Toward the end of the match, I was just laughing and shaking my head in disbelief. We had some great points, but I always ended up on the losing end of those points.

"I've lost love and love [6-0, 6-0] before and knew that I played really badly and probably deserved it. But in a way I didn't deserve it this time. I played quite OK, but he was just awesome. A few players who were there watching were laughing as well, saying, 'My God, I can't believe someone could play that well for so long and not lose focus.'"

Tami Jones was competing in a women's pro tournament at Brighton, England, when Agassi destroyed Woodforde. She watched the carnage on television.

"Agassi is one of the few players I've ever watched actually toy with another top player," said Jones, ranked 49th at the time. "It was unbelievable."

Jones said Agassi's stroke preparation impressed her most.

"Being a groundstroker, I watch him," she said. "It looks like he always has so much time. His preparation is so good. From the first point of the rally, he's got his opponent constantly off balance."

Agassi soared to a career-high No. 2 in the rankings, becoming the first player to reach that position from outside the top 20 in the same year.

The year ended on a sour note, though, when Agassi lost his temper in his last two tournaments.

Agassi swore, threw his racket and smashed a ball near a linesman during a 4-6, 7-6, 6-3 loss to Sampras in the semifinals of the $3 million ATP Tour World Championship at Frankfurt, Germany.

In December, Agassi was almost disqualified for swearing during a 6-3, 1-6, 6-0 loss to Magnus Larsson in the quarterfinals of the $6 million Grand Slam Cup at Munich, Germany. Agassi also whacked a return that almost knocked down umpire Mike Morrissey's microphone.

"That was very unfortunate, wasn't it?" Agassi dryly said later.

Agassi did apologize to Morrissey, though.

*　　*　　*

Nineteen ninety-five was a bittersweet year for Agassi. He:

- Won the Australian Open in his first appearance there.
- Seized the No. 1 ranking for the first time and held it for 30 straight weeks.
- Achieved career highs of 26 straight victories, a 73-9 (.890) match record for the year and seven titles.
- Helped the U.S. win the Davis Cup for the third time in six years.

After Agassi beat Sampras to win the Australian Open, there was talk of winning all four Grand Slam tournaments, the greatest achievement in tennis. The only men to win tennis' four biggest titles — the Australian, French, Wimbledon and U.S. championships — in one calendar year are Rod Laver (1962 and 1969) of Australia and Don Budge (1938) of the United States. Agassi had a chance to join them, but suffered heart-breaking losses in the last three Grand Slam tournaments of 1995.

"In a way it was a disappointing year," Agassi said. "It could have been a year of total domination for me. I could have played for the Wimbledon title and, if I had been able to be just a little sharper and fresher at the [U.S.] Open, I could have ended up having one of the best years any player has had in a long time.

"But you know, I don't really see it that way — as a disappointment. In fact, I went to sleep every night [in 1995] feeling that I was having the best year [of anyone] on the tour. And I still look back on 1995 as a great year for me."

Agassi continued: "In 1995, I proved to myself that I can go day in, day out, week after week after week, winning. I played every match with the same intensity — literally. It showed that I had the emotional stamina, the focus, the commitment, the strength, the ability.

"And let's face it, for someone who's been as up and down as I have, and who's had to deal with so much criticism because of that, that's a pretty good accomplishment. I'm not trying to talk myself into thinking I had a great year — I know I had one."

The rivalry between Agassi and Sampras blossomed into tennis' best since Bjorn Borg-McEnroe and Jimmy Connors-McEnroe. Agassi and Sampras met five times during the year, all in finals and two in Grand Slams, with Agassi winning three.

Agassi played in all four Grand Slam tournaments for the first time in his 9½-year career. He said he had never played in the Australian Open because he "never felt there was time to rest and refuel for the year. But I'm budgeting my time a lot better, and my priorities are in the right place. There's no place I'd rather be."

He showed up in Melbourne with closely cropped hair ("Van Gogh goes to prison," as Curry Kirkpatrick colorfully put it in *Newsweek*), long sideburns, a goatee and mustache and what appeared to be a paunch. He also wore a wild new Nike outfit featuring a magenta striped shirt and baggy plaid shorts.

Matt Slynn of the Oribe hair salon at Elizabeth Arden in New York cut Agassi's ponytail at Shields' brownstone in midtown Manhattan shortly before Christmas, according to *Sports Illustrated*. What did you expect, Supercuts? In attendance at the cosmic event were Shields, Perry Rogers and Wendi Stewart, who had remained a friend of Agassi's after their breakup.

There were rumors that Agassi had his hair cut at the request of Nike. The real reason was that it was thinning on top. The same had happened with Phillip Agassi in his 20s, and he began wearing a toupee. Andre, in contrast, decided to go for the natural look.

Attention quickly turned from Agassi's appearance to his game in the Australian Open as he breezed to the final without losing a set. Awaiting Agassi was Sampras, the defending champion.

Sampras was physically and emotionally drained entering the final. He had rallied from two sets down in the fourth round and quarterfinals and won in four sets in the semifinals. Sampras' coach, Tim Gullikson (Tom's twin brother), had suffered an apparent stroke during the first week, and Sampras cried for his stricken friend during his quarterfinal victory over Jim Courier. Gullikson was later diagnosed with a brain tumor and died in 1996.

Sampras, as gritty as he is talented, fought hard in the final, but Agassi survived a 28-ace onslaught to win 4-6, 6-1, 7-6 (8-6), 6-4 for his second straight Grand Slam title. Agassi wore down Sampras with punishing groundstrokes in a tremendous match.

The final illustrated the fine line between winning and losing at the top level of pro tennis. The key was the third-set tiebreaker. If Sampras had won it, he very well could have gone on to retain his title.

But Sampras, who lost all five tiebreakers he played in the tournament, fell behind 3-0 in this one. He won the next four points and served for the set at 6-4 with a stunning reflex volley. But Agassi then ripped a forehand return that nicked the net cord and skipped past Sampras for a winner. Had the ball been a fraction of an inch lower, Agassi would have lost the set and probably the match.

"When you've got Pistol Pete at set point, you've got to go with your hunch," Agassi said. "because you can't sit there and hope that he misses. He knows, with one execution of the racket head, the set's over."

Agassi won the next three points, closing out the set with a backhand volley drop shot.

Sampras, fighting fatigue, managed to blast 13 aces in the fourth set. Three of them came in the ninth game, but Agassi still broke him with a backhand passing shot. Agassi closed out the match with an ace of his own.

"If he stays healthy, he's a threat to win every major tournament of the year," Sampras said.

Addressing the crowd after the match, Sampras choked back tears while discussing his coach, who had flown home to Wheaton, Ill.

"I just want to let him know I keep thinking about him and that I wish he was here," Sampras said. "I've been praying for him the last couple of weeks."

Agassi praised Sampras' perseverance under extraordinary stress.

"I have to say what I witnessed Pete do in the past two weeks, with the difficulties about his coach, his courage on the court and off the court is abolutely inspiring," Agassi said. "We can all learn from what he did. He's a class act. I think he's shown these past couple of weeks why he is No. 1 in the world."

For Agassi, the Australian Open was a turning point.

"All of a sudden, I went from somebody who's won some championships to a champion," he crowed.

Agassi eagerly anticipated the next Grand Slam tournament, the French Open.

"Ironically, the one I haven't won yet is the one I was favored in in both finals," he said. "I want it."

Pancho Gonzalez watched the Australian Open final on television at home in Las Vegas. Afterward, he said Agassi and Sampras were the best players in history.

"I think these two guys would beat the pants off anybody in the past," said Gonzalez, who died six months later. "Pete has the most complete game of anyone I've ever seen. Andre has made a complete turnaround in the last five, six months and is on the same level as Pete. It's going to make for some damn interesting matches."

Las Vegan George MacCall, the U.S. Davis Cup captain from 1965 to 1967, said the Australian Open final "might have been the best match I've ever seen. I saw Gonzalez-[Charlie] Pasarell, [Tony] Roche-Laver, Borg-McEnroe, but none of them had this consistency on both sides. This was hammer, hammer, hammer. Agassi was a wall."

Agassi remained hot after the Australian Open, winning the title at San Jose, Calif. After beating Chang in a three-set final, Agassi poked fun at himself. When asked about comments he had made two years previously concerning yet another alleged improvement in his outlook, Agassi said with a straight face: "That was my new, new attitude. This is my new, new, new attitude."

Whatever attitude it was, Agassi was playing the best tennis of his life. But he said that wasn't the biggest difference in his game.

"I'm definitely playing well, but my worst game is nowhere near as bad as it used to be," Agassi said. "Now my 75 percent is much better than my 75 percent a couple of years ago. That's a big difference. It's easy to win when you're playing 100 percent."

Agassi credited Gilbert with the improvement.

"He showed me that even 60 percent of my game can get me through matches," Agassi said. "I've always had a good record against the top players. Unfortunately, I didn't get to play them enough because I was losing too early."

Agassi said he was more concerned with sharpening his game than gaining the top ranking.

"No. 1 is a byproduct," he said. "I want it like I want an 'A' on an exam, but there are a lot of things I've got to do to get that 'A.' "

Agassi extended his 1995 winning streak to 15 matches, the best start of his career, before losing to Thomas Enqvist 7-6, 5-7, 6-2 in the semifinals at Philadelphia.

After the Enqvist match, Agassi was fined the relatively hefty sum (by tennis standards) of $2,350 for slamming a ball at a linesman and hurling his racket 45 feet. Also, after umpire Carlos Bernardes of Brazil failed to overrule a call in Agassi's favor, Agassi turned his rear end toward Bernardes and scratched himself. Agassi was not punished for that brazen act.

Agassi did not tell anyone, but he learned before the Enqvist match that his father was to undergo heart bypass surgery in several weeks.

Agassi had won 37 of 40 matches since August 1994 and the last two Grand Slam tournaments.

"It would be a crime if he didn't do what he's doing — give it his best shot without all the image stuff," said Kelly

Jones, a former world No. 1 doubles player who lives with his wife, Tami, in the Las Vegas suburb of Henderson. "That's what Brad Gilbert has helped him do. . . .

"Agassi has grown up a lot in the last couple of years. He's really turned himself around. He got too much too soon. He needed the right person to bring out the best in him instead of people sucking up to him."

Chang agreed with Jones about Agassi.

"He's a much better player now," Chang said. "He's done a few things that have helped. Having a break for wrist surgery gave him more desire to play, and Brad Gilbert has helped him become a more patient player. Brad was known for being patient and making the most of his opportunities. That's something Andre lacked."

Agassi defeated Chang 6-3, 6-3 in a March 1995 exhibition before an announced crowd of 9,290 in the 11,400-seat MGM Grand Garden in Las Vegas. Even though Agassi and Chang live only 10 miles apart in the Las Vegas area, the exhibition marked the only time they have seen each other in Southern Nevada since Chang moved there six years ago from Southern California.

*   *   *

Agassi and Chang don't dislike each other, although Agassi has expressed some irritation with Chang. Rather, they have less in common than one would think.

"They are as opposite as you can get," Jones said. "Andre has a flamboyant personality. Michael is reserved, non-conformist, very sheltered."

Added Ken Flach, also a former No. 1 doubles player and a former U.S. Davis Cup teammate of Agassi and Chang's: "Michael is very disciplined. That's the best word to describe him. Andre is more free-floating. He needs someone around him to discipline him, or he runs to Taco Bell."

Agassi was once asked if he got along with Chang.

"How do you *not* get along with Michael Chang?" Agassi said. "He never says a word."

Agassi has, however, criticized Chang occasionally in print. Agassi once referred to Chang as "he of the deep pockets and short arms." Agassi has also been quoted twice in the past two years in *Tennis* complaining about Chang's lack of commitment to the Davis Cup. Chang has played in the Davis Cup only once since 1990 (as of July 7, 1997).

Concerning Chang's decision not to play in the Davis Cup quarterfinals against Italy at Palermo, Sicily, in 1995, Agassi cracked, "Maybe he had to go make a million or two over in Asia."

Chang said he was planning to play in the first round against France until the USTA chose Florida, instead of a West Coast site.

The 1997 Davis Cup quarterfinals against the Netherlands were played at Newport Beach, Calif., a few miles from where Chang grew up, but he passed in favor of "commercial requirements" in Hong Kong.

Agassi responded: "To my way of thinking, if you're asked to play [Davis Cup], you've got to play. It's too hard to do what Jim [Courier] does, what Todd [Martin] does or what I do [in terms of Cup commitment] to not get on those who refuse to support the effort."

Author John Feinstein recently offered his opinion about the Davis Cup feud.

"I think Agassi is absolutely right about Chang not playing Davis Cup," Feinstein said.

Chang, on the other hand, has several virtues Agassi doesn't. Chang always plays his hardest, doesn't swear on the court (at least audibly and probably not at all) and doesn't skip post-match interviews.

Rarely playing Davis Cup is not all that bothers Agassi about Chang. According to David Granger in *Gentleman's Quarterly*, it also annoys Agassi that Chang has patterned his game after Agassi's and moved to Southern Nevada to avoid paying California taxes.

What really bugs Agassi, Granger added, is that the 5-foot-9-inch, 150-pound Chang is always improving and therefore forces Agassi to keep improving. But Agassi also admires Chang's perseverance on the court.

"It's his determination and competitiveness that always makes him a threat to win the match even if you are playing your best tennis because he makes you do it over and over again, whether it's two hours or five hours," said Agassi, 11-7 professionally against Chang as of July 7, 1997. "He's one guy who, if you're not playing your best tennis, becomes almost unbeatable at times because you can't seem to end the point and mentally stay on top of him. His strength is his mind and quickness. I would take quickness in any sport over any other weapon."

The more pressure there is on Chang, the better he seems to play.

"This guy should pretend he's behind when he starts the match," Agassi said. "I've never played anyone who plays so much better when he's behind. He's a good closer, too.

"You can't run out the clock in tennis. You've got to end that last point, and nobody is better at keeping you from doing that than Michael."

Agassi, meanwhile, is exactly the opposite.

". . . Against Andre, you have to get on top of him fast," Chang said. "He doesn't play as well when he is down. He is a much better player when he is a front-runner."

Chang says there's no friction between him and Agassi. When they see each other, they engage in "small chit-chat, nothing in great depth," Chang said. "Andre and I are friends but not the closest of friends, to be honest with you."

Superficially, Agassi and Chang have many similarities. They are close in age (Agassi 27 and Chang 25), grew up 300 miles apart, became top-10 tennis players and are born-again Christians.

However, it's very rare for rivals to be good friends. Ken Flach said Agassi and Chang "tend to stay to themselves. They're going to play each other in big matches.

They don't want to practice with each other and give each other information."

Ironically, given their personalities, Chang is evangelistic and Agassi discreet about his faith. In Chang's tennis interviews, it's always "The Lord this" or "The Lord that." Agassi never mentions his faith after matches.

"Michael is very serious about his faith, reading the scriptures and studying," said Flach, also a born-again Christian. "Andre has a strong faith, but he's not a daily studious type of person."

Agassi, in fact, bristles at the word "religion."

"I don't believe in people being judgmental, and religion connotes that feeling," he said.

Nor do Agassi and Chang have similar interests. Agassi is an avid golfer, and Chang loves to fish (although he throws the fish back).

When asked if he could see himself going fishing with Chang, Agassi said, "I don't think I could see myself going fishing, period. I don't believe in messing with something that's not messing with me."

*   *   *

After the Chang exhibition, Agassi went to Indian Wells, Calif., for the $1.8 million *Newsweek* Champions Cup. For the first time in his nine-year career, Agassi had a mathematical chance — albeit a slim one — to gain the No. 1 ranking.

Agassi, ranked No. 2, would overtake Sampras if Sampras lost early at Indian Wells and Agassi won the title and earned enough bonus points by beating highly ranked players.

Agassi, however, said the week before Indian Wells that No. 1 wouldn't be on his mind.

"It would be easy to think I'm just avoiding the pressure by saying that," Agassi said. "But the bottom line is that you've got to play the best tennis on the tour for close to a year to have a shot at being No. 1. I've done it for seven months. I just want to maintain that level for the next two or three years.

"If I don't get to No. 1 before the French Open or the U.S. Open, it's not like at this time next year I still won't be striving for that.

"It could happen next week, and that would be a wonderful thing. But it's not anything I spend any time thinking about."

Agassi admitted it would be special to attain the No. 1 ranking in the Palm Springs area, a five-hour drive from Las Vegas. He made his Grand Prix main-draw debut there in 1986.

"I love the tournament," Agassi said. "It's almost like a home event to me because it's so close. I drive there, and there's the desert sun. It would be nice [to become No. 1] there, but it will feel great wherever it happens."

It would have to wait a few more weeks.

Agassi showed up at Indian Wells in what Bill Dwyre of *The Los Angeles Times* called "his garish pajama-like tennis outfit and a bandanna that made him look like a greeter for Pirates of the Caribbean [at Disneyland]." Agassi marched to the final before losing to Sampras, 7-5, 6-3, 7-5. Mike Agassi was scheduled to have surgery at UCLA Medical Center the next day.

After the final, Andre peered into the ESPN camera and said: "I love you, Dad. And don't worry . . . next time, I'll kick his ass."

The surgery went well, and Andre kept his promise. Sort of. In his next tournament, he edged Sampras 3-6, 6-2, 7-6 (7-3) to win the $2.25 million Lipton Championships at Key Biscayne, Fla.

Agassi, still ranked No. 2 behind Sampras but gaining fast, reluctantly agreed to play in the Davis Cup quarterfinals March 31 through April 2 against Italy, on clay, at Palermo, Sicily, and convinced Sampras to join him. It marked the first time the world's top two players had played on the same team since McEnroe and Connors competed for the U.S. in 1984. Agassi beat Andrea Gaudenzi, the world's top-ranked junior in 1990, in straight sets in the opening match, and the U.S. rolled to a 5-0 victory.

On April 10, 1995, Agassi became the 12th player in the 22-year history of the men's computer rankings to reach No. 1. Nineteen days before his 25th birthday, Agassi ended Sampras' reign of 82 weeks at No. 1.

Agassi was playing in the $1.06 million Japan Open at Tokyo when he took over the top spot.

"You get to No. 1, and there's a huge amount of excitement to it," said Agassi, who, playing with a strained lower back, lost to Courier 6-4, 6-3 in the Japan Open final. "I wasn't sure what they were saying [in Japanese during the introductions]. All of a sudden, I heard, 'No. 1,' and then 'Andre Agassi.' It was like, wow, OK. . . . I can't wait to be in Atlanta [for the AT&T Challenge] and hear it."

Mike Agassi called Andre's No. 1 ranking "a dream come true. When a kid is 2 years old, you think he'll be No. 1 in the world someday, and then 22 years later he's No. 1. It's something a handful of people do in a lifetime."

The novelty soon wore off for Andre, though.

"When your career is all said and done, you want to win the Slams," Andre said in September after losing to Sampras in the U.S. Open final. "Being No. 1 is great, but after the first hour it doesn't make any difference because you've still got every guy in the tournament trying to beat you."

After Japan, Agassi began his clay-court preparation for the French Open. He lost in the Atlanta final to Chang 6-2, 6-7 (6-8), 6-4 and in the quarterfinals of the German Open at Hamburg to Bruguera, 6-3, 6-1.

Agassi received a warning for making an obscene gesture in the last game of the Bruguera match and got in an argument with a fan afterward. According to *The Associated Press*, Agassi was packing his bags and getting ready to leave center court when a fan commented loudly on the poor quality of the match.

Agassi cursed the spectator and retorted, "Are you gonna get a knife and [inaudible] me now?" before swearing at the man again. Agassi was referring to the April 1993 stabbing of top-ranked Monica Seles by a fan on the same court. Agassi left without further incident.

Then came the French Open. With the title, Agassi would become only the fifth player to win all four Grand Slam singles titles in his career.

"Winning the French is the ultimate goal for me," Agassi said. "Pete and I have won three of the four. Jim [Courier] has won two of the four. Pete and I both want to be the first American [in the Open era] to win all four Grand Slams."

In addition to Budge and Laver, the only players to win all four Grand Slam singles titles in their careers are Fred Perry of England and Roy Emerson of Australia.

When Agassi was asked about the possibility of winning all four Grand Slam titles in 1995, he answered thoughtfully, with both tact and candor.

"I can't legitimately look at the profession I'm in and expect it or even go out on the court and demand myself to accomplish it," Agassi said. "To accomplish something so great is a wonderful freak of nature that could happen to somebody, but to assume that you can is disrespectful to the profession you're in and also to your peers.

"But I do feel I can win on all surfaces, which leaves me the possibility to go out there and do it. I've won two in a row, so that helps my confidence.

"The French and Wimbledon will be the tough ones. There are experts on clay, and there are experts on grass. I kind of try to do everything a little well."

Everything was going according to plan in the French Open as Agassi won his first four matches in straight sets to set up a quarterfinal against ninth-seeded Yevgeny Kafelnikov. Many felt Agassi was playing well enough to win the title, but he apparently strained a hip muscle in the first set and lost to the 21-year-old Russian, 6-4, 6-3, 7-5.

"It's really disappointing," Agassi said. "You come in here to play well and to give it everything. And for it to end like that is extremely disappointing."

Kafelnikov lost in the semifinals to eventual champion Thomas Muster, but won the French Open in 1996.

Agassi also began well at Wimbledon only to suffer a shocking loss. He lost only one set, to Wheaton in the third round, in his first five matches.

Agassi wore a new all-white outfit featuring baggy, knee-length shorts and a white bandanna with the Nike logo. When a reporter asked Agassi if he was aware that his shorts were transparent, Agassi retorted, "Obviously, you are."

Agassi suffered perhaps the worst collapse of his career in the Wimbledon semifinals as he fell to Boris Becker, Bollettieri's new disciple, 2-6, 7-6 (7-1), 6-4, 7-6 (7-1). Agassi, who had beaten Becker eight straight times, led 6-2, 4-1 before Becker stormed back.

"I was playing somebody from outer space," Becker said of the first set and a half. "I was hitting first serves hard, and he kept passing me. He kept hitting low on my first volleys, and I had to half volley all the time. On his service games, when I had break points, he aced me, or he played a forehand or running shot down the line. He played unbelievable."

Agassi probably got overconfident, a fatal mistake against someone as talented and determined as Becker, especially on his beloved Centre Court at Wimbledon.

"When that lead slipped away," Agassi said, "Boris started playing more aggressively, and when he got back on serve, I never quite had the confidence again. I didn't break his serve after that."

Sampras defeated Becker in the final for his third straight Wimbledon title.

Becker alleged afterward that Agassi received preferential treatment at Wimbledon, British newspapers reported. Becker, a former three-time Wimbledon champion, complained that he played only once on Centre Court before his semifinal victory over Agassi, whereas the top-ranked American played five of his six matches there.

"It cannot be just a coincidence that it is always Agassi at 2 P.M. on Centre Court," Becker said. "It would be interesting to see how he played if he was always on Court 2 at noon."

Becker charged that Nike was involved.

"The other companies just can't compete with them" Becker was quoted as saying. "The company puts pressure on the tournaments, and money plays a big role. You saw it at the French Open, and I am worried it will happen at the U.S. Open. I fear it will be like playing in a Nike house."

Nike spokesman Keith Peters called Becker's allegation "preposterous" and noted that two-time defending champion Sampras had played only once on Centre Court before the semifinals.

"I think it's absurd to suggest that Nike would try to influence what court players play on," Peters said. "I don't know how the tournament organizers manage things.

"I will point out that Agassi is currently ranked No. 1 in the world. It probably makes sense for him to play on Centre Court where more people can see him."

Agassi has a 10-year endorsement contract with Nike worth a reported $100 million to $150 million.

"They do not have enough money to buy me," said Becker, who has a contract with rival company Lotto. "I wouldn't want my son wearing the things Agassi does."

Agassi, added Becker, is not popular with the other players.

"Agassi is not someone the players like very much," Becker said. "He is always on his own and doing his own thing. He doesn't have much in common with us.

"He never opens up to the rest. Perhaps that's one of the secrets of his success. If he were to open up more, perhaps fewer players would fear him."

Agassi embarked on his 26-match winning streak after Wimbledon, capturing the titles at Washington, D.C., Montreal, Cincinnati and New Haven in sweltering heat.

Agassi threw up during his 6-4, 2-6, 7-5 victory over Stefan Edberg in the final at Washington because of exertion in the oppressive humidity.

Looking ahead to the U.S. Open, Mike Agassi was asked what advice he might give his son if Andre met Sampras in the final.

"Why should I tell him anything?" Mike said. "He hasn't listened to a thing I've said for three years."

One year after being unseeded at the U.S. Open, Andre was top-seeded in the 1995 event. He avenged the Wimbledon loss to Becker by beating him 7-6 (7-4), 7-6 (7-2), 4-6, 6-4 in the semifinals on Saturday night. Agassi broke Becker for the match, reeling off three straight brilliant returns of serve.

"He just played typical Andre Agassi shots to finish off the match," Becker said. "I didn't even see the ball."

Agassi, stung by Becker's comments at Wimbledon, gave Becker a perfunctory handshake afterward and refused to look at him.

"It is hard for me to respect anybody who says things that are not only wrong but are meant to hurt . . ." Agassi said. "He just made so many comments about players not liking me, me not hanging out in the locker room, me not practicing with the guys.

"I couldn't understand it. I take a lot of pride in how I handle myself off the court. I certainly don't want to speak for anybody else, but I go to sleep feeling like I am respected and liked."

Becker was somewhat apologetic after the match.

"I may have said a few things which aren't right; he has said maybe a few things which aren't right," Becker said. "But we are not all perfect."

Agassi had less than 24 hours to prepare for the final against Sampras.

*   *   *

It's especially rare for rivals to get along if they come from the same country. Go down the list from the past and present. McEnroe and Jimmy Connors were bitter enemies. Argentines Guillermo Vilas and Jose Luis Clerc bickered. Austrians Muster and Horst Skoff can't stand each other. Germans Becker and Stich go their separate ways. It must be a clash of egos, something about each stealing the other's thunder.

Agassi and Sampras are different. They are by no means bosom buddies, but neither are they at each other's throat. In tennis, that's saying something.

"These guys show it's possible to have a great rivalry without hating the other guy," said Tom Gullikson. "For too long in tennis, we never had that."

The relationship is based on mutual respect. They are in a class of their own in terms of talent, although Sampras leads the head-to-head series 12-8 (as of July 7, 1997) with a four-match winning streak.

"I don't care if we are playing on clay or grass or hardcourt," Agassi said, "Pete is the guy that I can potentially have no say so in how the match goes because he is that good."

Sampras, meanwhile, said of Agassi: "He is someone that I feel like I have to be at my best to beat. If I am not, then I am not going to beat him. He can return my serve as well as anyone. He might be the best returner of all time, so I have a lot of respect for him."

It's true that at a 1993 Nike promotion in Paris, Agassi said of the long-armed Sampras, "Nobody should be ranked No. 1 who looks like he just swung from a tree."

Agassi insisted he was only making an innocent joke that was taken out of context.

"He has amazing reach," Agassi said. "There aren't too many people who know what it's like to play him, but he's a 6-foot [actually 6-foot-1-inch] guy who looks like he's 6 feet 9 inches when he's serving. I consider Pete a friend of mine. . . . He knows as well as anyone I wouldn't do anything to hurt him."

The controversial comment came during an interview, nationally televised in France, with Agassi, Courier and McEnroe.

"The whole concept of the show was to make fun of the questions asked and not give normal answers," Agassi said. "The point was to attract attention and get Nike going."

Courier, for example, sarcastically said journeyman Christo Van Rensburg was a threat to win the French Open, according to Agassi.

After Sampras won his first-round match in the French Open that year, most of the questions at his news conference focused on Agassi's remark.

"It's best for me not to get into any verbal words with Andre," Sampras said. "I was a bit surprised. I consider Andre a pretty good friend. When I heard about it, my feelings weren't really that hurt. Maybe he didn't mean it."

Also, Agassi reportedly suggested at a 1994 Nike shareholder convention that company engineers design something to keep Sampras' tongue in his mouth.

In each case, Agassi quickly faxed an apology to Sampras, who accepted. Perhaps wanting to make amends, Agassi gave Sampras an extra hour to recover from food poisoning before the 1994 Lipton final.

The worst Sampras has done is mimic Barbra Streisand cheering for Agassi at Wimbledon in 1993 on the *Late Show With David Letterman*. In an impressive imitation, Sampras said with a lisp, " 'Dre. Let's go, 'Dre, c'mon, 'Dre."

Not only are Agassi and Sampras rivals, they are opposites in almost every way — on and off the court.

Sampras has the best serve, running forehand and leaping overhead in tennis. Agassi has the best service return, down-the-line backhand and topspin lob.

Sampras, from his conservative tennis attire to his short black hair to his stoicism, is as understated as Agassi is flamboyant.

"Both of us would be miserable if we had to live like the other," Agassi said.

When Sampras was asked what he likes about Agassi, Sampras hesitated, then said, "I like the way he travels," referring to Agassi's private jet.

*   *   *

Sampras ended Agassi's 1995 winning streak with a 6-4, 6-3, 4-6, 7-5 victory in the U.S. Open final.

"I'd give up all 26 to have that one back," Agassi lamented. "It's been a long summer."

The toll of a successful summer could be one reason no No. 1 seed had won the men's title at the U.S. Open since Lendl in 1987. (Sampras broke the streak in 1996.) It didn't help Agassi that he had to play the final so soon after beating Becker. During the rest of the U.S. Open, players had at least one day off between singles matches.

"I had a couple days off before I played Boris, and that really helped me a lot," Agassi said. "But coming back and playing today, I felt it in my legs after that long set point we had [in the final]. It was way too early in the match to be feeling that way."

With Agassi facing set point on his serve in the first set, he and Sampras traded blistering groundstrokes. Each shot seemed to be belted harder and at a greater angle than the last, the players showing how desperately they wanted another Grand Slam title.

Finally, Sampras nailed a sharply-angled cross-court backhand that Agassi couldn't reach. The crowd of 19,950 in the 20,000-seat Louis Armstrong Stadium roared its appreciation of the spectacular 22-stroke point.

"That was probably one of the best points I've ever been a part of," Sampras said. "I certainly hope it makes the Play of the Day."

Paul Annacone, coaching Sampras while Tim Gullikson underwent chemotherapy, watched the point in awe.

"Before the match, I told Pete to try to get into as many athletic points as he could," Annacone said. "And I think that was about as quintessentially athletic a point as you could have."

Agassi was less thrilled.

"That point really sucked," he snarled.

After the U.S. final, Agassi trudged back to Las Vegas to play for the U.S. with Sampras against Sweden in the Davis Cup semifinals at Caesars Palace. After pulling a chest muscle in his victory over Mats Wilander, Agassi played only one match the rest of the year. He accompanied the U.S. team to the Davis Cup final against Russia at Moscow in December, but was unable to play.

Sampras regained the No. 1 ranking on November 6, and Agassi finished the year at No. 2 for the second straight time.

The Early Years

ANDREE AGASSI

Photo courtesy Intermountain Tennis Association

Andre Agassi appears on the cover of the 1983 Intermountain Tennis Association yearbook. Note the misspelling of Agassi's first name.

Photo courtesy Hans Riehemann

Agassi (front row, far left) poses with his youth basketball team in 1980. Agassi was 9 years old at the time. Rich McKee (front row, second from right) would go on to accompany Agassi on the pro tennis circuit as a friend and helper.

Agassi (third from right) poses with future pros Ann Grossman (far left), David Wheaton (third from left), Martin Blackman (fourth from right) and other junior players at Bradenton, Fla., in 1985.

(Left to right) Blackman, Agassi, Nick Bollettieri, Jim Courier and Wheaton pose near Rye, N.Y., in 1986. Agassi and Courier would go on to reach No. 1 in the world, Wheaton No. 12 and Blackman No. 158.

Photo by James Bollettieri

Agassi receives instructions from Bollettieri.

Photo by James Bollettieri

Agassi thanks God after a victory.

AP Photo by Lionel Cironneau

A dejected Agassi receives the runner-up plate in the 1990 French Open final. Ecuador's Andres Gomez defeated Agassi, 6-3, 2-6, 6-4, 6-4.

AP Photo by Denis Paquin

Agassi sinks to his knees after defeating Goran Ivanisevic to win the men's singles final on Centre Court at Wimbledon in 1992.

AP Photo by Dave Caulkin

Agassi and his girlfriend at the time, Wendi Stewart, display the championship cup to fans before leaving Wimbledon.

Photo by James Bollettieri

Agassi practices during a tournament in Orlando, Fla.

AP Photo by Denis Paquin

Barbra Streisand exults as Agassi takes a point from Pete Sampras during the men's singles quarterfinals on Centre Court at Wimbledon in 1993. At left is Phillip Agassi, Andre's brother, and at right is Perry Rogers, Andre's best friend since childhood and business manager.

Photo by James Bollettieri

(Left to right) Phillip Agassi, coach Brad Gilbert, Rogers and Brooke Shields cheer for Andre during the 1994 U.S. Open.

Photo by James Bollettieri

Agassi in 1994 became the first unseeded player to win the U.S. Open since Fred Stolle in 1966.

Modern-Day Agassi

Photo by Cynthia Lum

Agassi and Sampras leave the court after the final of the 1995 Lipton Championships at Key Biscayne, Fla. Agassi won, 3-6, 6-2, 7-6 (7-3).

AP Photo by Oscar Honda

Agassi returns the ball to Sampras during the final of the 1995 U.S. Open in New York. Sampras won, 6-4, 6-3, 4-6, 7-5.

Photo by James Bollettieri

Agassi ponders Ivanisevic's default during the final of the 1996 Lipton Championships.

Shields cheers during Agassi's 6-4, 6-4 victory over Slovakia's Karol Kucera in the second round of the 1996 Olympic tennis tournament at Stone Mountain near Atlanta.

Agassi shares a moment with his father, Mike, after defeating Spain's Sergi Bruguera in the gold-medal match at the 1996 Centennial Olympic Games.

Agassi displays his gold medal after the Olympic singles final.

Agassi and Shields leave St. John's Episcopal Chapel in Monterey, Calif., after exchanging wedding vows Saturday evening, April 19, 1997. Agassi and Shields were married in front of 150 guests.

Virtual Andre

Agassi suffered one of the worst years of his career in 1996. Yes, he won the Olympic gold medal in singles, but the field was weak. Yes, he won singles titles at Key Biscayne and Cincinnati, but he had an easy draw at Key Biscayne and Goran Ivanisevic quit at 0-3 in the final with a stiff neck. Yes, Agassi reached the semifinals of two Grand Slam tournaments, but he lost in straight sets to Michael Chang each time.

More telling was that Agassi failed to reach a Grand Slam final for only the second time in seven years, the other time being in 1993 when he battled tendinitis. And that he lost all three of his matches against Sampras in straight sets, winning an average of only 4.3 games in each. And that he lost in the second round of the French Open and the first round at Wimbledon. And that he sank from No. 2 at the beginning of the year to No. 8 at the end. Whatever success Agassi had was a tribute to his sheer talent.

As always, the year was marked by volatile behavior by Agassi and controversy.

Agassi went into the Australian Open with his fragile confidence shaken by the loss to Pete Sampras in the 1995 U.S. Open final and his game rusty from his injury-induced layoff. As the defending champion, though, Agassi willed himself to the semifinals.

He survived three five-set matches, including one against qualifier Gaston Etlis of Argentina in the first round, to reach the semis before losing to Chang, 6-1, 6-4, 7-6. Against Jim Courier in the quarters, Agassi came back from two sets down for the first time in his career.

*   *   *

The careers of Agassi and Courier have been intertwined from the time they met at a national 12-and-under tournament in San Diego to the Bollettieri academy through professional tennis.

Agassi and Courier feuded at the 1989 French Open, when Courier beat Agassi in the third round and then said that he had always felt he was playing "second fiddle" to Agassi.

"Second fiddle?" Agassi responded. "Sounds like an insecurity problem to me."

"*I'm* insecure?" Courier snapped.

They later reconciled, however. Winning Grand Slam titles helped. Courier won the French Open twice and the Australian Open twice between 1991 and 1993. After Agassi broke through at Wimbledon in 1992, he felt secure enough to open up to Courier during the Davis Cup final at Fort Worth, Texas, that December.

Sitting with Courier on the U.S. team bench during the crucial doubles match, Agassi turned to him and said: "I really want to say that I'm very happy for you and the success you've had. I really am. I couldn't bring myself to tell you that until after I'd won Wimbledon, and I'm sorry for that. I should have realized sooner that you deserved every bit of it."

Courier defeated Agassi six straight times before Agassi won in the 1996 Australian Open.

"[Agassi has] more talent than I have, frankly, as far as his hands and stuff, but maybe I want it more than he does," Courier said in February 1992.

Courier remains one of the few players with a winning record against Agassi (7-5 through July 7, 1997). But Courier has been unable to recapture his championship form, an apparent victim of burnout. Courier actually read a book during changeovers at the 1993 ATP Tour World Championship in Frankfurt, Germany.

For one of the few times in his career, Agassi was asked about *someone else's* unusual behavior.

"I won't make any negative comments," Agassi said of Courier's actions at the season-ending tournament, "but there's a good chance he's not where he wants to be. I've been there a few times."

Agassi said in January 1995 that he and Courier "are at two ends of the spectrum [mentally]. He talks about relaxing and getting away from the game, but my problem was I was too relaxed and too happy, and I had to start getting more into the game."

*   *   *

Agassi regained the No. 1 ranking with his victory over Courier in the 1996 Australian Open, but surrendered it to Thomas Muster two weeks later. Muster, in turn, held the top spot for one week before Sampras recaptured it by routing Agassi 6-2, 6-3 in the final indoors at San Jose, Calif.

After edging Chang 6-2, 5-7, 6-4 in the semifinals at San Jose, Agassi showed his frustration in the final. Agassi knocked a ball into the upper deck in anger and was penalized a point for cursing.

"I don't feel good about the fact that I lost my temper," Agassi said. ". . . But the heat of competition brings out the competitor in me. And all I really wanted to do was break his damn serve."

Even though Sampras won easily, Agassi was the star of the show.

"He's bigger than McEnroe and Connors at their height," said tournament director Barry MacKay.

San Francisco Chronicle columnist Scott Ostler put it another way.

"He's Reggie Jackson, and Sampras is Harmon Killebrew," Ostler aptly wrote.

After San Jose, though, Agassi was more like *Michael* Jackson. Agassi, apparently playing with a stomach ailment, lost to Luke Jensen, ranked No. 419 in singles, 6-2, 6-4 in the second round at Memphis. Agassi then caved in against Chang in the quarters at Indian Wells 6-7, 6-2, 6-1 and skipped the mandatory post-match news conference.

Muster entered Indian Wells ranked No. 1. He had won the title at Mexico City the previous week, but lost to Romanian Adrian Voinea, ranked 40th and playing with tendinitis in his shoulder, in the second round at Indian Wells. Muster, who had drawn a bye in the first round, was unable to make a quick transition from the 7,000-foot altitude and clay surface in Mexico City to sea level and hard courts at Indian Wells.

The upset added fuel to the raging debate over whether Muster, who had won all but one of his 12 titles in 1995 on clay, deserved to be ranked No. 1.

Agassi adamantly denied having said that Muster was unworthy, despite reports to the contrary.

"Like I have always said, he has worked hard to get [to No. 1], and he deserves to be there," Agassi said. "Based on the ranking system, it is an incredible accomplishment.

"All I have stated about it was that long before Muster was No. 1, I have complained about the ranking system [in which only a player's best 14 tournaments in the past year count]. I think it is ridiculous that you can step on the court and have it potentially not count. . . ."

Muster, meanwhile, insisted that Agassi had criticized him.

"I don't understand why Andre, who is a champion himself and knows what it takes, would say what he did," said Muster, whose win-at-all costs attitude and perceived arrogance make him perhaps the most disliked player in men's tennis. "It's a little disappointing in one way; we had a friendship. Suddenly, I'm ahead of him, and now it's changed. But the only language that counts on the court and in the locker room is winning. Who wins is right, who loses fails."

Always the pragmatist, Muster defended the ranking system.

"Whatever the computer prints out, that's the No. 1," he said. "There is nobody No. 1 who doesn't deserve it. It's not like you buy your points in the supermarket and say, 'I want to be No. 1.' "

After Indian Wells, Agassi became the first player to win the Key Biscayne title three times, but then lost to 16th-seeded Alberto (now Albert) Costa of Spain 6-2, 6-1 in the third round on clay at Monte Carlo.

Agassi's troubles continued at the French Open and Wimbledon.

In the first round at Paris, he was given a point penalty, one step from default, for obscene language during a four-set victory over qualifier Jacobo Diaz of Spain. An overweight Agassi, seeded third, then lost to No. 72 Chris Woodruff in the second round 4-6, 6-4, 6-7 (7-9), 6-3, 6-2. Agassi didn't even chase balls late in the match.

"He's simply given up," British commentator David Mercer said during the telecast. Agassi again skipped the post-match news conference, incurring a $2,000 fine.

Wimbledon was worse. Agassi, again seeded third, fell to American qualifier Doug Flach, ranked No. 281, 2-6, 7-6 (7-1), 6-4, 7-6 (8-6) in one of the biggest upsets of the Open era.

Commentator John Lloyd said on the Home Box Office telecast: "I think he has taken 1996 off so far. He was desperately disappointed when he didn't win Wimbledon and the U.S. Open [in 1995]. He lost his motivation."

The match against Flach was played on Court 2 (Becker must have been smiling), known as "the graveyard of champions," and Agassi said he had come down with the flu a few days beforehand.

At least Agassi showed up at the news conference this time. He offered no excuses — or explanations.

"I'm trying to kind of get myself at the top of my game again," Agassi said unconvincingly. "You know, when you've been there, and then all of a sudden your game is a little off, there's more frustration to it."

Agassi revived his game for the Olympics and kept his momentum for the $1.95 million ATP Championship the following week at Cincinnati.

Agassi's game and temper were in top form at Cincinnati. He smashed one racket, incurring a $500 fine, during a three-set victory over fellow American Alex O'Brien in the third round. Agassi then defeated three top-five players in a row — No. 4 Yevgeny Kafelnikov, No. 2 Muster and No. 3 Chang — for the title. It was the first time Agassi had beaten three top-five players in one tournament since the 1990 ATP Tour World Championship at Frankfurt.

Agassi's 11-match winning streak ended dramatically when he was disqualified from a tournament for the first time in his career.

After drawing a bye in the first round at Indianapolis, Agassi met Daniel Nestor of Canada in the second round. Agassi was leading 6-1, 2-2 when he lost his serve. According to *The Associated Press*, he hit a ball into the stands and was cited for ball abuse by chair umpire Dana Loconto. Agassi then shouted an expletive at Loconto, who in turn called for ATP supervisor Mark Darby. After conferring with Agassi, Darby instructed Loconto to default the player.

The crowd reacted by booing and throwing paper towels and water bottles onto the court. Then the fans cheered Agassi as he departed.

"I got a warning, then he went straight to a default," Agassi said. "I felt I had an argument for not getting a point penalty [in between]. . . . It's something I've said a thousand times, and today they decide that crossed the line."

The default dropped Agassi to No. 8 in the rankings, leading to a seeding fiasco at the U.S. Open. Had Agassi been seeded No. 8, he could have met top seed Sampras in the quarterfinals. That would have meant a weeknight matchup on the USA Network rather than a blockbuster semifinal or final over the weekend on CBS, which pays an estimated $31 million per year to televise the tournament.

Presto! Agassi was seeded No. 6, guaranteeing he could not meet Sampras before the semifinals. The USTA also shifted some other seeds around and, defying the rules, placed the 16 seeds into the men's draw after the other 112 players.

Many players were irate.

"It's like cheating," said Muster, ranked No. 2 but seeded No. 3. "It's just so Agassi won't face Sampras in the quarters."

Amid rumors of a boycott, the USTA remade the draw for the first time in tennis history. The seedings stood, however.

"I just try not to get caught up in it at all, really," Agassi said. "I don't worry about where I'm seeded."

Agassi faced none other than Muster in the quarters. After two days of denying there was bad blood between them, Agassi prevailed 6-2, 7-5, 4-6, 6-2 in a ferocious night match as the players traded punishing groundstrokes.

"It was just a war," Agassi said, after evening his career record against Muster at 4-4.

Muster and Agassi couldn't even agree on that. Muster insisted it "wasn't a war," but blasted Agassi's entourage for yelling from its courtside box during the match.

"The Agassi fan club is not the nicest, it's not a secret," Muster said. "I don't care. They comment on every shot while I am playing. They were behaving like a bunch of idiots. It's nothing new."

Muster singled out Brad Gilbert.

"Gilbert doesn't like anybody, that's not a secret," Muster said. "Gilbert never liked me; that's not a secret, either. I think Andre is the same. That's always been his problem. If you have somebody talking to you like a radio all day, you must get nuts."

Agassi took a swipe at Muster afterward, saying, "Next time, I wish he would look me in the eye when we shake hands. I felt like we had a battle out there."

Incredibly, Agassi could not get motivated for the U.S. Open semifinal and mailed it in against Chang, 6-3, 6-2, 6-2.

"I felt flat," Agassi said in an understatement. "I missed a lot of second-serve returns. I felt like I was 40 percent of the player that I have been. I never found my game."

Mike Lupica, one of the top sportswriters in the country, called Agassi's performance against Chang "disgraceful" in a *Tennis* column.

"I have heard [Agassi's] spin on the day, heard everybody talk about how high Chang's tennis was that Saturday afternoon," Lupica wrote. "And I saw what I saw. We all did. Agassi got behind and didn't want to play anymore. Two years from when he was the Open champion, he looked like a quitter."

Agassi was so listless against Chang that it's hard to believe he simply suffered a letdown after beating Muster. Could it be that Agassi knew he couldn't beat Sampras in the final and didn't want to endure that much emotional pain again?

Sampras went on to roll past Chang 6-1, 6-4, 7-6 for his fourth U.S. Open title.

Agassi was no more motivated for the fall European circuit. After winning two matches in Stuttgart, Germany, he ended the year with four straight losses.

Agassi was assessed a $50,000 fine, one of the biggest fines in the seven-year history of the ATP Tour, for skipping the draw ceremony and a mandatory round of interviews on the eve of the $3.3 million ATP Tour World Championship in Hanover, Germany. Agassi reportedly was in town and practiced later that night. After losing to Sampras 6-2, 6-1 in the first round amid boos and whistles, Agassi withdrew with flu symptoms.

Agassi's year ended mercifully two weeks later with a 6-3, 6-4 loss to Mark Woodforde in the first round of the $6 million Grand Slam Cup in Munich. Agassi had beaten Woodforde 6-0, 6-0 in Vienna in 1994.

"I thought another severe defeat could be in the cards," Woodforde said. "But I noticed he hadn't been practicing much at all. We walked onto the court, and it was different. I don't think he was highly motivated [for the Grand Slam Cup]. He had never lost to me. . . . What's he got to prove against me? I know that he is one of the best players of today and maybe that have played the game. You're playing for a whole lot of money at that tournament, and he already has a whole lot of money. He's not going to improve his ranking at all [because the non-ATP Tour tournament doesn't count in the rankings]. I think he had been sick two weeks before at the ATP [Championships], so maybe he was still suffering some effects from that. A lot of [players] pulled out before [the Grand Slam Cup] began, and he still showed. So I give that to him."

After losing to Woodforde, Agassi said: "It's been a struggle most of the year. I thank God that I won the gold medal. But outside that, it's been a struggle.

"I just want to put it behind me and get ready to move on. I don't need any miracle cure. I just need to go back to good old fundamentals."

Gilbert, meanwhile, was doing his best to cope with Agassi's apathy.

"Yes, it bothers me, but I can't call time out, pull the guy out and put myself in," Gilbert said.

*   *   *

Just when Agassi appeared to regain his motivation, injuries sabotaged the first half of his year in 1997. He lost a career-high five straight matches at one point and plum-

meted to No. 31 in the rankings, his lowest since falling to
No. 32 in February 1994 after undergoing wrist surgery.

Agassi skipped the Australian Open in January to
rest physically and, more importantly, mentally. He had
planned to play for the U.S. in the first round of the Davis
Cup February 7 through 9 at Brazil, but withdrew after
spraining his left ankle in practice. Led by Courier's two
victories, the U.S. defeated Brazil and a promising player
named Gustavo Kuerten 4-1 in a tense series that was much
closer than the score indicated.

After a layoff of more than two months, Agassi returned to the circuit at San Jose, Calif., in early February.
Seeded third, he reached the semifinals before being upset
by hard-serving Englishman Greg Rusedski, the seventh
seed, 6-3, 6-4.

Agassi received a bye in the first round at Memphis
the following week. He re-sprained the ankle, much more
severely this time, in the second round during a 6-2, 6-4 loss
to the 83rd-ranked Kuerten, 20. Agassi, ranked 14th, was
trailing 3-1 in the second set when he fell behind the baseline and aggravated the sprain.

Kuerten used the victory, his first over a top-20
player, as a springboard to his stunning French Open title
3½ months later.

Agassi tried to come back too soon and lost to unseeded Javier Sanchez of Spain 6-3, 6-3 two weeks later in
the first round at Scottsdale, Ariz.

Agassi had one of the worst possible first-round
draws at Indian Wells the following week when he met 20-
year-old rising star Mark Philippoussis of Australia for the
first time. Philippoussis, built more like a linebacker than a
tennis player at 6 feet 4 inches and 202 pounds, had won his
second ATP Tour title the previous week at Scottsdale and
set a tour record with a 142-mph serve.

Philippoussis is nicknamed "Scud" because his powerful serve is reminiscent of the missile used in the 1992 Per-
sian Gulf war. Never mind that the nickname glorifies the
killing and maiming of countless people. Early in Boris

Becker's career, he was nicknamed "Boom Boom" for similar reasons. To his everlasting credit, however, the German asked the media not to use the nickname because he didn't want to be associated with the atrocities of World War II.

The Philippoussis-Agassi match, featuring the hardest server in tennis against the best returner, was unquestionably the most anticipated of the tournament, even though it occurred in the first round. It had the atmosphere of a final as 11,500 fans packed the stadium court at the beautiful Hyatt Grand Champions resort. In the background, the majestic Santa Rosa mountains towered over the Coachella Valley.

Looking extremely fit and eager, the 10th-seeded Agassi fought hard, but lost to the unseeded Philippoussis, 7-6 (7-5), 7-6 (7-5). Philippoussis fired 23 aces, many in the 130-135 mph range, in the one-hour, 40 minute match.

When asked what it was like to face Philippoussis' serve, Agassi replied tongue in cheek, "It's not difficult to get your racket on it."

Getting it back, of course, was another matter.

As rusty as Agassi was, he had done well to play Philippoussis so closely. But Agassi took a step backward in his next tournament, the Lipton Championships at Key Biscayne. After drawing a bye in the first round, he lost to 79th-ranked Scott Draper of Australia, 7-6 (7-5), 6-1.

Afterward, Agassi denied that motivation was a problem.

"I'm not tired," he said. "I'm not through."

Agassi admitted, however, that "the year has gone about as bad as you could expect it to. It's not good. When you're committed to going down a road and persevere, you can't expect it to be easy. I anticipated a struggle — certainly it's been more than I would have preferred. But I'm committed to this. I hope I get through it."

Agassi fell back on his old standby, the Davis Cup, to end his losing streak, winning both of his matches against the Netherlands in the quarterfinals April 4 through 6 at Newport Beach. He struggled to beat 20-year-old Sjeng

Schalken, playing only his second Davis Cup singles match, 7-6 (8-6), 6-4, 7-6 (7-2) in the opening match, and clinched the Americans' 4-1 triumph with a stirring 3-6, 3-6, 6-3, 6-3, 6-3 victory over Jan Siemerink.

It was only the second time in Agassi's career that he had won after losing the first two sets. Siemerink also led Courier two sets to none on the first day and lost. Agassi, meanwhile, extended his Davis Cup singles winning streak to 15, one short of Bill Tilden's record for consecutive victories by an American.

After marrying Brooke Shields on April 19 at Monterey, Calif., Agassi lost to 81st-ranked Magnus Norman of Sweden 7-6 (9-7), 3-6, 6-3 in the second round on clay in Atlanta.

Agassi was fined $1,000 for skipping the post-match news conference, bringing to eight the number of times he had been fined or penalized in 15 months. Peter Alfano, vice president/communications for the ATP Tour, said the amount of Agassi's career fines is "confidential." Suffice it to say the sum is considerable.

Ominously, Agassi felt a twinge in his surgically repaired right wrist during his quarterfinal doubles loss with Sargis Sargsian, an Armenian like Mike Agassi, in Atlanta. Andre subsequently withdrew from the German and French Opens and Wimbledon. He had missed the year's first three Grand Slam tournaments.

"His absence hurts the game," Sampras said. "He is one of the more popular players, and he brings a lot of attention to the game. And the game definitely needs him."

Sampras added that he missed his rivalry with Agassi.

"When I played Andre quite a bit a couple of years ago, he made me a better player, " Sampras said.

Strokes Of Genius

13

Agassi is famous for his forehand, but it's not the best in tennis. Agassi's backhand, in fact, is better than his forehand.

Those are the biggest surprises in Tom Gullikson and Richey Reneberg's analysis of Agassi's game.

Few people are as qualified to assess Agassi's game as Gullikson and Reneberg.

As captain of the U.S. Davis Cup team since 1994 and coach of the 1996 U.S. Olympic team, Gullikson has worked periodically with Agassi and observed him in countless tournaments.

Gullikson played professionally from 1975 through 1986, winning 12 doubles titles and one singles crown. He reached the 1983 Wimbledon doubles final with twin brother Tim before losing to John McEnroe and Peter Fleming and was ranked as high as No. 9 in doubles.

Tom Gullikson was no slouch in singles either, attaining a career-high ranking of No. 38 in 1981 and advancing to the U.S. Open quarterfinals in 1982. Gullikson had career singles victories over Bjorn Borg, Jimmy Connors, Vitas Gerulaitis, Ilie Nastase and Stefan Edberg.

Reneberg has probably seen more of Agassi than he'd like, winning only one set in eight career singles matches against his illustrious countryman.

Mind you, Reneberg has reached No. 20 in singles (1991 and 1996) and No. 1 in doubles (1993), won two Grand Slam doubles titles (the 1992 U.S. Open with Jim Grabb and the 1995 Australian Open with Jared Palmer) and earned $4 million in prize money.

Reneberg has been a teammate of Agassi's three times — twice in the Davis Cup (1993 and 1994) and once in the Olympics (1996).

Gullikson and Reneberg were asked to rate Agassi on his strokes and several intangibles on a scale of 1 (lowest) to 10 (highest). Although Gullikson and Reneberg were interviewed separately, their ratings were amazingly similar. The only major difference was on Agassi's first and second serves. Gullikson rated Agassi's first serve higher than his second, while Reneberg did the reverse.

Forehand

Gullikson (9) — "He's got a great forehand. He's a little bit vulnerable to the wide forehand. He doesn't hit the running forehand as well as he does the inside-out forehand or the standing forehand. But it's obviously a great shot. He can hit it with power, and he can also hit with a lot of angle. He can also create a lot of spin, a real high heavy looping ball. So he's got some variety off the forehand.

"I think [Pete Sampras'] forehand is probably overall a little better. He certainly hits it better on the run, and he hits it equally as hard, if not harder, than Andre."

Reneberg (9) — "In years past, I probably would have given him a 10. Nowadays, a lot of these guys — the Spaniards — maybe have a little more kick and spin on their forehands. But his forehand is still one of the best.

"He has very good eye-hand coordination. It's very hard to get him to move off the baseline. It's hard to push him back. That's why he's so good. He dictates play because he has such good eye-hand coordination that he's able to stay close to the baseline. He makes it look very easy, but even for professionals, it's very difficult. He takes the ball so early, he's able to stay in control of the point.

"The only reason I would give him a 9 and not a 10 is a guy like Sampras ends a lot of points with his forehand. I don't think Andre ends quite as many points as he used to with his forehand. A lot of other guys hit the ball a lot harder. I'd give Sampras a 10 on his forehand."

Backhand

Gullikson (9.5) — "One of the best. He can rip the backhand down the line better than anyone just about, he can hit angles cross-court, and he's very accurate. He's probably one of the best two-handers ever to play the game.

"I think his backhand is underrated. It's not quite as powerful a shot [as his forehand], but he's a little more solid off his backhand. He doesn't make as many errors on the backhand as he does on the forehand."

Reneberg (10) — "I think he's got one of the best backhands in the game. He can put it anywhere. He takes the ball early. He's very good at hitting up the line, he's able to hit angles, he loops the ball very well.

"He's got a *great* backhand. It's textbook perfect. If you had a kid, and you were going to try to teach him how to hit a two-handed backhand, you'd go watch him."

Return of Serve

Gullikson (10 backhand, 8.5 forehand) — "Probably the best in the game . . . the best the game has ever seen, really, on both sides.

"His forehand return is huge. He can hit winners off first serves, which is pretty unusual. He stands in and takes the ball early, so he's got great eyes. He rips that backhand return as well.

"I would have said Connors had the best return of serve I ever played against, but I think Agassi actually returns better because he hits the ball harder. He maybe misses a few more returns than Connors did — Connors used to get every ball in play — but Agassi definitely is more dangerous on the return.

"I think his backhand return might be a little more solid [than his forehand return]. He'll miss a few more forehand returns."

Reneberg (10 backhand, 10 forehand) — "Eleven, actually. He's the best returner in the game, period. He may be the best ever. He and Connors are the two guys who come to mind. Who knows who returns better?

"[Agassi] can take it early; he very rarely mis-hits it. He can take huge serves and hit them back just as hard, and he's very consistent at doing it. It's remarkable. He's got something special. A lot of guys are good tennis players, or they work hard or whatever, but Sampras and Agassi talent-wise are the best two in the game.

"Obviously, Andre's ranking has fluctuated a little bit more, but in my book, if you had to have someone out there playing a match, not including Pete, I'd pick Andre — even when he's ranked 20.

"A good argument can be made that Pete's the best player ever. That's not to take anything away from Andre. When Andre's at his best, they give tennis a real boost. It's a perfect contrast in styles, personality, everything. It would be nice if those two guys could play a little more often in a few more finals. Andre is struggling a little bit, but he'll be back, I'm sure."

First Serve

Gullikson (7) — "It's very effective. He doesn't have the big heater like a lot of the players have today. He can serve 110 [mph], 115 [as opposed to 130 to 140]. That's more his range. He *can* win some free points with his first serve, but he tends to win more with his groundstrokes."

Reneberg (6) — "He's improved it. When you're shorter [like the 5-foot-11-inch Agassi], your first-serve percentage fluctuates a little bit more. It's hard to be as consistent. You see that with [5-foot-9-inch] Michael [Chang].

"He'll win a few points on his first serve, but he's not Goran Ivanisevic. He's not looking to win a bunch of free points on his serve. He has to work for the points on his serve, and he does that with great groundstrokes."

Second Serve

Gullikson (5) — "I think his second serve is a little bit of a weakness at *times* when he's not confident. He can hit it a little too short, and the guy's gonna take advantage of his second serve. But when he's confident, his second serve is pretty good. When he's confident, his second serve is more like a 7. He's hitting it a little deeper and a little harder."

Reneberg (8) — "I think he has a very good second serve. That has also improved a lot. It used to be you might be able to take control of the point on his second serve, but now he's really improved it. He uses his legs a lot better. He goes up to the ball better. He has a lot of spin on his second serve. He's able to get you off the court sometimes with it, particularly on the ad side. Then he's standing on the base-line, he's ready for the return, and you're on the run the rest of the point usually."

Volley

Gullikson (forehand 5, backhand 5) — "Very aver-age. He's got quick hands. He can volley, but he certainly isn't looking to volley. He's not a great volleyer, obviously, like a Stefan Edberg.

"Because he doesn't come to the net very often, he doesn't cover the net that well. His movement at the net and how he covers the net probably need more work than his actual volley.

"He doesn't need to be a great volleyer because he hits the ball so well. He doesn't need to come to the net on average shots. He doesn't have to chip and charge. He can get the guy way out of position and pretty much have an easy volley to win the point.

"He never would have to be a great volleyer. He only needs to be a pretty competent volleyer to hit those finish-ing volleys. He doesn't need to come in and dig out low volleys and half-volleys like Edberg used to."

Reneberg (no ratings) — "It's hard to [rate]. He doesn't volley very much. I've seen days where he volleys very well and other days where he doesn't volley well at all. I don't know how to read that."

Overhead

Gullikson (8) — "He's got a very good overhead, especially the bounce overhead. He's got one of the best bounce overheads I've ever seen where he takes that high, deep lob, and the ball bounces, and he can put it away.

"His other overhead is pretty good, too. But once again, he doesn't hit *that* many because he doesn't come in that much."

Reneberg (8) — "There are very few guys these days with bad overheads. The overhead is pretty easy. It seems like everyone these days has a good overhead."

Lob

Gullikson (8.5) — "He has a very good topspin lob off both sides. Because he's such a great shotmaker with the passing shots, he probably underutilizes the lob a little bit. But he certainly has great hands and can generate a lot of topspin, and he has good disguise with the forehand and backhand lob.

"He doesn't hit the defensive lob that often. When he's on the run, he likes to go for a winner. He doesn't particularly like to play defense. He's much more of an offensive-minded player.

"The offensive lob is a good shot in his arsenal. Once again, he's playing guys who are rallying a lot more from the back. There are not a lot of net-rushers left. The lob is not as big a factor."

Reneberg (9) — "He has a great topspin lob. Once you do get to the net — if you get an opportunity — he's able to do so many things. He can lob, he can hit great angles off the pass, he can hit it hard and get it by you as well."

Drop Shot

Gullikson (5) — "Once again, he'd rather bludgeon that forehand or backhand. He can hit a drop shot. I wouldn't say it's his strength."

Reneberg (no rating) — "He has a very good drop shot. That's another one that's hard to rate. He does this, and Jim Courier does this — they're very consistent with their drop shots. [Agassi] doesn't use it often enough to really know."

Quickness

Gullikson (7) — "He can move very well. It just depends more on his commitment to moving. Sometimes when he doesn't want to run, he doesn't run.

"He's not the fastest guy on the tour, but he doesn't need to be because he dictates play. A lot of guys who play more defensively have to run more than he does. It's more important for counter-punchers to be faster because they're defending themselves more."

Reneberg (rating varies) — "When he's playing well, his movement is a 10. He doesn't have Michael Chang speed, but his footwork around the baseline when he's playing well and controlling the point is amazing. I think a lot of people don't really appreciate it. They think he just has great talent. Because of his footwork, he is able to move less during a point than anyone else because it's so hard to get him off the baseline. If you hit an angle, he gets over there and runs you back [and forth]."

Conditioning

Gullikson (rating varies) — "It comes and goes. It's in line with his motivation. If he's motivated to play well and have a good year and really go after it like he did after he was injured and got to No. 1 and won the U.S. Open, his motivation then was a 10. From the U.S. Open last year until [early 1997], I'd say his motivation was very low, a 2 or 3.

"Everybody's motivation goes through stages, but his goes up and down more than most guys'. He gets really excited about playing, and then he doesn't want to be there."

Reneberg (rating varies) — "Again, it depends on when. At times I think he's in great shape, and at other times I think he shows up at some tournaments in not as great shape.

"That's another thing that goes back to how well he's able to control points. Thomas Muster is fitter than anyone else. Michael Chang might be fitter than Andre.

"Andre works hard for his points because he has to hit a lot of shots, but the other guy is always doing all the running. That helps Andre as much as anything as far as conditioning. That's hard to rate. You see him at some tournaments, and he's probably a 5. At other tournaments, he's an 8 or 9. Muster and Courier would be the only 10s."

Mental Toughness

Gullikson (rating varies) — "Once again, when he wants to play, he can be very tough, like at the Olympics last year. He competed very well. His mental toughness is definitely tied into his fitness level and also his commitment level. He can be very mentally tough, and other times he doesn't really care to be out there.

"When he wants to play, and when he's really eager, he can be pretty good mentally. When he doesn't want to play, he can be pretty bad mentally, too."

Reneberg (rating varies) — "If his mental toughness was a 10, I think he would consistently be the No. 1 or No. 2 player in the world — probably No. 2 behind Pete. I think Pete's the best.

"I think [insufficient mental toughness] sometimes is what hurts him. At times his confidence in his game fluctuates a little more than Pete's. He also does a lot of stuff not related to tennis — the [charitable] foundation, Brooke and her career. . . . He's great when he's focused, but sometimes the focus seems to be gone. There are times when he's a 10, and there are times when he's a 3 or 4."

Winning At Love

14

Agassi, one of the richest, most glamorous athletes in the world, didn't have a girlfriend.

"And I'm not going to for a while," he said (erroneously, as it turned out). "I need to deal with me."

It was December 1993. Agassi was about to undergo wrist surgery. Wendi Stewart had broken up with him. Agassi and Barbra Streisand were just good friends, he said. Agassi had been communicating by fax with Brooke Shields for three months, but they had not met.

For all of Agassi's wealth and fame, there have been only four women in his life — Amy Moss, Stewart, Streisand and Shields.

Not that there haven't been plenty of opportunities.

"He had anything and everything [offered to him]," Stewart said. "It could have been served on a silver platter to him."

Weller Evans, the longtime ATP Tour executive, has observed Agassimania throughout the tennis star's career.

"When Andre walks by, heads turn — not just young girls, but mothers — as Andre returns from the practice court without his shirt on," Evans said.

It's all relative, though.

"Having been to five NBA All-Star weekends and hanging out at the hotel," Evans said, "I can tell you it makes the scene at the hotels at any of our tour stops seem like a nursing home, a library."

Agassi never took advantage of his opportunities, according to Stewart.

"That's just who he is," she said. "He's not about that. I have my own views on why people do that, but I don't think Andre needed it. He didn't have anything to prove. People are crazy what they'll do . . . absolutely amazing. I don't want to get into examples. It was never anything we dealt with."

What *is* Agassi "about?"

"Monogamous, meaningful relationships," Stewart said.

*   *   *

Agassi and Moss began dating during the 1988 U.S. National Indoor Championships at Memphis, Tenn. Moss was a Mississippi State student and volunteer driver for the tournament, which Agassi won, earning his second career title and first title in North America. He was only 17.

"He found out that I was a born-again Christian, and I found out that he was one," Moss said. "That was a big deal to both of us. He had said that he was looking for that in a girl, and I was looking for that in a guy."

Agassi, Moss, Agassi's parents (who were in town for the tournament) and Bill Shelton went to dinner at Grisanti's, an Italian restaurant.

"He said, 'Suggest someplace we can go that's quiet and we can just talk,' " Moss said. "And *please* put ' . . . So we can just talk.' That's *all* he wanted, just to talk. We just talked for a few hours and got to know each other."

At that point in the interview for this book, Moss said her boss told her to get off of the phone. She wanted Phillip Agassi's approval to talk further anyway.

Moss wouldn't divulge her telephone number or say where she worked, but she promised to call back regardless of Phillip's answer. Moss never did, and further attempts to reach her were unsuccessful.

In any case, born-again Christianity was not enough to sustain the relationship between Agassi and Moss. They broke up in 1990, and Agassi turned to his old friend.

*   *   *

Agassi and Stewart met at the old Cambridge Racket Club in Las Vegas.

"We had crushes on each other when we were 8 years old," Stewart said. "He was really cute. We were friends all through high school, and he'd come home from [the Bollettieri academy]. We'd hook up and go hang out. It wasn't very often at the time. He could only come home about once a year."

Agassi and Stewart didn't become an item, however, until they were both 20. They began seeing each other in Las Vegas, and then Stewart joined Agassi on the circuit.

"I didn't really think of anything when we hooked up and started hanging out," Stewart said. "We were just together all the time, and it just happened."

Stewart was a sophomore at Brigham Young University in Provo, Utah, when she began traveling with Agassi in the summer of 1990.

"I tried to go to school the first semester we were together, and it was just nearly impossible," Stewart said. "By Thanksgiving, I didn't go back. It was just too tough. I'd fly in for a test . . . it just wasn't working well."

Stewart dropped out of BYU and accompanied Agassi on the circuit full time. She jetted around the world, rode in limousines and stayed in the finest hotels with the multimillionaire pop icon.

"We were young kids, and we had a blast," Stewart said.

Agassi, she added, treated her "like an angel . . . always."

Millions of women would have traded places with Stewart. But the glamour soon wore off.

"I wanted more for myself than to just travel around with him," she said. "I wanted an education and a stable life of my own, because my life was pretty much his when you're traveling as much as we did.

"We didn't really have roots anywhere. We'd come home to Vegas for three or four days at a time, and I'd see my family, and that's really about it. I didn't have my own social circle. I really needed my own identity, separate from him. I loved his friends, but I needed to figure out what I was all about."

Stewart also found that she and Agassi didn't share many interests.

"He's very smart, but he hasn't had a chance to have any interests," Stewart said. "That was a big problem for us. We were so different. I like to go [snow] skiing and water skiing, and I like to read books. We just didn't do the same things."

Stewart said she "was *dying* to go to museums and stuff wherever we were, and it's just not easy for him. . . . He has to get geared up to go out in public. It's too much for him to get geared up to play a match and then get geared up to go somewhere."

Agassi and Stewart did go to a museum together once, but there was a catch. Agassi sat out of the 1993 French Open with wrist tendinitis, but he had to go to Paris anyway for the Nike promotion. Stewart and Agassi had broken up at the end of 1992, but she accompanied Agassi to Paris while they tried to patch up their relationship. During their stay, they went to the Louvre.

"He loved it," Stewart said. "We were really excited to see the Mona Lisa because his agent [at the time], Bill Shelton, has this *amazing* voice. He would sing that song all the time. We both had an interest in it because [Shelton] would sing that song ['Mona Lisa']."

Stewart struggled to identify any of Agassi's interests.

"He liked cars for a while, then he was fascinated with planes," Stewart said. "He liked four-wheeling. He got the Hummer, and he liked doing that. He would do that every night [in Las Vegas]."

Agassi said in December 1993: "My interest in life is personal growth. Faith in God is the strongest part of my life."

Meanwhile, Agassi had trouble understanding why Stewart was unhappy.

"It was hard for a *lot* of people to figure out why," she said. "They look at what I had and the life I led, and it's like, 'How could you not be happy?' It's like, it wasn't *my* life. So I was miserable. . . . I learned at a very early age that money can't buy happiness or love.

"He tried to fix things many times, but nothing worked. I wanted to move away [from Las Vegas], and we got a place in Seattle. He would go with anything I would mention that I thought would help fix things. But little patches weren't fixing it."

Stewart finally broke up with Agassi for good in late 1993. Agassi cried for weeks over the split.

"It was kind of a sad ending . . . not sad, but when you are together that long, nobody really wins," Stewart said. "I wanted to move on and finish school and started seeing other people."

Stewart attended the University of San Francisco for one year and graduated from New York University in broadcast journalism in May 1997. She said she hopes to work in San Francisco or Washington, D.C., with a national service organization such as Big Brothers or Big Sisters. She rarely sees Agassi anymore.

*   *   *

By the time Agassi and Stewart broke up, he had become friends with Streisand. There were reports that this caused friction between Stewart and Agassi. One report had Stewart flinging one of the singer's CDs out of the window of Agassi's limousine during the 1992 U.S. Open and telling him: "That woman's old enough to be your mother. She's trying to rip us apart."

Stewart, however, denied that account and said she never objected to Agassi seeing Streisand.

"Absolutely not," Stewart said. "Never. That got turned into a circus because it sounded good for the press. We'd read the tabloids, 'Andre was leaving [Streisand's] house late at night.' Well, yeah, that was true, but they failed to mention that I was staying there, too. It just wasn't as juicy. We'd go stay at her house in Malibu [Calif.]. It *never* bothered me, ever.

"That U.S. Open she went to, I was there with Andre, staying with Andre every night. He was not with her. I could tell you where he was every night. . . . I wouldn't count Barbra [as a girlfriend]."

Nor, apparently, did Agassi.

"We're just real good friends," he said. "The media is getting a kick out of making more of it than there is."

Streisand agreed.

"What I find is that the media destroys relationships before they can even begin," she said. "They write terrible things, they assume things. Because I go to see Andre Agassi play at Wimbledon, they write that I'm his girlfriend. Then they say he 'left' me for Brooke Shields. It's ridiculous."

Stewart described Streisand as "very bright, incredibly bright . . . incredibly talented . . . and [strange]. She just sees things that most people don't see. You're at a restaurant, and she has to change tables around so the lighting is correct. . . .

"I think too that when you're so protected from the public, you lose a sense of what reality is. I think that's the scariest part of the whole business and world that they live in."

Streisand said her reputation as a harsh, demanding diva is unfair.

"There are so many myths in the media, lies perpetuated over and over again — about my being a perfectionist, being difficult, all those negative words — usually not from people who've really worked with me. . . ."

Like Agassi, Streisand rose from a difficult childhood to achieve stardom. In an interesting coincidence, their fathers have the same first name — Emanuel Streisand (now deceased) and Emmanuel Agassi.

There is, of course, one big difference between Andre and Barbra. Streisand is 28 years older than Agassi. Her son with ex-husband Elliott Gould, Jason Gould, is four years older than Agassi.

Whereas Andre said his childhood was not abusive, Barbra's was — emotionally and physically. When she was 1, Emanuel died suddenly at age 35 from an improperly treated epileptic seizure following a mysterious, though not fatal, head injury. Barbra's mother, Diana, was shattered. She withdrew and became overprotective.

"Emotionally, my mother left me at the same time [as my father]," Streisand later reflected. "She was in her own trauma."

They moved in with Diana's parents, and Barbra (who was born "Barbara") rarely received affection or approval from her mother or grandparents.

When Barbara went to her first day of kindergarten, Diana gave her a brown paper bag lunch and a litany of *don'ts*. Don't talk to strangers. Don't cross the street. Don't go near the water. Don't do this, and don't do that.

"I was raised to be frightened of everything," Barbra said.

Matters got worse when Diana married Louis Kind when Barbara was seven. Kind was anything but. Randall Riese wrote in his 1993 biography, *Her Name is Barbra*, that Kind physically abused Diana and Barbara. When Kind wasn't hitting Barbara, he was ignoring or castigating her.

According to Riese, Kind once told Barbara she couldn't have an ice cream cone because she was too ugly.

She was nothing of the sort, but she was unusual looking with a crooked nose and big, blue eyes spaced too far apart. Kind also told Barbara she "would never amount to anything," a friend of the family told Riese.

Television and movies provided two of Barbara's few escapes from her grim existence. She began to act out commercials and found that she had a good singing voice.

Barbara decided that the best way to fight her mother's indifference and her stepfather's cruelty towards her was to succeed, to become a star.

"I'll show them," she said to herself as she practiced her repertoire of facial expressions in front of the bathroom mirror.

Show them she did. Streisand had an estimated gross income of $63 million in 1994 and 1995 combined.

Agassi was a fan of Streisand's long before they met. He and Shelton used to debate who was the better singer, Carly Simon or Streisand. Shelton favored Simon. Agassi insisted Streisand was more versatile and the better overall entertainer.

"Andre will say, 'Listen to this note, Bill. Can Carly get that note?' And maybe she can't. But there are other notes Carly can hit that Streisand can't either. So it's a matter of taste," Shelton said in 1989.

Agassi and Streisand met shortly after Agassi saw the 1991 movie *The Prince of Tides*, directed by and starring Streisand. It is a serious love story about a psychiatrist (Streisand) and a football coach (Nick Nolte), both of whom are unhappily married and lonely. They meet after Nolte's sister, played by Melinda Dillon, tries to commit suicide. Nolte and Dillon were the victims of abusive childhoods in the movie.

"What Streisand establishes, with admirable patience as both a director and actress here, is that the people can heal best by learning to build and trust relationships," film critic Roger Ebert wrote. "And by making those relationships tentative learning experiences, she leads up to an extraordinary payoff in which Nolte does finally at last reach back to touch the demons that torture him."

Agassi was so moved by the film that he telephoned Streisand. They talked for two hours and eventually went on a dinner date.

Streisand and Stewart watched Agassi from the stands during his fourth-round victory over Carlos Costa in the 1992 U.S. Open. Streisand sat near an exit so she could make a quick getaway, Stewart said. Stewart sat in Agassi's box.

One television announcer said Barbra looked at Andre like "an ice cream cone with a cherry on the top."

Streisand, meanwhile, described Agassi as "very intelligent, very, very sensitive, very evolved — more than his linear years. And he's an extraordinary human being. He plays like a Zen master. It's very in the moment."

Agassi's game may have been "in the moment," but he was out of the tournament when Jim Courier beat him in a four-set quarterfinal.

Streisand attended another match of Agassi's in Los Angeles later that month, and Agassi reportedly gave her several private tennis lessons.

Streisand promised to come to Wimbledon in 1993 if Agassi, the defending champion, reached the quarterfinals. When he did, Streisand flew to London from Greece, where she had been vacationing, and showed up in a sailor suit and cap.

When Courier was asked whom he was cheering for, he said, "I'm cheering for Barbra."

"To win or lose?"

"I just want to meet her," he said.

Streisand was an emotional wreck as Agassi battled Pete Sampras. She jumped up and down, screamed out Andre's name and nervously bit her nails. After Agassi lost in five sets, Streisand cried for her "special friend."

The next day, the *Daily Mirror* ran a front-page photo of a dejected Streisand with the headline "Barbra Cry-Sand."

Agassi tactfully answered questions afterward about his relationship with Streisand.

"How special is this friendship we hear about with Barbra?" Agassi was asked.

". . . Important . . ." he said.

"Above others?"

"Above some."

"How about Stewart? Is she still in the picture?"

"Absolutely. She's in school right now in Salt Lake City, and I'll be seeing her in a few days. . . . I've spoken to her a lot during the tournament. . . ."

Agassi was also quoted in *London Today* as saying provocatively of his relationship with Streisand: "I've been learning about the sweet mysteries of life, and this is one of them. I'm not sure I can fully explain. Maybe she can't either. But it doesn't matter. We came from completely different worlds, and we collided, and we knew we wanted to be in each other's company right then."

Agassi was evasive on ESPN's *Up Close* when host Roy Firestone asked him if there there was a romance between him and Streisand.

"It depends what you consider 'romance,'" Agassi said.

Firestone then let Agassi off the hook, asking, "What do you consider romance?"

"Anytime you're with somebody, and you share a piece of who you are, whether it's something that you would say is more than friends or not, it's giving yourself to somebody," Agassi said cryptically. "And you do that with everybody. You do that with your friends, with your girlfriend, with your family. You run into that a few times in your life.

"Me and Barbra have a very special relationship. We are very intimate — in the sense of how we handle each other and how we share with each other and talk to each other. Anything you have with a good friend, and that's what she is — a good friend."

In an interview with *Inside Tennis*, Agassi said Streisand "taught me an incredible amount. She has shown me what it means to face fears. She didn't perform live for a long time, and I spent a lot of time talking to her about the feelings that are involved in that, as well as things I go through.

"It's great to see her address her life based on what she wants for herself, not what she feels that she's a victim of. That's quite an incredible, incredible lesson. I have the utmost amount of respect for Barbra."

Stewart said it would "shock" her if Agassi and Streisand had an affair.

"I don't know if it's so much their age [difference] or what it is, but it seems so unlikely," Stewart continued. "Anything's possible, but I'd find it hard to believe."

Agassi and Streisand went their separate ways after Wimbledon in 1993. Agassi broke up with Stewart for good and began dating Shields. Streisand became engaged to actor James Brolin, who played Dr. Steven Kiley on *Marcus Welby, M.D.*, in January 1997.

* * *

Agassi and Perry Rogers were talking one night in Rogers' bedroom in Las Vegas when they were teenagers.

"He was going away to college," Agassi said. "I was about to turn pro, I was 16, and I was getting very sad. Life was so safe and so secure, and that was all changing. Perry was assuring me we'd stay close. And I said, 'Yeah, but it's not the same. I mean, talking about girls and who we want to date.' And I swear this is a true story. He looks at me, and he says, 'Andre, you don't understand. One day, instead of talking about which girl you want to go out with at Gorman High, we're gonna be talking about you dating Brooke Shields.'"

If there are a few similarities between Agassi and Streisand, those between Agassi and Shields are uncanny. It's no wonder they eventually got married.

"We've both gone through a lot of the same things," Agassi said in 1995. "We were both celebrities young. We both were thrown into a strange lifestyle young, and we both got bad raps when we were young, so we have a similar history together. And I think both of us haven't maximized our abilities. But that's changing."

Shields' mother, Teri, a former model and cosmetologist, and father, Frank, a Revlon executive, separated five months after Brooke was born. They later divorced.

Shields began modeling at 11 months, doing an Ivory soap commercial. Under her alcoholic mother's direction, Brooke continued to model throughout her childhood.

Frank opposed his daughter's career.

"He rejected it all," Brooke said.

Frank was so intent on protecting Brooke from the spotlight that he would tell her not to pose in family pictures.

Teri forged ahead anyway. Brooke became a celebrity at 13 when she played a child prostitute in the highly acclaimed *Pretty Baby*. She starred in *The Blue Lagoon*, about the growing love and sexuality of two children stranded on a South Sea island, at 15, and *Endless Love*, the story of a teenage love affair, at 16.

Also at 16, Shields starred in a breakthrough Calvin Klein jeans advertising campaign ("What comes between me and my Calvins? Nothing.")

Teri has been widely portrayed as the quintessential stage parent, but Brooke staunchly defends her.

"I never felt pushed by her," Brooke said. "Countless times I'd say I didn't want to do something, and she listened. There were no other kids, no husband. It was just us, and we formed a little team."

Shields, however, developed a reputation as being more style than substance. Her 1992 movie, *Brenda Starr*, flopped.

"The movies were convenient," she said. "They fit into my summer schedule, and they were fun. I wasn't a serious or committed actress at the time."

Remind you of anybody?

Shields entered Princeton in 1983 and wrote a book, *On Your Own*, at 20 in 1985, in which she advises young women on how to succeed after leaving home. Ironically, given her provocative modeling and acting roles, Shields admitted she was a virgin.

"I basically wrote about not being ashamed to be a virgin — it's not a stigma to wait," Shields said. "It was an honest thing to say, but I'm sure it was confusing because of my image."

Shields returned to Teri after graduating from Princeton with a degree in French literature, but her career fizzled.

Shields wasn't faring much better in her personal life. She was linked to John F. Kennedy Jr., Michael Jackson, Liam Neeson, George Michael, Michael Bolton and others, but none of those relationships worked out.

Agassi and Shields were set up by Lyndie Benson, a mutual friend and the wife of saxophonist Kenny G, in 1993.

Shields was anything but a tennis fan, even though her grandfather, Frank Shields, reached the U.S. Open final in 1930. Because she felt pressured to play, she avoided the game.

Shields, bored while filming *Running Wild* in South Africa, faxed Agassi a lighthearted introductory note in September 1993. Agassi replied with a long, sincere letter about the importance of being vulnerable. Shields wrote back at length, too.

Agassi and Shields communicated by fax for three months before Agassi took her to dinner at Pasta Maria in Los Angeles on December 26, 1993, six days after he had undergone wrist surgery. Shields was wary.

"It all looked good on paper," she said. "Sure, he was smart and nice and called when he said he'd call. He even remembered things I'd told him. All these things — but I was so afraid."

Agassi and Shields, who's five years older than he, talked until the restaurant was ready to close.

Agassi, however, later confessed that the meeting was awkward after corresponding for so long.

"[It wasn't easy] to take this person you feel like you know so well and stick this person inside the face of something you've seen for so long," he said. "It was very uncomfortable. I will say I handled it better than she did. I didn't get much eye contact for the first hour, but I got some blushing cheeks. So I felt like my chances were good."

One month later, Shields entered a New York hospital for an operation of her own. Agassi stood by as Shields had all of her toes broken and realigned to reverse damage caused by dancing. Agassi stayed with Shields for 10 days while she recuperated and felt unattractive.

"I was just expecting roses that said, 'Get well soon.'" Shields said. "Normally, guys are like, 'When you look good, give me a call.'"

Agassi, however, "was there all the way," Shields said. "Even when I looked my worst and was puking [in reaction to some medication], he never left my side. He carried me from my bed to the bathroom."

Meanwhile, Agassi and Shields decided to commit themselves to their careers. With Agassi's support, Shields confronted her mother and severed their professional relationship. Agassi had done much the same with his father.

Shields watched at courtside as Agassi won the 1994 U.S. Open.

"... The more time I spend with him, my opinion of him and my feelings toward him only improve," Shields said. "I mean everyday, I am amazed at the quality of the human being that he really is."

The actress described Agassi as "extremely sensitive and thoughtful, honest and open, and warm and unaffected ... very down to earth."

Shields is also remarkably down to earth. At Agassi's first fund-raiser for his charitable foundation, at Planet Hollywood in Las Vegas three weeks before the 1994 U.S. Open, she volunteered to be interviewed by a newspaper reporter. Then again, she might have just wanted to help publicize Agassi's foundation.

Shields soon landed the lead role of Rizzo in the Broadway revival of *Grease*. Agassi attended more than 30 performances.

After *Grease*, Shields was offered a guest appearance on NBC's *Friends* on Super Bowl Sunday in 1996. She displayed a flair for comedy, leading to her starring role in the NBC hit comedy *Suddenly Susan*. Shields plays Susan Keane, a sweet, klutzy columnist for a San Francisco magazine.

Back in the spotlight, Shields appeared on the cover of every magazine except *Guns & Ammo* in 1996.

Agassi has had enough success himself that he wasn't threatened by Shields'.

"I've known a lot of men who were intimidated by a woman's strength," Shields admitted. "But he's the opposite. He's not just strong for me, he encourages me to be strong."

Shields, said Agassi, is "the sweetest, kindest, warmest, strongest human being that I know, and without her, life would take on a new meaning to me. I cannot even imagine the thought of living life without her."

Shields was getting impatient when Agassi, trying to find the right moment, finally proposed in February 1996 while the two were vacationing in Hawaii.

"He had talked a lot about getting engaged," Shields said. "But I'd heard that kind of talk before. As far as I was concerned, it was a daydream."

But it wasn't. More than 80 of their friends — including Streisand, Kevin Costner and Paul Reiser — attended an engagement party at the Malibu home of Grammy-winning producer David Foster, who has produced two fund-raising concerts in Las Vegas for Agassi's foundation.

Agassi and Shields were married April 19, 1997, at St. John's Episcopal Chapel in Monterey, Calif. Agassi was 26 and Shields 31.

People reported that Agassi and Shields rented the Stonepine Estate Resort, a sprawling compound with 17 rooms, a restaurant and stables in nearby Carmel Valley,

Calif., for five days. The estimated price for lodging alone was $50,000. Agassi and Shields stayed in separate buildings before the wedding.

At the rehearsal dinner at Stonepine the night before, Shields' father reportedly gave Agassi a medal that Brooke's grandfather had been awarded as a member of a U.S. Davis Cup team.

Agassi, wearing a black tuxedo, arrived at the rust-colored wooden church at 6:15 P.M. in a chauffeured Lincoln Town Car with a police escort. Shields wore a white, low-cut gown.

Among the 150 guests at the wedding were *Susan* costar Judd Nelson; actress Nastassja Kinski; Brad Gilbert; David Pate, Agassi's longtime friend from Las Vegas and a former doubles star; and George Fareed, the doctor for the U.S. Davis Cup team. There were no active professional tennis players at the wedding, Fareed said.

Rogers, the manager for Agassi and Shields, served as best man, and Lisa Sansone, a Princeton classmate of Shields', was the maid of honor. The two groomsmen were Phillip Agassi and Gil Reyes. Shields' stepsister Diana Cunningham and friend Audrey Rose were the bridesmaids.

Father Charles Gard, a Catholic priest from Glendale, Calif., and longtime friend of Shields', presided over the ceremony. Agassi and Shields exchanged vows and platinum rings (Shields' had 16 diamonds) as paparazzi helicopters hovered overhead.

The newlyweds arrived at the reception at Stonepine in a horsedrawn carriage at 8 P.M. Agassi and Shields spent the night in a suite at Stonepine.

Mindy Weiss' Beverly Hills party consulting company planned the wedding.

"They were very easy to work with, very cute and romantic," Weiss said. "Whenever they saw each other in the morning, it was like the first time they met. I do weddings every weekend — it's so nice and refreshing to see that."

It says much about Agassi's character that he married someone older, taller (Shields is 6 feet and Agassi 5 feet 11 inches) and better educated than he. For someone who can be so insecure on the court, Agassi can be very secure off of it.

After the wedding and a short honeymoon at an undisclosed location, Agassi tried to resurrect his tennis career, and Shields prepared for another season on *Suddenly Susan*. Money, it's safe to say, wasn't a problem.

Agassi Means Business (Sometimes)

If Agassi retired tomorrow — and there has been much speculation about his doing just that — he'd have plenty of money for the rest of his life. And then some.

Agassi signed a 10-year contract worth a reported $100 million to $150 million with Nike in 1994. Nike spokeswoman Robin Carr Locke would not say whether Agassi would receive all the money if he suddenly retired.

"We don't comment on contracts, and we can't get into speculation," she said. "It's something we would deal with if and when it happens."

Agassi has had no discussions with Nike about retirement, Carr Locke added.

Lawrence Fleischman of Tucson, Ariz., helped Agassi negotiate the Nike contract while serving as a Pima County Superior Court judge. Perry Rogers, Agassi's manager and best friend since childhood, was a law clerk for the judge.

Fleischman resigned in January 1997 after a state judicial ethics panel recommended that he be suspended for two months without pay for practicing law while being a judge. Fleischman said he was simply advising a friend, but a document showed he could earn $2 million.

Fleischman refused to fully disclose his contract with Las Vegas-based Agassi Enterprises, citing a confidentiality clause. However, the Arizona Commission on Judicial Conduct subpoenaed it, and the Arizona Supreme Court released it against Fleischman's wishes. The contract showed that Fleischman was to get $175,000 up front, 2.1 percent of the first $100 million paid to Agassi under the contract and 3.5 percent of all money in excess of $100 million.

Agassi ranked seventh on *Forbes'* annual list of the world's highest-paid athletes, with earnings of $15.2 million, including prize money and endorsements, in 1996. That's $60,800 a day before taxes, based on a five-day work week and two-week vacation.

"I'll tell you exactly what money means to me," Agassi said in 1993. "It's given me the chance to live without worrying about where my next dime is coming from, and it's let me help out my friends. I've probably bought some 30 or 40 cars for people, no exaggeration. At times in the past, I did find myself a little too concerned about [money], but I pulled back and thought it through. . . . "

Mike Tyson topped the Forbes list for 1996 with $75 million. Following Tyson were Michael Jordan ($52.6 million) and auto racer Michael Schumacher of Germany ($33 million).

Of Agassi's $15.2 million, $13 million came from endorsements, according to *Forbes.* Included in the $13 million are exhibition and appearance fees. Agassi can command $300,000 or more just to play in a tournament. Whatever prize money he earns is additional.

Only three athletes had more endorsement income in 1996 than Agassi: Jordan ($40 million), Shaquille O'Neal

($17 million) and Arnold Palmer ($15 million). Pete Sampras, who's perceived as bland, managed to earn $8 million in endorsement income.

That doesn't mean Agassi is the fourth most-popular athlete in the world, said Nye Lavalle, managing director of the Dallas-based Sports Marketing Group.

"Endorsement income does not have any direct relationship to how popular an athlete is," said Lavalle, who was involved in professional tennis for more than 10 years, as an agent, administrator, promoter and businessman. "It has a direct relationship to how interesting an athlete is to commercial advertisers and marketers. There are dozens and dozens and dozens of athletes far more popular than Andre Agassi. . . .

"Here's the real interesting thing: A guy like Sampras is actually what Americans find most popular, but it's not what Madison Avenue finds most popular. Americans like the girl, the boy next door. They like the Mary Lou Rettons, Dorothy Hamills, Peggy Flemings, Scott Hamiltons, Dan Jansens and Bonnie Blairs.

"Americans turn off to bravado, cockiness, egotism, arrogance and showmanship. The vast majority don't like that. However, Madison Avenue likes that — like Dennis Rodman. The persona there makes great creative execution, it makes great copy, it makes great awareness.

"Andre's image over the years — the Goldilocks hair, the bandanna, the flair — really created a personality in tennis, so it's great for Madison Avenue, but does that make him really popular among the public? Absolutely not. In fact, that type of personality turns a lot of people off."

There's no question, though, who the biggest — perhaps only — star is in tennis. Even when Agassi is not entered in a Grand Slam tournament, he's often the star of the show on television because of his commercials throughout the event.

Other players appear on TV only when their match happens to be shown. As soon as they lose, they cease to exist, as far as television is concerned, until the next tournament. Not Agassi. He's playing tennis with Sampras in the streets of San Francisco in a Nike ad. Or dangling from a helicopter in a Mountain Dew ad. Or splashing paint all over the place in a Canon ad. Or umpiring a match as a robot in Nike's "Virtual Andre" ad.

Agassi also dominates tennis in print. The first chapter of a 1996 biography of Sampras begins with the words "Andre Agassi." The title of the first chapter of Nick Bollettieri's autobiography is "Raising Andre." Would Bollettieri have written a book if he hadn't coached Agassi? Would anybody read about Bollettieri (although he's produced other champions)?

"I think [Agassi] is very important to men's tennis because unlike years past, men's tennis today is lacking in terms of personalities and stars," Lavalle said. "He's probably one of the last remaining stars. A lot of players today are kind of human androids, devoid of emotion, devoid of flair. When John McEnroe hung it up, he was the last of our generation. . . .

"When we played [with wooden rackets], you had to have good strokes, you had to have speed, you had to have agility, you had to have a lot of talent. Today all you have to do is be very physical. With the [composite, oversized] rackets, with the sweet spots, you can just bang your way to being a top player."

Bill Shelton, Agassi's former agent, once said his client received six to eight endorsement offers a day. Agassi, though, has accepted only a handful.

"I won't be a whore," Agassi said on ESPN's *Outside The Lines*. "It has to be something I believe in. It's called integrity."

Agassi's most visible endorsements are with Nike (tennis shoes and clothes), Head (rackets) and Canon (cameras).

Agassi has been affiliated with Nike since he turned pro in 1986. Nike, launched as a running-shoe manufacturer, entered the tennis market in 1973. Trying to make a name for itself, the Beaverton, Ore.-based company signed

brash, temperamental stars Ilie Nastase and McEnroe to endorsement deals.

The strategy worked as Nike expanded into other
sports and became the industry leader. Today, Jordan, Tiger
Woods, Agassi and Sampras, to name a few, are under
multimillion-dollar endorsement contracts with Nike.

Agassi has been a trendsetter throughout his association with Nike. He first made fashion news when he
stepped on the court in 1988 in denim shorts. McEnroe actually suggested the idea but balked when he saw the finished product. Agassi gladly obliged.

At the U.S. Open in 1990, Agassi showed up in lime
bicycle shorts underneath his tennis shorts with a black,
white and lime shirt and a headband. The wildest outfit of
all — a magenta number featuring baggy plaid shorts and
a striped shirt — came in early 1995. Agassi told the *Toronto
Globe and Mail* that he wanted the new collection to be
"something that guys could wear skateboarding."

Agassi broke new ground again at the 1996
Olympics by wearing a long-sleeve zip-up shirt in Atlanta's
muggy heat. When his sanity was questioned, Agassi explained that the material, called "Dri-F.I.T.," cooled him off
as he sweated.

Agassi is heavily involved with the design of his
clothes and shoes, according to Carr Locke.

"He comes up here [to Beaverton, outside Portland,
Ore.] two or three times a year and works with our designers and gives his specifications on both footwear and apparel . . . whether he wants the shoe a certain cut. . . . He's
kind of an aggressive, quick, cat-like player," she said. "Our
designers determine, based on what he needs, what to put
technically into the shoe. He tries it on, and he tweaks a little bit. He's one of our more involved athletes. It's the same
with apparel. . . ."

Nike introduced an Agassi logo and line of clothing
in January 1996.

"It sells out everywhere, beyond just tennis," Carr
Locke said. "Kids just like to wear it. Whenever he goes on

the court, he certainly makes a statement. He's very particular about the color. He wants it to be bold."

Nike supplies Agassi in several ways, Carr Locke explained. Agassi or his brother might stop by Nike's camp at the major tournaments, one of them might call Nike with an order, Andre might fly to Oregon or Nike might send a representative to Las Vegas.

"It's very informal," Carr Locke said.

Representatives from Canon and Head would not disclose the length or amount of their contracts with Agassi.

Canon's "Image is Everything" advertising campaign was a public relations disaster for Agassi. As he lost his first three Grand Slam finals, the slogan reinforced the public's perception of Agassi as all style and no substance.

Agassi admitted on *60 Minutes* in 1995 that he regretted making the commercial.

"I think if I didn't regret it, I'd be somewhat . . . ignorant," he said. "It's brought a lot more grief than anything else."

Rogers insisted in 1994 that Canon replace the "Image is Everything" slogan with the much more favorable "Express Yourself."

Agassi expresses himself on the court not only with his outrageous outfits but with a Head Radical Performance racket with twin-tube construction.

Agassi and Byron Black of Zimbabwe are the only men on the tour who use a combination of Kevlar and gut strings, said racket stringer David Mindell of Palm Springs, Calif. Agassi and Black use Kevlar, a synthetic fiber, on the main (vertical) strings for durability and cow gut on the cross (horizontal) strings for playability.

Seventy percent of the men in the top 100 use all gut strings, Mindell explained, and the rest use all nylon. The percentages drop to 40 percent gut and 60 percent nylon for pros ranked 100 to 500. Nylon ($4 to $5 per set of strings) is cheaper than gut ($28 to $34 per set) and lasts longer, but provides less "feel."

"Andre would find [all gut] too explosive," said Mindell, who strings rackets at the *Newsweek* Champions Cup at Indian Wells, Calif., each March.

Casey Maus, who co-owns Star Stringing in Palm Springs with Mindell, added that Agassi "generates a lot of racket head speed. He creates the power."

Mindell, who strung Agassi's rackets at the Champions Cup from 1990 through 1992, tells an interesting story about how Agassi started using Kevlar and gut.

"He used to use a product called Zyex, a semi-metallic string," said Mindell, looking like a pharmacist with reading glasses sitting on the edge of his nose. "Bollettieri wasn't with him at the 1992 *Newsweek*. [Coach and former pro] Brian Teacher is a friend of ours and was with him. I said to Brian, 'Why is he using Zyex? The string has a tendency to relax, to go dead. He's in the court; he's hitting the ball so early.'

"[Brian] said, 'Well, what do you think?' I said, 'Well, if he went with Kevlar in the mains and gut in the cross strings, it would give him the stiffness that he wants and give him some playability because the gut would act like a trampoline, like a springboard.'

"He said, 'Well, string one up.' The next thing you know, that's what [Agassi] won Wimbledon with. Did we ever get a thank you for that?"

Agassi's rackets these days are strung by Jay Schweid, who either sets up shop at the tournament hotel or ships the rackets by overnight mail from his New York office to the tournament site. Schweid declined to be interviewed.

The string tension on Agassi's rackets is 64 pounds per square inch, which is about average. In this high-tech era, it's quaint that Agassi uses a rubber band from the post office as a vibration dampener.

*   *   *

It was obvious in 1993 that Shelton's days as Agassi's agent were numbered. He was a friend of Bollettieri's, and

Bollettieri had abruptly resigned as Agassi's coach. Also, Shelton was based in Arlington, Va., and Rogers was graduating from the University of Arizona School of Law.

Agassi set up Agassi Enterprises in August 1993 to handle his tennis and business interests. The company occupies a suite of offices on the 11th floor of the U.S. Bank Building on Sahara Avenue, several miles west of the Strip.

Agassi employs 13 to 15 people at any given time.

"The greatest experience I've ever had in business is offering somebody a job," he said.

Many of those jobs have gone to family and friends. Agassi serves as chief executive officer, Rogers as chief operating officer and Phillip Agassi as vice president. Rich McKee worked on one of Agassi's Porsches at an auto shop and thereafter accompanied Agassi on the circuit as a friend and attendant.

Agassi is certainly an equal-opportunity employer. His former agent (Shelton) is black, his coach (Brad Gilbert) is Jewish and his strength and conditioning coach (Gil Reyes) is Hispanic.

It's difficult to imagine a more muscular person than Reyes, the strength and conditioning coach at the University of Nevada Las Vegas before Agassi hired him. But Reyes is a kind, gentle soul.

Rogers manages the careers of Agassi and Shields. Like Agassi, Rogers grew up with a demanding father. Jim Rogers, also an attorney, is the president and owner of 11 television stations throughout the West, the largest of which is NBC's affiliate in Las Vegas. Perry's mother, Janet, is yet another attorney.

"My dad gave me the worst work in the world because he wanted to teach me the business from the ground up," said Rogers, who's raspy-voiced, soft-spoken and clean-cut. "I was a janitor, then worked construction. I cleaned his law firm every Wednesday night, and it took me all night. Any other time, I was supposed to be studying."

Phillip Agassi handles media requests, schedules exhibitions for Andre and helps Rogers.

It is often difficult to deal with Phillip. An incident in 1995 is typical. Andre was holding a news conference at the MGM Grand Hotel to promote a fund-raising concert for his charitable foundation. The *Las Vegas Review-Journal* sent two reporters to the news conference: an entertainment writer to cover the concert angle and a sports writer to try to talk to Andre about tennis because Andre almost never makes himself available to the local sports media.

Phillip refused to allow the sports writer to ask Andre any tennis questions, saying the news conference was strictly to promote the concert. The reporter finally said, "OK, but I hope I don't turn on the TV news tonight and hear Andre talking about tennis."

Guess what? Andre appeared on the TV news that night and talked about tennis. When the sports writer called Phillip and asked him to explain the double standard, Phillip said it was OK for the TV reporter to ask tennis questions because he also asked about the concert. It didn't matter to Phillip that the *Review-Journal* had also sent an entertainment writer there for that purpose. When the sports writer complained that he "got screwed," Phillip blew up. The message seemed to be, "How dare anyone criticize an Agassi?"

One couldn't help but contrast Phillip's attitude with Arthur Ashe's during Ashe's December 1992 visit to Las Vegas. The dignified, scholarly tennis Hall of Famer had contracted AIDS after receiving a contaminated blood transfusion during open-heart surgery in 1983. Ashe came to Las Vegas to speak on "AIDS Awareness and Bias — A Personal Perspective."

After his speech at UNLV, Ashe repaired to a side room and fielded questions from a small group of invited guests. A sports writer from the *Review-Journal* was allowed to join them. After the sports writer apologized for changing the subject from a life-and-death issue such as AIDS to tennis, he asked Ashe to comment on the direction of

Agassi's career. If anyone were ever justified in losing his temper and refusing to answer a question, it was Ashe at that moment.

Ashe's response?

"I've been waiting for someone to ask me that," he said with a smile.

Ashe proceeded to give a typically candid, thoughtful answer, after which the subject of the discussion returned to AIDS.

Pure class to the end.

Ashe died two months later at age 49.

In defense of Phillip, he is devoted to Andre. Bollettieri wrote in *My Aces, My Faults* that Phillip has done more for Andre than anyone, sacrificing "a large part of his own life for his brother."

Wendi Stewart, Andre's former girlfriend, has had her own disagreements with Phillip. But even she called him "a good guy" who "loves Andre with all his heart and would do anything for him."

*   *   *

Nobody can accuse Andre of simply raking in his millions and giving nothing back. He and Rogers founded the Andre Agassi Foundation in March 1994 to benefit underprivileged children in Las Vegas.

"I can't just take the wonderful life I've had without striving to make a difference," Agassi said.

Agassi admitted that his childhood was "compromised in many ways," but denied that it motivated him to start the foundation.

Agassi donated $1.25 million in 1994 for the renovation of a Boys and Girls Club in Las Vegas and raised a combined $4.2 million from his Grand Slam for Children concerts at the MGM Grand Garden in 1995 and 1996. Performers have included Elton John, Robin Williams, Michael Bolton, Kenny G, Oleta Adams, Wynonna Judd, Seal, Vanessa Williams, Faith Hill and Tim McGraw.

In addition to the Boys and Girls Club, beneficiaries of Agassi's foundation are:

- The National Junior Tennis League (NJTL), which offers tennis to underprivileged children and promotes self-esteem.
- Child Haven, a shelter that provides temporary care for abused, neglected and abandoned children under protective custody of the court system in Southern Nevada.
- The Assistance League of Las Vegas' Operation School Bell, which provides clothing and hygiene packs to needy children to encourage school attendance and build self-esteem.
- The Cynthia Bunker Memorial Scholarship Fund, a perpetual scholarship at the College of Performing Arts at UNLV. Bunker, Agassi's friend and hair stylist, was killed in a car accident in 1994.

*   *   *

So much of the foundation's expenses are underwritten by Agassi and others that almost all money raised goes to charity.

In January 1996, *USA Weekend Magazine* named Agassi one of five winners of its "Most Caring Athlete Award."

After the September 1996 "Grand Slam for Children" concert, Agassi took out a full-page ad in the *Review-Journal* to thank Rogers for his help with the foundation. It read:

"As boys we talked about giving back to this community. As adults I was scared and unsure. You stayed strong and continued to lead. With every decision and every step, the children of Las Vegas rested safely in your ability and passion to protect them and to ensure them a brighter tomorrow.

"Thank you for the Andre Agassi Foundation. You are the cornerstone that made it possible.

"Thank you for then. Thank you for now. Thank you for a lifetime!

"I love you,
Andre Agassi."

One Of A Kind

Agassi has accomplished almost everything in tennis. He's won Wimbledon, the U.S. Open, the Australian Open, the Olympics and the ATP Tour World Championship — all once each. He's been ranked No. 1. He's been a member of three Davis Cup championship teams. All that's missing is the French Open.

Throw in his celebrity status, and there's little doubt that Agassi is a future Hall of Famer. Nominated players must be five years removed from being a "significant factor" in competitive tennis.

"There's no way he could be kept out," said Richard Evans, a British member of the Hall of Fame nominating committee who has covered professional tennis as a writer and radio commentator since 1960. "He's not only won Grand Slams all over the place, but he's definitely one of the most remarkable players of this era without any doubt at all. He's certainly one of the most talented.

"We judge these things on a list of different criteria. He certainly makes it on [being a] great player, he makes it on the personality level — he's not a bad guy, he's a good guy. There's no reason at all why he should be kept out."

The only possible objection is that Agassi has won "only" three Grand Slam singles titles (through July 7, 1997). Tracy Austin was inducted in 1992 with two, but back and foot injuries virtually ended her career at 21.

Pilloried early in his career for showboating, skipping Wimbledon for three straight years and losing his first three Grand Slam titles as the favorite each time, Agassi has made amends in all three areas and won over many of his critics.

"When he first came onto the scene, I thought he was very brash and immature, almost like a smart ass," recalled Australian veteran Mark Woodforde. "He was almost trying to put down his opponent, trying to make fun of him. If [Agassi] missed a shot, he'd make a big deal of it. If he was winning easy, he'd be joking with the crowd.

"He's certainly progressed past that. Now he knows he has to concentrate because he can't get away with all of that sideshow. His focus is on beating the other person with his game. Forget the crowd, the linesmen and the umpire. He's a lot better person, a very nice guy now."

John McEnroe, once incensed at Agassi for tanking a set against him, became a good friend of his and helped Agassi win Wimbledon in 1992.

Even John Feinstein, who had little that was good to say about Agassi and even less about his entourage in *Hard Courts*, has changed his view of the American star.

"He's ended up carving out a good career for himself," Feinstein said. "I wish he'd gotten different advice earlier in his career; I wish he'd started playing Wimbledon earlier; I wish he'd avoided some of the tantrums and blowups that he's had. But overall I'd say he's come a long way and deserves credit. He *easily* could have said — especially in that 1993-94 period when he'd won a Wimbledon and had all the money you could possibly hope to have —

'Aw, the heck with it. I'm a millionaire. I'm outa here.' And he didn't."

Agassi still has some detractors, though.

One tennis writer who requested anonymity described him as "a very disingenuous person. He reinvents himself every few years. He has a short attention span. He's an American kid. When he's not interested, he's an awful tennis player. When he is, he's a great tennis player. He's not highly professional."

Agassi remains an enigma to Evans.

"He happens to be the only Wimbledon champion I've never had a serious conversation with," Evans said, "and that goes back to Budge Patty in 1950. It's strange.

"I find [Agassi] very difficult to approach, and indeed so do many other people. I'll preface this by saying I think he's probably a very nice guy. I've seen him in press conferences, and there's obviously a very soft, good side to Andre. But he does himself no favors with this what I call sort of 'Las Vegas aura' that he cloaks over himself."

As an example, Evans mentioned an incident in the players' lounge in Barcelona in the early 1990s. The lounge was bustling with activity when Agassi, sandwiched by Gil Reyes in front and another burly man in back, entered the room.

"They march in, pick up three chairs and go off into the farthest corner and sit down and talk among themselves," Evans said. "It was just a very incongruous sight, as if [Agassi were saying], 'Don't come near me, and if you do, these two guys are going to. . . . '

"I don't know what he thinks. I don't know what his problem is, but somewhere in there he's desperately insecure. That's the only way I can come up with any rational solution to it."

Veteran player Richey Reneberg has a different perspective.

"At the tournaments he pretty much stays with his group of people, but that's not to say that he's not friendly," Reneberg said. "If I talk to him, he's very friendly, but he doesn't waste a lot of time at the courts. After the match, he takes off pretty quickly. I think that stems from who he is. Everywhere you go, people are asking you for stuff or wanting your autograph or whatever. You can't spend a lot of time hanging around."

Several journalists who were interviewed agreed that Agassi has not reached his potential.

"He's had moments where he has," Feinstein said. "He should have won the French. I don't think there's any question about that — at least once, maybe twice. There was no excuse for losing that match against [Andres] Gomez in 1990. That was pathetic. They were both awful that day . . . and Andre was awful-er. He probably would have won the match against [Jim] Courier if not for the rain delay in 1991, but that's part of the deal.

"If I look back on Andre Agassi, I would say he's a guy who probably should have won six or seven majors, just as I look back on John McEnroe and say he should have won 12 [rather than seven]."

Evans said flatly, Agassi "was definitely a huge talent — he's maybe still a huge talent — and he should have won more [Grand Slam titles]."

*   *   *

You don't have to be Bud Collins to recognize that Agassi's career has followed a pattern.

"He has a good year, and I should lay down bets that the next year he'll have a bad year," said Wendi Stewart, Agassi's former girlfriend. "It's usually the odd years that are bad. That's the way he works."

To describe Agassi as streaky is an understatement.

"It used to give me cardiac arrest sitting there and watching him, because I didn't know if he'd walk out and tank or if he'd walk out and just be *unbelievable*," Stewart said. "At the time I was traveling [with him, from 1990 through 1992], it was either one or the other. There was no middle ground."

Since his wrist surgery in December 1993, Agassi has been on a two-year cycle. After his five-month layoff, he regained his love for the game and produced two good years. But since his loss to Pete Sampras in the 1995 U.S. Open final, he's had two bad years.

Interestingly, Agassi's history of inconsistency does not apply to the Davis Cup, in which he has won 15 straight singles matches (through July 1997). He often needs something extra to motivate him, such as playing for his country, and he doesn't want to let his teammates or his country down (at least not after the debacle against Carl-Uwe Steeb of Germany in 1989).

The simple reason for Agassi's erratic play concerns his baseline game and lack of a dominating serve.

"It takes an incredible amount of intensity for me to play my game," he said. "If Pete and Boris [Becker] are a little off, they can hold serve long enough, and maybe something good will happen. If I'm a little off, it's tougher. I've got to break guys down. To do that day in and day out, week in and week out, year in and year out, is difficult."

But Agassi's inconsistency goes far deeper than that. Mike Agassi deserves great admiration for devoting his life to his children's tennis careers. If not for him, Andre wouldn't be where he is. But Mike's obsession with producing a champion had many unfortunate consequences.

1. It created a fundamental conflict in Andre. He desperately wants to live up to expectations and please his father, but he also desperately wants his own identity. He has never had a chance to develop one because he was programmed from birth for tennis stardom.

"He just fights himself," Stewart said. "He struggles to be more than just a tennis player, and the tour doesn't really allow that. When he's doing well, it's week after week after week after week after week. It has usually come from a place where everybody's kind of counting him out. It's almost like, 'Oh, you don't think I can do this? Just watch me.' Then the next year, it's like, 'He should win Wimbledon.' That's when he walks on the court and it's like, 'Oh yeah? Watch me piss it away.' It's like this fight.

"I think the tour gets boring to him, too. So it's like this little mind thing that he does. I don't think it's thought out. It's just kind of his nature. If you tell him he can't do something, lo and behold, he'll do it."

2. It linked Andre's self-esteem to winning.

"It's more than about a tennis match [for Andre]," Stewart said. "It becomes about him. If he wins, he's good, and if he loses, he's bad. It's almost like, 'How dare you?' It's almost like his way of saying 'Fuck you,' but nobody knows there's a fight."

Brooke Shields, meanwhile, told interviewer Steve Croft on *60 Minutes* in 1995 that "the times [Agassi] doesn't feel good about himself outweigh the times he does."

Croft logically countered: "He's the No. 1 tennis player in the world, he just signed a $150 million contract, he has his own private jet, he has you as his girlfriend. What's not to feel good about?"

Shields responded, "Unless you have a real sense of belief in yourself deserving those things, then they become very relative."

Agassi might feel undeserving as an adult because nothing he did as a child was enough to satisfy his perfectionistic father.

"[Andre] had it tough," Stewart said. "All he did was play tennis. If he didn't win, I mean, that was like the end of the world [to Mike]. I think [Andre] still carries that around a little bit. I think he's done much, much better in the last couple of years. He's learned how to tap in and take control a little bit better. He is *the* most gifted person I have ever watched, and I saw a *lot* of tennis . . . a *lot* of tennis. I saw everybody play, and there's nobody who can make the ball dance like he does. When he wants to, he could play with a baseball bat."

Agassi is more gifted than Sampras?

"Sampras is obviously gifted — don't get me wrong," Stewart said. "But Andre can do anything. He can hit any shot. His strokes are just beautiful. Sampras is obviously up there [in terms of talent], but I just don't think he's as beautiful to watch as Andre."

Why has Sampras won 10 Grand Slam singles titles (through July 7, 1997) to Agassi's three? One major reason is Sampras doesn't carry around the emotional baggage that Agassi does. Sampras knows he's a good person whether he wins or not. Agassi doesn't, even though he is. Sampras can just play tennis.

"It's a lot simpler for Sampras," Stewart said. "He's developed his talent, he's focused, he's determined. He's developed all those things that you need to have to be a consistent champion. I don't think Andre has, and I don't think he'll ever be like that. It's just not Andre."

It's as if Agassi is not obsessed with tennis precisely because his father was. And as if Sampras *is* obsessed with tennis it's because *his* father was not. Then again, maybe it's just a difference in personalities.

"[Sampras] only thinks about tennis and nothing else," said recently retired German tennis star Michael Stich. "That's the person he is, and that's great for him. I could have never done it. I cared about a lot of other things in life. He is a person who just focuses on tennis, day and night, and I think that's part of his success."

Another part is his dominating serve. Michael Chang said it's tougher for him to play Sampras than Agassi, even though Chang is 7-11 against each in the pros (through July 7, 1997).

"[Sampras'] serve is one of the most difficult to get back," Chang said. "With Andre, at least you're able to get into a rally. If Pete is serving well, it makes it very difficult."

Woodforde said without hesitation, though, that it's tougher for him to play Agassi than Sampras, even though Woodforde is 1-3 against the former and 0-9 against the latter.

"[Agassi's] return is better than my serve," Woodforde said. "I'm not too bad at covering the net, but he still has the firepower to get it by me. If I stay on the baseline, he can certainly run me around. I don't have the big fore-hand or the big backhand like he does. It's almost like every department, in my mind, he's stronger than me.

"Sampras, to me, doesn't have those huge ground-strokes. I feel like I can stay back and rally with him and work my way in [to the net]. He [might] blast me off the court with his serve, but if you can hang in there with him early in the match and hold your serve enough times, you can make a game of it. With Agassi, it has been very different."

Kelly Jones, the top-ranked doubles player in the world in 1992 and a Southern Nevada resident, offered a detached yet informed opinion about Agassi vs. Sampras.

"I believe if both players are at their best, Sampras will win because he's the most complete player," said Jones, who's 0-1 against Agassi in singles and has never played Sampras in singles. "He serves better, he volleys better, and he's got an all-around game. Agassi is pretty much a baseliner."

3. Mike's obsession put enormous pressure on Andre to succeed.

"There are land mines on the court of words like 'ex-pectation' and 'potential' and 'pressure' and 'doubts,' " Agassi told Croft on *60 Minutes*. "It seems like they're all over the place like land mines that you just step on and out of nowhere can just blow up, and everything can come crashing down in the middle of a match, in the middle of laying your heart on the line. That's scary because you come off the court, and you feel like . . . a failure."

Stewart said tennis "was always just crammed down [Andre's] throat. His whole life was set up to win, and if you don't, it's a pretty hard fall. . . .

"He was struggling with this whole 'Do I want it?' and it's a lot easier to go 'No, I don't want this. I'm going to tank,' than realize you don't have what it takes. And I think that scared him. Maybe he didn't have what it took. And here he had given his whole life and [was] forced [to play] his entire life, and maybe it was all for nothing."

4. It shook Andre's confidence.

"He had a habit of 'Oh, it's my footwork. That's what it is. My footwork's off,' " Stewart said. "Or it was, 'Oh, it's the stringing. That's what it is.' He'd always come up with the solution, but you could put him in the worst circumstances, and if his head was there, he would win. . . .

"It was like he needed a new coach for his serve or a new coach to help his footwork, and it was like, 'God bless it. You don't need any of this stuff. You gotta fix your head.' It was really hard to watch."

Even in the pros, Andre couldn't escape Mike's meddling.

"If [Andre] didn't serve well that week, sure enough . . . " Stewart said. "His dad has satellite [television] so he can see a tennis match anywhere in the world at any time. He'd have hours of videotape. He'd say, 'OK, [here's] Sampras' serve, you need to serve like this.' He'd just pick out some random person who served well that week, and it was like [imitating a Middle Eastern accent], 'No, you've got to do this. You've got to hit it like this and string your rackets like that.' I mean, do you know how many rackets we went through? How many different stringing ways we went through? How many service motions, because that was the big, hot topic?

"I mean, *every* week, it was something new. You wondered where Andre got this, 'Oh-this-must-be-the-solution' idea. It was because his dad would do the same damn thing. [Mike] drove me crazy. And Andre *knew* he was [wrong], but I think parents have access to that place that's so vulnerable, and [Mike] would just beat on that vulnerable part of Andre. It was bad."

And still nothing that Andre did was good enough, such as when he won Wimbledon and Mike reacted by asking him why he had lost the fourth set.

"That was the worst part to watch," Stewart said. "That would send me through the roof because I *knew* how it would just break [Andre] up inside. I saw it, and Mike couldn't see that."

It's no wonder that Andre said in 1995 of Sampras: "The one thing that Pete has over me — or I shouldn't say over me — but that I wish I had, is such a simple approach and raw belief that he is just better than everybody. With me, it's different. Even at the level of being No. 1 now for a while and winning tournaments and winning Slams, I still could convince myself that, Geez, maybe I'm just not as good as I think I am."

That's apparent to Richard Evans.

"He's the champion with the least self-confidence I've ever known," Evans said. "His confidence seems to hang on a [thread]. If he's really playing well, he thinks he can blast the world, which he can — no question. But if something isn't working, then all these doubts and frailties start to show themselves, and he becomes prey for anybody.

"I've seen it so often. I mean, Brad Gilbert came along and pumped him up and said, 'Andre, you're great, fabulous, wonderful.' And he believed it, and up his ranking went for a time. Then he lost to Sampras in the [1995] U.S. Open final, and it was like pricking a balloon. He's never been the same again. It has to be all about confidence because as a tennis player, he's great."

5. Mike's obsession made Andre fear losing.

When you're afraid of losing, it becomes a self-fulfilling prophecy. That's what happened in Andre's first three Grand Slam finals: the 1990 French Open against Gomez, the 1990 U.S. Open against Sampras and the 1991 French Open against Courier. Sampras probably would have won anyway, but not Gomez and Courier.

"You can look in Andre's eyes and tell if he's going to win or not," Stewart said. "When he walked out after the rain delay in the Courier match and when he walked out on the court with Gomez, it was like a deer caught in headlights. Those were pretty devastating."

A fear of losing is another reason for Agassi's history of tanking matches. After all, if you haven't tried, you haven't really lost, right? The opponent hasn't beaten the "real" Agassi.

6. It created in Andre a greater need than in other pros to get away from tennis.

Agassi wasn't able to do much else as a child. He wasn't able to do much else at the Bollettieri academy. And he's not able to do much else when he's on the year-round pro tour. Agassi is trying to make up for lost time, but the tennis circuit makes that almost impossible.

"It's tough to balance tennis with any life," Agassi said. "Because it's a year-long sport, it's not like you have all the time in the world to address the things that are also important to you. It's hard. It's a light switch that goes on and off.

"You play for three weeks and then are off for two. You have no life for three weeks, and then you have to figure out what you can catch up on and get it done now. Then it's back to playing again.

"Sometimes it can get a bit overwhelming, which is why I tend to have my moments of complete all-consumed intensity and then some amount of distance from it. It's not easy for me to keep it all balanced today."

Stewart understands all too well. The pro tennis circuit, she said, "is a rough, rough life. It's really hard on people. The way they have it structured, there's really no off-season. It's ridiculous. I guess for a workhorse like Jim Courier, you can grin and bear it and kind of go through the grind, but Andre doesn't function like that. I saw the tour just wear him out.

"One week you're in Paris, and people are chanting outside the hotel, and you can't go anywhere. There's really no time. We're in these wonderful places, and he never got to go see anything. You see a hotel room and the tournament site, and that's it.

"In smaller tournaments, you have a match almost everyday, so you can't go walking around a museum and then go play. It's just a rough life.

"There's just no room to have a life. That's what made it hard, because you try to have a life, but whatever life you have has to come with you. Or you don't see each other for a month at a time.

"He has a lot more options now. He has a plane and can fly whoever wherever. That's why he traveled with an entourage — to make some kind of life on the road. Otherwise, you don't have one."

Stewart described a typical day for Agassi when they traveled together on the circuit in the early 1990s:

- Wake up at noon or later.
- Leave the hotel and eat at a nearby coffee shop or International House of Pancakes. Agassi liked to order eggs and bacon or a chicken sandwich.
- Return to the hotel to rest and digest his meal.
- Practice for 20 minutes with hitting partner Raul Ordonez from the Bollettieri academy or players such as Aaron Krickstein and Luke Jensen.
- Return to the hotel, shower and chat with the members of his entourage (brother Phillip, Stewart, Bollettieri, agent Bill Shelton and conditioning coach Reyes) or watch television. Agassi had no favorite shows, Stewart said.
- Eat a light meal such as Frosted Flakes in the hotel room before his match. (Because Agassi is invariably the star attraction, most of his matches are at night.)
- Play his match.
- Shower and change at the hotel and go out to dinner with his entourage.
- Occasionally rent a movie. Agassi liked horror movies for a while, Stewart said. And after he went through that phase? "I don't know," Stewart said. "He wasn't really a big movie person."
- Go to bed at 2 or 3 A.M.

"The whole day was geared around a match," Stewart said. "He didn't like to go out and be bothered by people. Everywhere he'd go, it was just a scene. Doing any kind of sightseeing or walking around is tiring. It's hard."

Agassi did everything he could on the circuit to keep tennis from dominating his life, Stewart said. He rarely spoke to the other players. He stayed at different hotels from the other players. He showed up for his matches and left immediately afterward.

"He wanted to get out of there as quick as he could," Stewart said. "I think for him it was too much. He was eating and breathing tennis. He wanted to go away and forget about it for a little while. That's why we *never* stayed in the player hotel. He *hated* running into groupies or fans or other tennis players."

7. Finally, Mike's obsession might have led to tendinitis in Andre's wrist and subsequent surgery. Dr. Richard Scheinberg, who operated on Agassi in 1993, was asked if Agassi's wrist problem was caused by the millions of balls he slugged off machines as a child or by the wristy forehand that Mike taught him.

"It's a combination of both," Scheinberg said.

The surgery left a purple scar on the top of Agassi's right wrist. Is he emotionally scarred from his pressure-packed, one-dimensional upbringing?

"Everybody who's had a [difficult home life] — which is probably most people — has a certain amount of scars," Stewart said. "Life is kind of figuring out how to deal with them and put patches over them. That's what Andre's finally figured out how to do, or is working on it.

"Before, yeah, he was scarred, but I don't think it's going to do permanent damage. There was a good chance of that. He could have gone either way, but Andre's a survivor, and he's a fighter. He wouldn't settle for that."

*　　*　　*

For all Agassi's fame, Stewart didn't hesitate when asked if the public really knows him.

"No," she said. "I don't think they know the soft, good side. I think all they see is the cocky, emotional, flamboyant tennis player, and that's not really who he is."

Player and tennis commentator Luke Jensen agreed.

"Even though he's a very public figure, he's mysterious," said Jensen, a longtime friend of Agassi's.

So who is Agassi?

"He's a good-hearted person," Stewart said. "He's a good guy. He's honest and loyal, and he's got a big heart. Probably the most public [example] is his [charitable] foundation.

"But he does things on a personal level for people. Anybody who's worked for him — even if they're not useful anymore — he'll still keep around and support . . . find something for them to do. He takes care of his family and friends. . . . He put his best friend through law school, he has a bunch of college funds for friends' children. He built his parents a beautiful home — things like that."

Agassi is legendary on the pro circuit for his generosity. American doubles star Rick Leach said Agassi donated $50,000 to the St. Jude's Children's Hospital in Memphis in 1996. St. Jude's spokesman George Shadroui would not confirm or deny the figure, saying the hospital does not release donor information.

On a smaller scale, Leach recalled playing doubles with Agassi at Washington, D.C., in 1991. They lost to Nicolas Pereira of Venezuela and Jaime Yzaga of Peru, 6-4 in the third set, in the first round to earn $600 apiece.

"We played the feature match at night in doubles, and that never happens," said Leach, who has won four Grand Slam men's doubles titles (including Wimbledon in 1990 with Jim Pugh). "I had a great time.

"I came to the next tournament, and the ATP Tour rep came up to me with an envelope. Andre gave me his portion of the prize money just for playing with him, which was unbelievable. He didn't have to do that."

Reneberg remembered flying from Los Angeles to Sydney, Australia, on a 747 with two other players for the Australian Indoor Tennis Championships in 1991.

"The three of us were sitting upstairs in business class, and Andre was downstairs in first class," Reneberg said. "Before the plane took off, the stewardess came up to get us and brought us down to first class. We thought [Agassi] OK'd it to sit there. Actually, he paid for all of us to upgrade.

"When we were down there [in Australia], we went shark fishing one day, and Andre set all this stuff up. We all just went along: Scott Davis, David Pate, Luke Jensen. . . . "

Agassi wants to be liked. He is very sensitive, as illustrated by an incident at the Las Vegas Country Club in early December 1993.

Agassi was appearing with Jimmy Connors at the news conference to announce that their upcoming exhibition at the MGM Grand Garden had been delayed three months to give Agassi time to recover from wrist tendinitis. The news conference soon lapsed into typical public relations fluff. Agassi was great. Connors was great. The MGM was great. Life was great.

Then an intrepid sports writer asked Connors how he felt about Agassi's comment at the 1988 U.S. Open, that Agassi had expected to beat Connors, 6-3, 6-3, 6-3. Before Connors had a chance to answer, Agassi blew up. His eyes got red, as if he were about to cry — which might well have been the case.

"I knew one of you jerks would ask that," Agassi snapped. "I was 18 and thrown into an environment. Let's put your life under a magnifying glass."

Agassi admits that tennis is not his life. He said his priorities are: "First, my relationship with God. The loved ones in my life, second. Then, I'd say my ability within the game. In that order."

Agassi is liberal, at least fiscally, according to Jensen.

"He's a big Clinton fan. He likes a lot of government programs for the poor and education. I know he wanted

Clinton to win the last two elections. [Agassi] is a guy who could use a 15 percent tax cut, but the country is more important to him. I know whenever I brought up [George] Bush or [Bob] Dole, he gave me a hard time," Jensen said.

Agassi attended a speech by Clinton in Las Vegas on October 31, 1996.

Stewart said Agassi did not read books when they traveled together, but apparently that has changed. His taste runs toward religious and self-help books. He read Pope John Paul II's 1994 autobiography, *Crossing the Threshold of Hope*, several times because he was so fascinated by it.

In contrast to his flamboyant, rebellious image, Agassi prefers mellow music by performers such as Michael Bolton, Kenny G, George Winston, Nanci Griffith and James Taylor. Bolton and Kenny G are friends of Agassi's.

Agassi is not a big sports fan, according to Stewart.

"Every once in a while he'll follow something. I think he likes to go see hockey matches. . . . He loves March Madness. He has fun with big events, but he's not a real follower of sports," Stewart said.

Though not well-educated, Agassi apparently is very intelligent.

"I could read a whole book, but I can't really tell you what it's about," said Stewart, who nevertheless seems quite intelligent herself. "I'm not good at that at all. Andre could read probably the first five pages of the book and give you a complete dissertation on it."

Not only that, Agassi "is the most logical person you'll ever meet," Stewart said. "He can break anything down into logic."

Agassi has an *"un-bel-ievable* memory," Stewart continued. "He can remember *points* from junior tennis and how the match went. He remembers *everything*. Every match, he can tell you what was going on and why he hit that shot, from the time he was a tiny boy."

Agassi's memory extends beyond tennis.

"He remembers lyrics of songs," Stewart said. "[Or] we would talk about something, like some kind of heart-to-heart, and I would think, 'OK, he didn't really listen.' But it takes a minute or two to process, and he *remembers* that. He doesn't ever forget . . . anything."

Agassi is actually a mass of contradictions: supremely confident at times but a bundle of nerves at others, flamboyant on the court but low-key off of it, a born-again Christian who swears profusely on the court, reclusive yet generous, bright but regarded early in his career as stupid.

"He's a fascinating guy," Evans said. "He's been very good for the game."

*   *   *

Agassi's five-match losing streak, marriage and 2½-month layoff with wrist tendinitis in early 1997 fueled widespread speculation that he would announce his retirement at age 27. Agassi, though, scoffed at the idea as he prepared to return to the circuit in July at Washington, D.C.

"Believe me, I'm much more at risk of leaving this game when I'm on top than I am when I'm down and out," he said. "I don't like the feeling of being beaten by something."

Those are comforting words to Collins, the prominent tennis commentator, writer and historian.

"If he were to quit tomorrow, [tennis writers] would all miss the hell out of him because he's given us plenty to write about," Collins said. "He's the only [male] tennis player I've ever known who has painted his fingernails or dyed his hair or come up with a new outlandish outfit.

"I'm a fine one to talk about outlandlish outfits, but he'd leave a real void. I think it would be too bad for him because he was obviously put on earth to play great tennis, and it would be too bad for the game. I think he's got to get this all squared in his mind, where he wants to go."

Even assuming Agassi continues to play, tennis journalists said before the 1997 U.S. Open that they doubt he will win any more Grand Slam singles titles.

"I think he's probably finished," Feinstein said. "I'm always reluctant to write off someone who's more talented than 99.9 percent of the people at what they do. It's like with Greg Norman in golf. I think he's probably finished, but a talent like that can maybe just say, 'OK, I'm going to suck it up one more time and really work.'

"I think the whole question with Andre is, does he want to do the work again, the work that he obviously did, especially in that '94-'95 period when he played so well — to practice, to be in shape, to play enough tournaments, to dig in, to start playing tough matches again. There's so much involved, and there are so many hungry guys out there.

"He doesn't have the intimidation factor anymore. Guys get ahead of him in a match, and they figure they're going to win, whereas when you're 1-2-3-4 in the world, guys get ahead of you, and they start figuring out how they're going to lose. He doesn't have that right now.

"Also, if you look back historically in tennis, a lot of players are done in their late 20s. He's 27 now. McEnroe never won another major after 25. [Bjorn] Borg never won another major after 25. So [Agassi] certainly wouldn't be the first player to stop winning big events in their mid- to late-20s."

Indeed, of the 31 men's Grand Slam tournaments in the 1990s through Wimbledon in 1997, 26 (83.9 percent) have been won by players 25 years old or younger.

Collins also does not foresee Agassi winning another Grand Slam title.

"I hope I'm terribly wrong," Collins said. "I'm happy to laud him for what he's done, but there's so much more that I think he *could* do . . . if he wants to. Now, maybe he doesn't want to, and that's all right, too, because he's spent really half his life as a professional tennis player.

"Once his father sent him to Nick's, that turned him pro as far as I'm concerned, even though he didn't actually become a pro until 16. When you go there, that's what you're there for. You're like a big-time college athlete. They might call you an amateur, but you're not. I think he's been a pro since the age of 13. That's a long time — it's half his lifetime.

"We see what happens to a lot of these players — Gabriela Sabatini [who retired in 1996 at 26] the same way. She ran out of steam. It looks like Arantxa Sanchez Vicario is running out of steam, and [Steffi] Graf. They start awfully young, and they don't last very long."

As Stewart said, though, if there's one thing Agassi likes to do, it's prove people wrong. He lives for challenges, and there are two left: the French Open and Sampras.

With the French Open title, Agassi would join Rod Laver, Don Budge, Fred Perry and Roy Emerson as the only men to win all four Grand Slam singles titles in a career. Borg didn't do it. Nor did Bill Tilden, Ken Rosewall, Connors, Ivan Lendl or McEnroe. Not even Sampras has done it.

Can Agassi still win the French?

"It's up to him," said recently retired Frenchman Guy Forget. "He definitely has the ability. He should have won it already. He came close a couple of times. It takes a lot of work."

Forget was a two-time doubles runner-up in the French Open, with countryman Yannick Noah in 1987 and Jakob Hlasek of Switzerland in 1996. Noah is the only Frenchman to win the French Open singles title since Marcel Bernard in 1946, accomplishing the feat in 1983.

"For three full months, Noah went to bed thinking he was going to win the French Open," Forget said. "He ate, slept and played only to win the French Open. If [Agassi] does that a couple of times, he'll be able to say he did everything he could. If I were him, it would be the only thing that would still excite me. He has a lot more of a chance of winning the French Open than Wimbledon [again] — by far."

Agassi, meanwhile, has lost to Sampras four straight times (as of July 1997) — the last three in routs — beginning with the 1995 U.S. Open. Will Agassi reassert himself in the rivalry? Or will Sampras drive him out of the game, the way he did to Becker and McEnroe to Borg?

Time is running out on Agassi. Thirty, give or take a couple of years, is retirement age in men's professional tennis. The last player over 30 to win a Grand Slam singles title was Arthur Ashe, who was 31 when he won Wimbledon in 1975. Not that conventional standards have ever applied to Agassi . . .

After tennis, then what? For the first time in his life, Agassi will be able to choose what he wants to do. It's exciting but frightening, too. Acting, business and broadcasting are possibilities. He probably won't be content just to play golf.

". . . My mind has not gone beyond tennis," Agassi said before his marriage. "My mind is still inside the lines. I still want to experience being a great tennis player. That's my fantasy. I love tennis. I'm good at it, and I wouldn't change that for the world — at least not for the next few years — because when I do change it'll be because I'm forced to."

Funny, isn't it? Forced to play for so many years, Agassi says he'll have to be forced to quit.

If Agassi should have won more than three Grand Slam singles titles as of July 1997, he also could have won none like Jennifer Capriati or only one like Mary Pierce.

Like Agassi, Capriati was groomed from birth by her father for tennis stardom. Considered the next Chris Evert, Capriati signed a $5 million dollar endorsement contract at the age of 13 and appeared on the cover of *Sports Illustrated* at the same age. After reaching three Grand Slam semifinals and No. 6 in the rankings by 15, however, Capriati was cited for shoplifting a $15 ring in 1993, was arrested for possession of marijuana in 1994, underwent a court-mandated drug treatment program in 1994 and dropped off of the tour for two years. She has never been the same.

Like Agassi, Pierce was driven by a fanatical father. Banned at various times from junior and professional tournaments for disruptive behavior toward Mary and her opponents, Jim Pierce has been described in print as "The Tennis Father From Hell." In 1993, Mary obtained a restraining order to keep her father at a safe distance.

It is a tribute to Agassi's perseverance that he has achieved more than Capriati and Pierce. Unfortunately, though, we'll probably never know how good Andre Agassi could have been.

Statistics

AGASSI'S CAREER AT A GLANCE

Year	Year-End Singles Ranking	Singles W-L	Total Prize Money	Grand Slam Singles Titles	Total Singles Titles	ATP Tour World Champ.	Davis Cup Singles
1986	91	5-6 .455	$24,938	0	0	—	—
1987	25	26-17 .605	205,555	0	1	—	—
1988	3	63-11 .851	822,062	0	6	—	3-0
1989	7	41-19 .683	478,901	0	1	—	4-2
1990	4	45-12 .789	1,741,382	0	4	**4-1 Won**	2-2
1991	10	39-17 .696	982,611	0	2	2-2 Semis	3-0
1992	9	42-14 .750	1,027,834	**1**	3	—	**7-0**
1993	24	33-11 .750	407,835	0	2	—	1-0
1994	**2**	51-13 .797	1,941,667	1	5	3-1 Semis	—
1995	**2**	**73-9 .890**	**2,975,738**	1	7	—	2-0
1996	8	38-14 .731	1,629,928	0	3	0-1 RR	—
1997 Thru 7/7	30	6-6 .500	44,915	0	0	—	2-0
Total	—	462-149 .756	$12,946,246	3	34	9-5 .643	24-4 .857

RR—Round Robin
Career best in boldface

AGASSI'S CAREER SINGLES TITLES
(Through July 7, 1997)

1987 (1)

$516,000 Sul America Open, Itaparica, Brazil, hardcourt. Defeated Luiz Mattar in final, 7-6, 6-2.

1988 (6)

$415,000 Volvo/U.S. Indoor National Championships, Memphis, Tenn., indoor hardcourt. Defeated Mikael Pernfors in final, 6-4, 6- 4, 7-5.

$220,000 U.S. Open Men's Clay Court Championships, Charleston, S.C., clay. Defeated Jimmy Arias in final, 6-2, 6-2.

$677,500 Eagle Tournament of Champions, Forest Hills, N.Y., clay. Defeated Slobodan Zivojinovic in final, 7-5, 7-6, 7-5.

$305,000 Mercedes Cup '88, Stuttgart, Germany, clay. Defeated Andres Gomez in final, 6-4, 6-2.

$592,500 Volvo International, Stratton Mountain, Vt., hardcourt. Defeated Paul Annacone in final, 6-2, 6-4.

$123,400 Mennen Cup, Livingston, N.J., hardcourt. Defeated Jeff Tarango in final, 6-2, 6-4.

1989 (1)

$415,000 Prudential-Bache Securities Tennis Classic, Orlando, Fla., hardcourt. Defeated Brad Gilbert in final, 6-2, 6-1.

1990 (4)

$225,000 Volvo Tennis, San Francisco, carpet. Defeated Todd Witsken in final, 6-1, 6-3.

$1,200,000 Lipton International Players Championships, Key Biscayne, Fla., hardcourt. Defeated Stefan Edberg in final, 6-1, 6-4, 0-6, 6-2.

$420,000 Sovran Bank Classic, Washington, D.C., hardcourt. Defeated Jim Grabb in final, 6-1, 6-4.

$2,000,000 ATP TOUR WORLD CHAMPIONSHIP, Frankfurt, Germany, carpet. Defeated Edberg in final, 5-7, 7-6, 7-5, 6-2.

1991 (2)

$225,000 Prudential Securities Tennis Classic, Orlando, Fla., hardcourt. Defeated Derrick Rostagno in final, 6-2, 1-6, 6-3.

$465,000 Sovran Bank Classic, Washington, D.C., hardcourt. Defeated Petr Korda in final, 6-3, 6-4.

1992 (3)

$235,000 AT&T Challenge, Atlanta, clay. Defeated Pete Sampras in final, 7-5, 6-4.

$3,654,296 THE LAWN TENNIS CHAMPIONSHIPS, Wimbledon, England, grass. Defeated Goran Ivanisevic in final, 6-7, 6-4, 6-4, 1-6, 6-4.

$1,025,000 Player's Ltd. International Canadian Open, Toronto, hardcourt. Defeated Ivan Lendl in final, 3-6, 6-2, 6-0.

1993 (2)

$275,000 Volvo Tennis-San Francisco, indoor hardcourt. Defeated Gilbert in final, 6-2, 6-7, 6-2.

$275,000 Purex Tennis Championships, Scottsdale, Ariz., hardcourt. Defeated Marcos Ondruska in final, 6-2, 3-6, 6-3.

1994 (5)

$288,750 Nuveen Men's Tennis Championship, Scottsdale, Ariz., hardcourt. Defeated Mattar in final, 6-4, 6-3.

$1,470,000 Player's Ltd. International Canadian Open, Toronto, hardcourt. Defeated Jason Stoltenberg in final, 6-4, 6-4.

$4,100,800 U.S. OPEN, Flushing Meadows, N.Y., hardcourt. Defeated Michael Stich in final, 6-1, 7-6, 7-5.

$375,000 CA Tennis Trophy, Vienna, carpet. Defeated Stich in final, 7-6, 4-6, 6-2, 6-3.

$2,000,000 Open de la ville de Paris, carpet. Defeated Marc Rosset in final, 6-3, 6-3, 4-6, 7-5.

1995 (7)

$3,720,800 FORD AUSTRALIAN OPEN, Melbourne, Australia, hardcourt. Defeated Sampras in final, 4-6, 6-1, 7-6, 6-4.

$303,000 Sybase Open, San Jose, Calif., indoor hardcourt. Defeated Michael Chang in final, 6-2, 1-6, 6-3.

$2,250,000 Lipton Championships, Key Biscayne, Fla., hardcourt. Defeated Sampras in final, 3-6, 6-2, 7-6.

$550,000 Legg Mason Tennis Classic, Washington, D.C., hardcourt. Defeated Edberg in final, 6-4, 2-6, 7-5.

$1,545,000 du Maurier Ltd. Open, Montreal, hardcourt. Defeated Sampras in final, 3-6, 6-2, 6-3.

$1,545,000 Thriftway ATP Championship, Cincinnati, hardcourt. Defeated Chang in final, 7-5, 6-2.

$915,000 Volvo International Tennis Tournament, New Haven, Conn., hardcourt. Defeated Richard Krajicek in final, 3-6, 7-6, 6-3.

1996 (3)

$2,300,000 Lipton Championships, Key Biscayne, Fla., hardcourt. Defeated Ivanisevic in final, 3-0, retired.

OLYMPIC GAMES, Atlanta, hardcourt. Defeated Sergi Bruguera in final, 6-2, 6-3, 6-1.

$1,950,000 Great American Insurance ATP Championships, Cincinnati, hardcourt. Defeated Chang in final, 7-6, 6-4.

Titles by surface:

Hardcourt (outdoor and indoor)	25
Carpet	4
Clay	4
Grass	1
Total	**34**

CAREER SINGLES TITLES
Open Era (1968-present)
(Through July 7, 1997)

1. Jimmy Connors	109
2. Ivan Lendl	94
3. John McEnroe	77
4. Bjorn Borg	62
4. Guillermo Vilas	62
6. Ilie Nastase	57
7. Boris Becker	49
8. Pete Sampras	48
9. Rod Laver	47
10. Thomas Muster	44
11. Stefan Edberg	41
12. Stan Smith	39
13. ANDRE AGASSI	**34**
14. Arthur Ashe	33
14. Mats Wilander	33
16. John Newcombe	32
16. Manuel Orantes	32
16. Ken Rosewall	32
19. Tom Okker	31
20. Michael Chang	30

CAREER PRIZE MONEY
(Over $10 million)
(Through July 7, 1997)

1. Pete Sampras	$27,073,925
2. Boris Becker	24,087,955
3. Ivan Lendl	21,262,417
4. Stefan Edberg	20,630,941
5. Goran Ivanisevic	15,484,687
6. Michael Chang	14,610,829
7. Jim Courier	13,112,782
8. ANDRE AGASSI	**12,946,246**
9. Michael Stich	12,628,890
10. John McEnroe	12,539,622
11. Thomas Muster	10,331,754
12. Sergi Bruguera	10,299,619

WEEKS AT NO. 1
Open Era (1968-present)
(Through July 7, 1997)

1. Ivan Lendl	270
2. Jimmy Connors	268
3. Pete Sampras	181
4. John McEnroe	170
5. Bjorn Borg	109
6. Stefan Edberg	72
7. Jim Courier	58
8. Ilie Nastase	40
9. ANDRE AGASSI	**32**
10. Mats Wilander	20
11. Boris Becker	12
12. John Newcombe	8
13. Thomas Muster	6

AGASSI HEAD-TO-HEAD RECORDS
(All opponents listed are Grand Slam singles champions)
(Through July 7, 1997)

Vs. Boris Becker
(Agassi, 9-4)

Year	Tournament	Surface	Round	Winner	Score
1988	Indian Wells	Hard	SF	Becker	4-6, 6-3, 7-5
1989	Davis Cup	Carpet	SF	Becker	6-7, 6-7, 7-6, 6-3, 6-4
1989	Masters	Carpet	2	Becker	6-1, 6-3
1990	Indian Wells	Hard	SF	Agassi	6-4, 6-1
1990	U.S. OPEN	Hard	SF	Agassi	6-7, 6-3, 6-2, 6-3
1990	ATP Champs.	Carpet	SF	Agassi	6-2, 6-4
1991	French Open	Clay	SF	Agassi	7-6, 6-3, 3-6, 6-1
1991	ATP Champs.	Carpet	1	Agassi	6-3, 7-5
1992	WIMBLEDON	Grass	QF	Agassi	4-6, 6-2, 6-2, 4-6, 6-3
1994	Key Biscayne	Hard	3	Agassi	6-2, 7-5
1995	Indian Wells	Hard	SF	Agassi	6-4, 7-6
1995	WIMBLEDON	Grass	SF	Becker	2-6, 7-6, 6-4, 7-6
1995	U.S. OPEN	Hard	SF	Agassi	7-6, 7-6, 4-6, 6-4

Vs. Sergi Bruguera
(Agassi, 6-2)

Year	Tournament	Surface	Round	Winner	Score
1989	Italian Open	Clay	SF	Agassi	6-3, 6-4
1993	Barcelona	Clay	QF	Bruguera	6-3, 6-1
1994	Canadian Open	Hard	QF	Agassi	4-6, 7-6, 6-1
1994	Paris Indoor	Carpet	SF	Agassi	6-4, 6-4
1994	ATP Champs.	Carpet	RR	Agassi	6-4, 1-6, 6-3
1995	German Open	Clay	QF	Bruguera	6-3, 6-1
1995	New Haven	Hard	QF	Agassi	6-4, 6-1
1996	OLYMPICS	Hard	F	Agassi	6-2, 6-3, 6-1

Vs. Pat Cash
(Agassi, 1-0)

Year	Tournament	Surface	Round	Winner	Score
1987	Stratton Mtn.	Hard	2	Agassi	7-6, 7-6

Vs. Michael Chang
(Agassi, 11-7)

Year	Tournament	Surface	Round	Winner	Score
1988	Tourn. of Champ.	Clay	3	Agassi	6-2, 6-4
1988	U.S. OPEN	Hard	4	Agassi	7-5, 6-3, 6-2
1990	FRENCH OPEN	Clay	QF	Agassi	6-2, 6-1, 4-6, 6-2
1990	Washington	Hard	SF	Agassi	6-3, 6-1
1990	Canadian Open	Hard	QF	Chang	4-6, 7-5, 7-5
1992	Grand Slam Cup	Carpet	1	Chang	6-4, 6-2
1993	Canadian Open	Hard	3	Agassi	7-6, 6-3
1993	Cincinnati	Hard	SF	Chang	7-5, 1-6, 7-5
1994	U.S. OPEN	Hard	4	Agassi	6-1, 6-7, 6-3, 3-6, 6-1
1994	ATP Champs.	Carpet	RR	Agassi	6-4, 6-4
1995	San Jose	Ind-hard	F	Agassi	6-2, 1-6, 6-3
1995	Atlanta	Clay	F	Chang	6-2, 6-7, 6-4
1995	Cincinnati	Hard	F	Agassi	7-5, 6-2
1996	AUSTRALIAN OPEN	Hard	SF	Chang	6-1, 6-4, 7-6
1996	San Jose	Ind-hard	SF	Agassi	6-2, 5-7, 6-4
1996	Indian Wells	Hard	QF	Chang	6-7, 6-2, 6-1
1996	Cincinnati	Hard	F	Agassi	7-6, 6-4
1996	U.S. OPEN	Hard	SF	Chang	6-3, 6-2, 6-2

Vs. Jimmy Connors
(Agassi, 2-0)

Year	Tournament	Surface	Round	Winner	Score
1988	U.S. OPEN	Hard	QF	Agassi	6-2, 7-6, 6-1
1989	U.S. OPEN	Hard	QF	Agassi	6-1, 4-6, 0-6, 6-3, 6-4

Vs. Jim Courier
(Courier, 7-5)

Year	Tournament	Surface	Round	Winner	Score
1989	Philadelphia	Carpet	3	Agassi	6-3, 7-6
1989	Tourn. of Champ.	Clay	3	Agassi	3-6, 6-3, 7-5
1989	FRENCH OPEN	Clay	3	Courier	7-6, 4-6, 6-3, 6-2
1990	Key Biscayne	Hard	QF	Agassi	4-6, 6-3, 6-1
1990	FRENCH OPEN	Clay	4	Agassi	6-7, 6-1, 6-4, 6-0

1991	Indian Wells	Hard	3	Courier	2-6, 6-3, 6-4
1991	FRENCH OPEN	Clay	F	Courier	3-6, 6-4, 2-6, 6-1, 6-4
1991	ATP Champs.	Carpet	SF	Courier	6-3, 7-5
1992	FRENCH OPEN	Clay	SF	Courier	6-3, 6-2, 6-2
1992	U.S. OPEN	Hard	QF	Courier	6-3, 6-7, 6-1, 6-4
1995	Japan Open	Hard	F	Courier	6-4, 6-3
1996	AUSTRALIAN OPEN	Hard	QF	Agassi	6-7, 2-6, 6-3, 6-4, 6-2

Vs. Stefan Edberg
(Agassi, 6-3)

Year	Tournament	Surface	Round	Winner	Score
1989	Masters	Carpet	2	Edberg	6-4, 6-2
1990	Indian Wells	Hard	F	Edberg	6-4, 5-7, 7-6, 7-6
1990	Key Biscayne	Hard	F	Agassi	6-1, 6-4, 0-6, 6-2
1990	ATP Champs.	Carpet	RR	Edberg	7-6, 4-6, 7-6
1990	ATP Champs.	Carpet	F	Agassi	5-7, 7-6, 7-5, 6-2
1992	Davis Cup	Clay	QF	Agassi	7-5, 6-3
1994	Key Biscayne	Hard	QF	Agassi	7-6, 6-2
1995	Washington	Hard	QF	Agassi	6-4, 2-6, 7-6
1995	U.S. OPEN	Hard	3	Agassi	6-4, 6-3, 6-1

Vs. Andres Gomez
(Gomez, 3-2)

Year	Tournament	Surface	Round	Winner	Score
1987	Japan Open	Hard	QF	Gomez	6-2, 6-0
1988	Stuttgart	Clay	F	Agassi	6-4, 6-2
1989	Boston	Clay	SF	Gomez	7-6, 6-7, 6-2
1990	Key Biscayne	Hard	4	Agassi	6-7, 6-2, 6-3
1990	FRENCH OPEN	Clay	F	Gomez	6-3, 2-6, 6-4, 6-4

Vs. Yevgeny Kafelnikov
(Tied, 2-2)

Year	Tournament	Surface	Round	Winner	Score
1994	Monte Carlo	Clay	1	Kafelnikov	1-6, 6-3, 6-4
1995	AUSTRALIAN OPEN	Hard	QF	Agassi	6-2, 7-5, 6-0
1995	FRENCH OPEN	Clay	QF	Kafelnikov	6-4, 6-3, 7-5
1996	Cincinnati	Hard	QF	Agassi	7-6, 3-6, 6-3

Vs. Gustavo Kuerten
(Kuerten, 1-0)

Year	Tournament	Surface	Round	Winner	Score
1997	Memphis	Ind-hard	2	Kuerten	6-2, 6-4

Vs. Richard Krajicek
(Agassi, 3-1)

Year	Tournament	Surface	Round	Winner	Score
1991	WIMBLEDON	Grass	3	Agassi	7-6, 6-3, 7-6
1993	Key Biscayne	Hard	4	Krajicek	6-2, 7-5
1993	WIMBLEDON	Grass	4	Agassi	7-5, 7-6, 7-6
1995	New Haven	Hard	F	Agassi	3-6, 7-6, 6-3

Vs. Ivan Lendl
(Lendl, 6-2)

Year	Tournament	Surface	Round	Winner	Score
1987	Stratton Mtn.	Hard	SF	Lendl	6-2, 5-7, 6-3
1988	U.S. OPEN	Hard	SF	Lendl	4-6, 6-2, 6-3, 6-4
1988	Masters	Carpet	RR	Lendl	1-6, 7-6, 6-3
1989	Tourn. of Champ.	Clay	SF	Lendl	6-2, 6-3
1989	Canadian Open	Hard	SF	Lendl	6-2, 3-6, 6-4
1989	U.S. OPEN	Hard	SF	Lendl	7-6, 6-1, 3-6, 6-1
1990	Canadian Open	Hard	F	Agassi	3-6, 6-2, 6-0
1993	New Haven	Hard	QF	Agassi	6-3, 6-4

Vs. John McEnroe
(Tied, 2-2)

Year	Tournament	Surface	Round	Winner	Score
1986	Stratton Mtn.	Hard	QF	McEnroe	6-3, 6-3
1988	Los Angeles	Hard	SF	Agassi	6-4, 0-6, 6-4
1989	WCT Dallas	Carpet	QF	McEnroe	4-6, 3-0, ret.
1992	WIMBLEDON	Grass	SF	Agassi	6-4, 6-2, 6-3

Vs. Thomas Muster
(Tied, 4-4)

Year	Tournament	Surface	Round	Winner	Score
1987	Key Biscayne	Hard	1	Muster	7-6, 7-5, 5-7, 0-6, 6-4
1988	Italian Open	Clay	3	Agassi	6-4, 7-5
1988	Boston	Clay	QF	Muster	6-1, 6-4
1990	Davis Cup	Clay	SF	Muster	6-2, 6-2, 7-6
1994	FRENCH OPEN	Clay	2	Muster	6-3, 6-7, 7-5, 2-6, 7-5
1994	U.S. OPEN	Hard	QF	Agassi	7-6, 6-3, 6-0
1996	Cincinnati	Hard	SF	Agassi	6-4, 6-1
1996	U.S. OPEN	Hard	QF	Agassi	6-2, 7-5, 4-6, 6-2

Vs. Yannick Noah
(Tied, 1-1)

Year	Tournament	Surface	Round	Winner	Score
1989	Indian Wells	Hard	QF	Noah	7-5, 6-4
1989	Davis Cup	Carpet	QF	Agassi	6-3, 7-6

Vs. Pete Sampras
(Sampras, 12-8)

Year	Tournament	Surface	Round	Winner	Score
1989	Italian Open	Clay	2	Agassi	6-2, 6-1
1990	Philadelphia	Carpet	3	Sampras	5-7, 7-5, ret.
1990	U.S. OPEN	Hard	F	Sampras	6-4, 6-3, 6-2
1990	ATP Champs.	Carpet	RR	Agassi	6-4, 6-2
1991	ATP Champs.	Carpet	RR	Sampras	6-3, 1-6, 6-3
1992	Atlanta	Clay	F	Agassi	7-5, 6-4
1992	FRENCH OPEN	Clay	QF	Agassi	7-6, 6-2, 6-1
1993	WIMBLEDON	Grass	QF	Sampras	6-2, 6-2, 3-6, 3-6, 6-4
1994	Key Biscayne	Hard	F	Sampras	5-7, 6-3, 6-3
1994	Osaka	Hard	SF	Sampras	6-3, 6-1
1994	Paris Indoors	Carpet	QF	Agassi	7-6, 7-5
1994	ATP Champs.	Carpet	SF	Sampras	4-6, 7-6, 6-3
1995	AUSTRALIAN OPEN	Hard	F	Agassi	4-6, 6-1, 7-6, 6-4
1995	Indian Wells	Hard	F	Sampras	7-5, 6-3, 7-5
1995	Key Biscayne	Hard	F	Agassi	3-6, 6-2, 7-6

1995	Canadian Open	Hard	F	Agassi	3-6, 6-2, 6-3
1995	U.S. OPEN	Hard	F	Sampras	6-4, 6-3, 4-6, 7-5
1996	San Jose	Ind-hard	F	Sampras	6-2, 6-3
1996	Stuttgart	Carpet	QF	Sampras	6-4, 6-1
1996	ATP Champs.	Carpet	RR	Sampras	6-2, 6-1

Vs. Michael Stich
(Agassi, 6-0)

Year	Tournament	Surface	Round	Winner	Score
1990	Canadian Open	Hard	2	Agassi	6-3, 6-7, 6-3
1991	Davis Cup	Clay	SF	Agassi	6-3, 6-1, 6-4
1991	ATP Champs.	Carpet	RR	Agassi	7-5, 6-3
1993	Cincinnati	Hard	QF	Agassi	6-3, 6-2
1994	U.S. OPEN	Hard	F	Agassi	6-1, 7-6, 7-5
1994	Vienna	Carpet	F	Agassi	7-6, 4-6, 6-2, 6-3

Vs. Mats Wilander
(Agassi, 5-2)

Year	Tournament	Surface	Round	Winner	Score
1986	La Quinta	Hard	2	Wilander	6-1, 6-1
1988	FRENCH OPEN	Clay	SF	Wilander	4-6, 6-2, 7-5, 5-7, 6-0
1994	FRENCH OPEN	Clay	1	Agassi	6-2, 7-5, 6-1
1995	Indian Wells	Hard	2	Agassi	6-0, 6-2
1995	Canadian Open	Hard	SF	Agassi	6-2, 6-0
1995	New Haven	Hard	SF	Agassi	6-3, 6-3
1995	Davis Cup	Hard	SF	Agassi	7-6, 6-2, 6-2

Totals

Of the 18 fellow Grand Slam singles champions Agassi has played, he has a winning record against nine and a losing record against five (.643). He is even against four. Overall, Agassi is 75-57 against them (.568).

Sources

I interviewed more than 50 people, including Rita Agassi and Wendi Stewart, exclusively for this book. Other quotes came from stories I wrote for the *Las Vegas Review-Journal*, *Japan Times* or *Reno Gazette-Journal*. The remaining quotes are listed below with the writer or broadcaster.

Foreword

- "... to not accept losing"
  Steve Croft, *60 Minutes*, September 17, 1995.

Chapter 1

- "... For tennis players ..."
  Julie Cart, *Los Angeles Times,* July 11, 1996.
- "With neither money ..."
  Joel Drucker, *Tennis,* July 1996.
- "Ferreira found out ..."
  Julie Cart, *Los Angeles Times,* July 31, 1996.
- "Bruguera is only interested ..."
  Gene Wojciechowski, *Chicago Tribune,* August 4, 1996.

Chapter 2

- "We'd start shoveling ..."
  Richard Hoffer, *Los Angeles Times,* May 24, 1988.
- "... Because it was tennis country ..."
  Ibid.
- "We loved the rain ..."
  Martha Sherrill, *Esquire,* May 1995.
- "She had a chance ..."
  Ibid.
- "I'd say, 'Shut up' ..."
  Sally Jenkins, *Sports Illustrated,* March 13, 1995.
- "... Always too lazy ..."
  Robert Sullivan, *Sports Illustrated,* October 26, 1987.
- "... Was one of the few ..."
  William G. Simons, *Inside Tennis,* June 1996.
- "... Confidence and self-esteem ..."
  Nick Bollettieri, *My Aces, My Faults,* 1996, p. 20.
- "... I've resolved my own ..."
  Sally Jenkins, *Sports Illustrated,* March 13, 1995.

Chapter 3

- "I put him . . ."
  Richard Hoffer, *Los Angeles Times*, May 24, 1988.
- "He just thought . . ."
  Ibid.
- "I've always wanted . . ."
  Matthew Tolan, *Racquet-Performance*, 1996.
- "Three thousand balls . . ."
  Robin Finn, *New York Times*, October 29, 1990.
- "Dad raised me . . ."
  Esquire, op cit.
- "Every time he played . . ."
  My Aces, My Faults, 1996, p. 23.
- "By any means an abusive . . ."
  Inside Tennis, op. cit.
- "He toyed with me . . ."
  Peter de Jonge, *New York Times Magazine*, August 27, 1995.
- "Kick (Andre's) ass . . ."
  David Higdon, *Tennis*, December 1994.
- "Don't feel bad . . ."
  Ibid.
- "I'm going there . . ."
  Ibid.
- "My father put a lot . . ."
  60 Minutes, op. cit.
- "Whatever makes Pete happy . . ."
  Thomas Bonk, *Los Angeles Times*, July 23, 1993.
- "If I wasn't behind . . ."
  Barry McDermott, *Tennis*, April 1988.
- "They made me . . ."
  Ibid.
- "He's changed now . . ."
  Curry Kirkpatrick, *Sports Illustrated*, March 13, 1989.
- "Mike is consumed . . ."
  Sally Jenkins, *Sports Illustrated*, March 13, 1995.

Chapter 4

- "We operate totally . . ."
  William R. Newcott, *National Geographic*, December 1996.
- "It's my home . . ."
  Playboy, August 1996.
- "My son doesn't . . ."
  David Clayton, *Las Vegas Sun*, October 19, 1993.
- "One of the realities . . ."
  Racquet-Performance, op. cit.
- "I took a couple of . . ."
  Sally Jenkins, *Sports Illustrated*, December 5, 1993.
- "Will be the most . . ."
  National Geographic, op. cit.
- "Slowly shaking the head . . ."
  Ibid.
- "In Nevada, they say . . ."
  Ed Vogel, *Las Vegas Review-Journal*, November 9, 1996.

Chapter 5

- "If I didn't leave . . ."
  My Aces, My Faults, p. 27.
- "I taught him to hit . . ."
  Ibid., p. 21.
- "Whatever it takes . . ."
  Ibid.
- "Me and school . . ."
  Robert Sullivan, *Sports Illustrated*, October 26, 1987.
- "It was like . . ."
  Curry Kirkpatrick, *Sports Illustrated*, March 13, 1989.
- "I had never met . . ."
  My Aces, My Faults, 1996, p. 24.
- "A nifty combination . . ."
  Curry Kirkpatrick, *Sports Illustrated*, March 13, 1989.
- "But let me put it . . ."
  Brian Hewitt, *Los Angeles Times*, April 2, 1989.

- "... I don't hide that ..."
  Linda Pentz, *Tennis* (France), July 1992.
- "A ticking time bomb ..."
  My Aces, My Faults, p. 25.
- "He was a bit of ..."
  Curry Kirpatrick, *Sports Illustrated,* March 13, 1989.
- "Might be dealing blackjack ..."
  My Aces, My Faults, p. 28.
- "Hated growing up in ..."
  Esquire, op. cit.
- "I told people ..."
  My Aces, My Faults, p. 46.
- "I faked it ..."
  Ibid., p. 47.
- "I wanted to be ..."
  Ibid., p. 48.
- "If anyone can ..."
  Ibid., p. 49.
- "The demand was suddenly ..."
  Ibid., p. 81.
- "... We made mistakes ..."
  Barry McDermott, *Tennis,* April 1988.

Chapter 6

- "When I beat Mayotte ..."
  Robert Sullivan, *Sports Illustrated,* October 26, 1987.
- "This isn't for me ..."
  Neil Amdur, *World Tennis,* December 1987.
- "(Agassi) did not fall ..."
  My Aces, My Faults, p. 112.
- "Emotional letdown"
  World Tennis, op. cit.
- "Two years ago ..."
  Jim Loehr, *World Tennis,* June 1988.
- "I had to go through ..."
  Ibid.
- "He earned my trust ..."
  Curry Kirkpatrick, *Sports Illustrated,* March 13, 1989.

- "In the juniors . . ."
  Sports Illustrated, September 19, 1988.
- "I've never seen anything . . ."
  Donna Doherty, *Tennis,* January 1989.
- ". . . All made decisions . . ."
  Peter Bodo, *Tennis,* February 1993.

Chapter 7

- ". . . Didn't care about playing . . ."
  Tennis, June 1990.
- "I just can't understand . . ."
  Ibid.
- ". . . It wasn't so much . . ."
  Ibid.
- "I realized that Nick . . ."
  My Aces, My Faults, p. 114.
- "It's too tough . . ."
  John Feinstein, *Hard Courts,* 1991, p. 22.
- "Tanking — giving up . . ."
  Ibid.
- "It shook me up . . ."
  Ibid., p. 423.
- "I'll take those . . ."
  International Tennis Weekly, November 30, 1990.
- "He was met there . . ."
  Alexander Wolff, *Sports Illustrated,* June 18, 1990.
- "A little shit"
  Hard Courts, p. 225.
- "You get out of . . ."
  Ibid.
- "I've never had . . ."
  Alexander Wolff, *Sports Illustrated,* June 18, 1990.
- "Any rumors that Agassi . . ."
  Hard Courts, p. 363.
- "When Farrar heard . . ."
  Ibid., pp. 399-400.
- "I'm sad anyone can . . ."
  Bruce Newman, *Sports Illustrated,* November 26, 1990.

- "I was out to prove . . ."
  Ibid.
- "A year ago, I would . . ."
  Nora McCabe, *World Tennis*, February 1991.
- "Agassi immediately called . . ."
  Hard Courts, p. 224.
- "This isn't soccer . . ."
  Hard Courts, p. 428.
- "The entourage situation . . ."
  Roy Firestone, *ESPN, Up Close*, August 26, 1991.
- "The pessimistic side . . ."
  Curry Kirkpatrick, *Sports Illustrated*, June 17, 1991.
- "We had bullshitted . . ."
  My Aces, My Faults, p. 120.
- "I can understand that . . ."
  Tennis (France), July 1992.
- "Old versus young. . . ."
  Curry Kirkpatrick, *Sports Illustrated*, September 9, 1991.
- "Wimbledon was my last . . ."
  Thomas Bonk, *Los Angeles Times*, March 27, 1992.

Chapter 8

- "I was getting away . . ."
  Ibid.
- "I've always been . . ."
  Ibid.
- "Most people have to . . ."
  Sally Jenkins, *Sports Illustrated*, May 11, 1992.
- "It felt so unfair . . ."
  Ibid.
- "I didn't believe . . ."
  My Aces, My Faults, p. 125.
- "Goran is . . ."
  Curry Kirkpatrick, *Tennis*, July 1993.
- ". . . His psyche is more . . ."
  Sally Jenkins, *Sports Illustrated*, May 11, 1992.
- "I studied Andre . . ."
  My Aces, My Faults, p. 129.

- "... You work so hard ..."
  Roy Firestone, ESPN, *Up Close,* December 28, 1993.
- "I don't think it ..."
  Alison Muscatine, *Washington Post,* July 16, 1992.
- "I'd get arrested ..."
  Ibid.

Chapter 9

- "I felt uneasy ..."
  My Aces, My Faults, p. 134.
- "Some people just look out ..."
  David Higdon, *Tennis,* December 1994.
- "I wanted to be sure ..."
  My Aces, My Faults, p. 135.
- "He's very gifted ..."
  Jim Greenidge, *Boston Globe,* August 30, 1993.
- "And to thank me ..."
  ESPN, *Up Close,* op. cit.
- "It was a fairly ..."
  Robin Finn, *New York Times,* December 22, 1993.
- "The pain was coming ..."
  Ibid.
- "I came to terms ..."
  Sally Jenkins, *Sports Illustrated,* March 13, 1995.
- "Once tennis was out ..."
  Inside Tennis, op. cit.
- "I sat there with ..."
  Diane Pucin, *Philadelphia Inquirer,* February 19, 1995.
- "I honestly didn't think ..."
  Sally Jenkins, *Sports Illustrated,* March 13, 1995.

Chapter 10

- "In my mind ..."
  Jerry Crowe, *Los Angeles Times,* March 3, 1994.

- "I thought we were . . ."
  Joel Drucker, *San Francisco Focus,* February 1995.
- "He had my game . . ."
  Esquire, op. cit.
- "I just told him . . ."
  Mark Preston, *Tennis,* April 1995.
- "Brad's got a good . . ."
  New York Times Magazine, op. cit.
- "You have to be . . ."
  Arthur S. Hayes, *Tennis,* June 1986.
- "(Brad) was a little . . ."
  Ibid.
- ". . . Work ethic and on-court . . ."
  Bob Hurt, *Arizona Republic,* October 6, 1987.
- "When Brad came to me . . ."
  Brad Gilbert, *Winning Ugly,* 1993, p. 159.
- "I went there thinking . . ."
  Arthur S. Hayes, *Tennis,* June 1986.
- "I'm a real fighter . . ."
  International Herald Tribune, August 22, 1989.
- "He's sort of the ultimate . . ."
  Ibid.
- "I don't overpower . . ."
  Winning Ugly, p. 69.
- "Always be asking yourself . . ."
  Ibid., p. 70.
- "I've never seen . . ."
  Ibid., p. 147.
- "First of all . . ."
  New York Times Magazine, op. cit.
- "We concentrated on two . . ."
  San Francisco Focus, op. cit.

Chapter 11

- "To me, that's the sign . . ."
  San Francisco Focus, op. cit.
- "In a way, it was . . ."
  Peter Bodo, *Tennis,* March 1996.

- "He of the deep pockets . . ."
  David Granger, *Gentleman's Quarterly,* July 1996.
- "Maybe he had to go . . ."
  Chris Clarey, *Tennis,* February 1996.
- "To my way of thinking . . ."
  Tennis, June 1997.
- "Why should I tell . . ."
  New York Times Magazine, op. cit.
- "These guys show it's . . ."
  Curry Kirkpatrick, *Newsweek,* July 3, 1995.
- "I like the way . . ."
  New York Times Magazine, op. cit.

Chapter 12

- "I really want to say . . ."
  Peter Bodo, *Tennis,* February 1993.
- "(Agassi has) more talent . . ."
  Roy Firestone, ESPN, *Up Close,* February 3, 1992.
- "He's bigger than . . ."
  Scott Ostler, *San Francisco Chronicle,* February 16, 1996.
- "He's Reggie Jackson . . ."
  Ibid.
- "I don't understand why . . ."
  Julie Cart, *Los Angeles Times,* March 13, 1996.
- "I have heard (Agassi's) . . ."
  Mike Lupica, *Tennis,* June 1997.
- "Yes, it bothers me . . ."
  Dave Albee, *Marin Independent Journal,* February 9, 1997.

Chapter 13

- Tom Gullikson and Richey Reneberg were interviewed at the
  Newsweek Champions Cup at Indian Wells, Calif., during the
  week of March 10, 1997.

Chapter 14

- "What I find . . ."
  James Spada, *Streisand: Her Life*, 1995, p. 512.
- "There are so many . . ."
  Lynn Elber, *The Associated Press*, November 9, 1996.
- "Emotionally, my mother . . ."
  Randall Riese, *Her Name is Barbra*, 1993, p. 22.
- "I was raised . . ."
  Nancy Collins, *Entertainment Tonight*.
- ". . . Would never amount . . ."
  Her Name is Barbra, p. 30.
- "I'll show them"
  Her Name is Barbra, p. 28.
- "Andre will say . . ."
  Brian Hewitt, *Los Angeles Times*, April 2, 1989.
- "What Streisand establishes . . ."
  Roger Ebert, *Roger Ebert's Video Companion*, 1997, pp. 613-614.
- ". . . Taught me an incredible . . ."
  Inside Tennis, op. cit.
- "He was going away . . ."
  Gentleman's Quarterly, op. cit.
- "We've both gone through . . ."
  Esquire, May 1995.
- "He rejected it all"
  David Wild, *Rolling Stone*, October 3, 1996.
- "I never felt pushed . . ."
  Gail Buchalter, *Parade*, September 1, 1996.
- "The movies were convenient . . ."
  Lisa Simmons, *Cosmopolitan*, December 1996.
- "I basically wrote . . ."
  Parade, op. cit.
- "It all looked good . . ."
  Esquire, op. cit.
- "[It wasn't easy] to take this person . . ."
  Rolling Stone, op. cit.
- "I was just expecting . . ."
  People, July 11, 1994.
- ". . . Extremely sensitive, and thoughtful . . ."
  Hello, 1994.

- "I've known a lot . . ."
  Cosmopolitan, op. cit.
- "The sweetest, kindest . . ."
  Inside Tennis, op. cit.
- "He had talked . . ."
  People, March 25, 1996.

Chapter 15

- "I'll tell you . . ."
  Peter Bodo, *Tennis*, February 1993.
- "My dad gave me . . ."
  David Higdon, *Tennis*, December 1994.

Chapter 16

- "It takes an incredible . . ."
  Joel Drucker, *Tennis*, April 1997.
- "The one thing . . ."
  New York Times Magazine, op cit.
- "First, my relationship . . ."
  Julie Cart, *Los Angeles Times*, April 4, 1997.
- "Believe me, I'm much more . . ."
  Robin Finn, *The New York Times*, July 15, 1997.
- "My mind has not . . ."
  Joel Drucker, *Tennis*, April 1997.

Bibliography

ATP Tour. *1997 Player Guide*. ATP Tour, 1997.

Blake, Benjamin and Erickson, Hannah. *Amazing Las Vegas Trivia*. Las Vegas Trivia, 1995.

Bollettieri, Nick and Schaap, Dick. *My Aces, My Faults*. Avon Books, 1996.

Bollettieri, Nick and McDermott, Barry. *Nick Bollettieri's Junior Tennis*. Simon and Schuster, 1984.

Collins, Bud and Hollander, Zander. *Bud Collins' Modern Encyclopedia of Tennis*, Visible Ink Press, 1994.

Corel WTA Tour. *1997 Corel WTA Tour Media Guide*. WTA Tour, 1997.

Ebert, Roger. *Roger Ebert's Video Companion*. Andrews and McMeel, 1996.

Famighetti, Robert. *The 1997 World Almanac*. World Almanac Books, 1996.

Feinstein, John. *Hard Courts*. Villard Books, 1991.

Gilbert, Brad and Jamison, Steve. *Winning Ugly*. Birch Lane Press, 1993.

Hassan, John. *1997 Information Please Sports Almanac*. Houghton Mifflin Company, 1996.

International Tennis Federation. *Media Guide: 1996 Olympic Tennis Event.* International Tennis Federation, 1996.

McCracken, Robert D. *Las Vegas: The Great American Playground.* Marion Street Publishing Company, 1996.

Reise, Randall. *Her Name is Barbra.* Birch Lane Press, 1993.

Shields, Brooke. *On Your Own.* Villard Books, 1985.

Spada, James. *Streisand: Her Life.* Crown Publishers, Inc., 1995.

Wallington, Mark. *UNLV Tennis '97.* Century Graphics, 1996.

Index